RULE # 1

HAVE AN ADVENTURE!

Ruthann Zimmer Faber

Published 2017.
Printed in the United States of America.

ISBN 978-1-943650-61-3

Library of Congress Control Number 2017961017

Cover background image by Can Stock Photo/Garsya.

Published by BookCrafters, Parker, Colorado.
www.bookcrafters.net

INTRODUCTION

Everyone has a life story to tell. This one is mine. The facts are correct to the best of my recollection; however, the story spans more than seventy years and I am relying on my memory for most of the details. I have kept journals throughout my life and my mother saved all the letters I wrote her, as did my good friends Ginger and Barbara, and this has been an enormous help in writing this story. I have used first names or initials for many of my friends, acquaintances, co-workers, and former students.

Most people I know do not "lead" their life, it just happens. To avoid this I have developed rules to live by, that I am using to begin each chapter of this book. My "Rule # 1 is to "Have an Adventure!" This has become a main priority in my life. I have spent ten years overseas, and in particular, I have loved the Middle East where I lived and worked in Iran and Saudi Arabia. I have fulfilled childhood dreams of traveling down the Amazon River, riding camels in the Sahara Desert, and walking on the snows of Mt. Kilimanjaro. I have visited about eighty different countries in search of adventure, exotica and first-hand knowledge.

I grew up in Wisconsin, "North of the McCarthy Line," as my Icelandic-born husband describes it. From a stereotypical childhood on a small family dairy farm, raised Republican and Lutheran, I am today a Democrat and a liberal Unitarian Universalist. I once had an "out of body experience," which changed my spiritual thinking, so I now study both science and reincarnation. I married at the age of forty-one and had a daughter at age forty-two, a miraculous event I believe was always meant to be.

I am a retired school superintendent with thirty-five years of experience in education. I have loved my career. As a teacher, I used to bemoan Fridays since I had to wait a whole weekend before I could teach again. As a school superintendent, I often said that I loved my job so much I just wanted to "kiss my desk"!

I wish everyone would write the story of his or her life for future generations to enjoy. I personally would much prefer to read the biographies of "ordinary" people rather than just the rich and famous. "Ordinary" people do not necessarily lead "ordinary" lives.

DEDICATION

I am dedicating this book to my descendants and all the students I have worked with. I have written my "story" with my descendants in mind (I wish I knew more about my ancestors!), and all the students I had the pleasure of knowing, hoping they will follow my Rule # 1: Have an Adventure!

ACKNOWLEDGEMENTS

To my friend, Natasha Reatig, for editing this entire book and offering numerous helpful changes which have made it much more readable. Thank you Natasha!

To my husband for encouraging me to write this book. It has taken me nearly eight years to complete and without his suggestions and continuous push to get it finished I would still not be done! Thank you Donald Gudmundur Faber!

TABLE OF CONTENTS

CHAPTER 1

RULE #1: Have an Adventure!

At least once in your life go out and have a real adventure. I am not talking about a vacation, like a week at the beach. A real adventure requires more than a few weeks. Take a risk! Do something no one you know would believe you actually did! Trek the Pacific Crest Trail from Canada to Mexico or vice versa. Move to a state, or better yet a country, where you do not know anyone, and just live for a while. Join the Peace Corps or some other volunteer organization where you can serve others in a Third World country. Become a scuba diver and explore the world's incredible coral reefs. Climb Mt. Kilimanjaro. Get the idea? And age does not matter. Having a big adventure when you are young is probably easier since you are less likely to have responsibilities to attend to and physical strength and health may be better. However, it is never too late and will bring personal benefits no matter what your age.

SYRIA, 1969

From the moment I got off the freighter in Istanbul and was greeted by a makeshift band of Turks playing "When the Saints Go Marching In," I knew that I had entered an "exotic" land. The band members were dressed in traditional baggy pants and tunic tops, fez-like caps, slipper-like

Entering Istanbul

shoes, and they were playing instruments which included concertinas, cymbals, and drums. Alongside the band was a live dancing bear dressed in a black muzzle, ankle bracelet attached to a heavy chain, and multi-colored tutu. The scene was stranger to me than any I had ever seen, and yet the music I was hearing was as familiar to me as Bourbon Street in New Orleans where I had recently spent a year.

Cappadocia Rock–Cut Site

Days after my arrival in exotic Turkey I was enjoying a warm summer evening on a rooftop in Goreme. Goreme is a small village in Nevsehir Province. It is in central Turkey near the Cappadocia Region, a major tourist attraction that I was interested in visiting. There are more than six hundred rock-cut churches that monks built and lived in beginning in the 4th Century. At this time, I was traveling with Judy, an American from Minneapolis, and Paul, a French Canadian from Quebec City. We had become a threesome somewhere in Greece and had been traveling together for a few weeks. Judy was very blonde and had blue, blue eyes so she was always the center of attention in the villages of Turkey. The children would try to touch her eyes to see if they were real or not. Paul was big, and he had a full beard, dark hair and dark eyes. We had arrived in

Goreme in the late afternoon, found a room in a small "otel," walked about the village, and then made our way to the "otel's" rooftop where tables and chairs awaited us and dinner was served. The village below was now alive with chatter as people returned from the fields to prepare dinner and rest for the evening. There was little electricity in the village so lanterns were lit, fires were built, water was carried from the village well, and soon there were small groups of people gathered in circles around small fires throughout the village. The smells of smoke and spices permeated the air, and as I looked out over this scene, I tried to soak in all that I saw and smelled; I promised myself that I would always remember this night, to recall it all whenever I needed a touch of "exotica" in my life.

We ate a simple yet very tasteful dinner of kebabs cooked on a grill served with aromatic rice and a salad dressed in olive oil and lemon juice. Drinks continued to be served throughout the meal amidst laughter and what I came to perceive as lust on the part of the host-owners of the place. The drink served was Arak, a common Middle Eastern drink which turned cloudy when water was added, and it had a licorice flavor. The Greeks call this drink Ouzo. I did not care for it, neither did Judy, but she had the amazing ability to drink a lot of alcohol without a noticeable effect. Paul, ever cautious and feeling somewhat responsible for our safety, drank sparingly. I had managed to finish one small glass when the host was already bringing out the second bottle. It was late and I was tired; alcohol definitely has that effect on me.

I decided to leave our little "party" and go to bed. Paul walked me to my room. We had rented three rooms, side by side, directly under the rooftop dining area. We had to insist on side-by-side rooms since originally they wanted to place Paul in a room across the hall. Our thought was that if ever Judy or I felt frightened we could bang on the wall to Paul's room and he would hear us. With this in mind, Paul had taken the room in the middle. As Paul and I reached my room, he told me that he was going to sleep in Judy's room for the night and give her his room. He felt as I did, that our hosts had a definite interest in Judy.

Switching rooms without the owner's knowledge proved to be fortuitous. I awoke once during the night and thought I saw shadows in the light coming from under the door to my room. I watched for a while and then fell back to sleep when I decided it was probably just a flickering lantern. In the morning we gathered for breakfast on the roof. Judy was her smiling, happy self with no signs of a hangover or any ill effects from consuming large amounts of Arak the night before. Paul proceeded to tell us that someone had tried to get into his room during the night. Someone with a key had quietly opened the door but Paul had been awake and saw shadows under the door and heard footsteps so he hid behind the door. When the key turned and the door opened he reached around and grabbed the hand and bent the thumb backwards before the person escaped and left. Paul had not seen who it was. After a leisure breakfast on the roof we gathered our belongings and went to the reception desk to check out. There was the owner's son, with a large bandage on his thumb!

We rode a large diesel bus from Ankara to Marvan, over the mountains on an all-night trip. There was a full moon that evening, which was unfortunate, because it gave us an all too clear view of the narrow winding roads without shoulders and the frightfully steep drop-offs and hairpin turns. Sharing the road with us, but going in the opposite direction, were numerous semi-trailer trucks carrying loads of watermelon up over the mountain to Ankara. We had front row seats, an honor often given to foreign visitors, and thus had a frightening view of the near misses on this harrowing ride. On this night I learned the art of "letting go," closing my eyes, and entrusting my well-being to Allah and the bus driver. I soon fell asleep and awoke hours later, at dawn, and saw that we were riding on a nice flat, straight road through a beautiful agricultural valley with fields and fields of vegetable crops where farmers were already at work.

We arrived in Marvan around 9 a.m. and discovered that there were no trains going across the border to Bagdad until 4 p.m. that afternoon. With nothing else to do, and being seasoned travelers with abundant patience, we sat down to play cards with the Turkish border guards. They spoke no English and we spoke no Turkish but they were friendly and knew how to play gin rummy. We played cards on and off all day, and by the time the train came at four we felt a bit sad to leave our new Turkish "friends."

We were a little nervous upon boarding the train since we knew we were about to cross the border into Syria. We had been told by an official at the American embassy in Ankara that Americans could ride this train to Bagdad even though it would pass through a corner of Syria. Since the 1967 Israeli War, the United States had no relations with Syria and therefore Americans were not allowed to travel to Syria. However, we were assured that this was an "international train" and as long as we stayed on the train we would be fine. We were warned that if the train stopped in Syria for any reason we were not to get off.

The train was crowded with Iraqi students, all male, on their way home. It was a tense summer in the region and their government had called them back to be prepared for military service in the ongoing border skirmishes with neighboring countries. They were friendly and proud to practice their English on us. They laughed a lot and didn't seem distressed to be returning to a possible dangerous situation.

A few minutes after crossing the Syrian border the train came to a halt and armed, uniformed Syrian soldiers boarded the train. They went from car to car and when they came to us they asked for our passports. One of them spoke English – he said that my passport was "fake" because there was no stamp inside indicating my religion. I was told to get off the train. Certain that there was some mistake, I told him no, it wasn't fraudulent, that I was an American citizen and that religion was not stamped in U.S. passports. He leaned over and showed my passport to two other guards, talking about it, loud and excitedly, in Arabic. Then with anger on his face and contempt in his voice he said that my name told him I was a "Jew." He put his hand on the pistol he was wearing in a holster around his waist, looked directly at me and told me I had to get off the train. He then told Judy to get off the train since she was traveling with a "Jew." Paul was free to go since he was a Canadian.

Now we truly began to protest, telling him that we knew Americans were not allowed in Syria, and that we had been told not to leave the train. Suddenly he pulled out his pistol and ordered us off, at once! Paul said he would not leave us, and they replied: "as you wish." And so, when the train pulled out of the station the three of us along with two young German men were left on the platform with the Syrian soldiers. The Germans were told they were not allowed in Syria, that Syria had no diplomatic relations with Germany and that they should turn around and walk back along the tracks and across the border to Turkey — which they immediately did. We had not met them on the train and no words were exchanged among us on the platform. They just picked up their backpacks and began walking. Judy and I were told to get into a car already filled with soldiers. Paul was ordered into a separate car behind ours. My level of fear kept growing. Both cars drove some distance down the road, but when we came to a fork our car turned right and Paul's car turned left. At that moment fear turned to a quiet panic. Judy and I looked at each other but did not speak. I knew she was feeling the same as I was, experiencing an adrenaline induced terror.

Twenty minutes later we found ourselves at a tiny border post, one small office building next to a fence with a gate. On the other side of the fence was a wide stretch of desert and in the far distance we could see the little Turkish town we had just left. There were nine Syrian border guards / soldiers, including the one who could speak English. There was one big tree next to the office building and a small field of green bell peppers surrounded by an irrigation ditch with muddy water. Judy and I sat in the shade of the tree and wondered, what next? We were told that Paul was on his way to Aleppo to get visas for us. They had taken our passports, our backpacks and all our belongings. What money we had we were wearing inside our clothes in money belts and we knew it would be a mistake to let them know we had cash on us.

Evening came and the guards began to build fires, cook food, and then started to eat and drink. We were told that we were welcome to share their food and the surprisingly abundant supply of alcoholic drinks, but also that we would have to "pay for it – somehow." We understood that they were suggesting we trade food for sex. That night we went to sleep hungry, under the stars, on the ground, with no cover and a growing, aching fear.

We awoke early, to a day already hot and uncomfortable. I realized that more than food, what I really wanted was a cigarette! I had been smoking over a pack a day and it had been nearly twenty hours since my last cigarette. I asked as politely as I could, but the guards were not about to give me cigarettes without "pay." Fear and disgust at the thought of that "payment" quickly quieted my cravings, and I sat back down.

The guards went about their daily routines, talking constantly in Arabic; we knew they were talking about us. Finally at mid-morning they asked if anyone was meeting us in Bagdad. We quickly lied and said that yes, friends were meeting us there and they would surely be wondering where we were. They said they didn't believe us, and anyway, if they didn't hear anything official after a few days they would know that we were lying. The sneers on their faces told us their intentions. At that point with adrenaline at a peak I said in a loud defiant voice, "If you touch us we will have you hung! There is a death penalty for rape in this country!" But our level of fear jumped enormously. We realized that no one, other than Paul, knew where we were. In fact, in our last letters to our families we had said that we would be flying from Beirut to Bagdad, The train had been an alternative that we had decided on at the last minute, without really giving it much thought.

The day wore on. We had eaten nothing since our last meal in the "otel" and by noon we were really very hungry and thirsty. We began to assess our surroundings for something edible. The one big tree happened to have a medium sized and quite unfamiliar looking yellow fruit. We decided to try it. Much to the amusement of the guards, we climbed the tree and began eating the fruit. With one bite we identified it as a fig. Neither of us had ever seen a live fig, only Fig Newtons where they are smashed into a dark brown sticky paste. Picked yellow from the tree, they were quite tasty. Our only available drink was the mud-brown irrigation water, home also to a number of small noisy frogs. Drinking it I knew we were probably picking up some sort of parasite, but there was no choice. The temperature was well over 100F by now and we needed water.

At dusk a Mullah was brought to us by the guards. He was dressed in the traditional robe and turban of an Islamic "holy man." Without any introduction or explanation he began to teach us about the Islamic faith. He spoke slowly, in a heavily accented English that was not easy to understand. Even more difficult to comprehend was the message he was relaying; which went something like this: When you die the Angel Gabriel will come and knock on your grave and ask you three questions which you must answer correctly in order to enter heaven. The first question is, "What sect of the Islamic faith do you belong to?" I don't remember the next two questions. About the status of men and women he had this to say: A good Muslim man will spend eternity with Allah, a bad Muslim man will only get to see Allah on Friday, the holy day. A good Muslim woman will get to see Allah once a year during a special Eid (holiday). Non-Muslims and "bad" Muslim women would be denied the sight of Allah. He described "bad" Muslim women as those who expose their ankles through a hole in their stocking or prostitutes. They are one and the same. When this lesson was over he said he would return the following day with further instructions in Islam.

After he left, Judy and I sat alone under the fig tree and discussed this amazing event. We wondered whether the reason for the lesson in Islam was that the guards had wanted to "cleanse" us of our "Jewishness" before touching us. We were now more terrorized. We believed that in time they would rape and kill us and that no one would ever find out what happened to us.

That evening we watched again as the guards ate and drank and again invited us to join them. We politely declined, and they laughed at us. They proceeded to get quite drunk once again and soon all were asleep, even the one who had been assigned to guard the camp. Judy and I stayed awake and discussed our options. We remembered that we both could speak Pig Latin "eryvay astfay." We now had a secret language that we could use and we knew "eythay ouldway otnay underay andstay!" We decided that we would try to sneak back across the border into Turkey. We hadn't driven very far and we could see the lights of the Turkish town from where we sat. The guards were heavily armed and there was also a machine gun on a swivel-tripod that faced the Turkish side of the border. We assumed it had a long firing range, and that if they woke up and saw us escaping to Turkey, they would very likely shoot us. In fantasy, we contemplated the possibility of spinning the machine gun around and shooting them all as they lay drunk and sleeping. Reason prevailed and this option was ruled out, not because we felt badly about the thought of their demise, but because neither of us knew anything at all about machine guns! We were afraid they would wake up, see us struggling with the gun and use that as a good justification to kill us. So we settled on an escape by foot and planned to go the following evening. Knowing that Judy could definitely out do them all in alcohol consumption, we thought we would encourage them to get really drunk by agreeing to drink with them. Then when we were sure they were all soundly asleep, we would sneak away and, very quietly walk back to Turkey. We wouldn't even try to locate and reclaim our passports or belongings. We knew that the Turkish border guards would recognize us, their gin rummy partners, and that they would let us cross the border. Once safely back in Turkey we would inquire about what happened to Paul.

At mid-morning on our third day in Syria, "escape day," the English speaking guard brought us a melon. I was sitting on the ground and he rolled it over to me with a sneer, saying, "Here, you can have this." It landed by my leg; I replied sarcastically, "And just *how* am I supposed to eat this?" Whereupon, he took out a knife and threw it at me. From a distance of about 10-12 feet, it landed right in the middle of the melon, just inches from my thigh. I was trembling inside and the thought of that sharp blade so close made my entire leg feel like mush. I tried calming myself by talking to Judy in Pig Latin and he became irate, saying, "I knew you were Jewish! I hear you speaking Hebrew!"

Later, in the afternoon, the Mullah returned to continue our lessons on Islam. We pretended to be interested, and became noticeably friendlier. The guards were pleased and soon began offering us food and alcoholic drinks. This time we accepted and "the party" began. We laughed and ate and drank and all of us, Judy and I and the guards, were so caught up in the moment that we failed to notice a tourist bus driving from the Turkish border in the direction of our border post until it was only thirty or forty yards away. Once we spotted it however, Judy and I immediately jumped up and ran toward it. We knew the guards would not shoot us in front of all these witnesses. The bus driver saw us coming and quickly let us aboard. Breathless and almost in hysteria, we told him and the bus full of amazed Austrian college students our situation. Instantly we were saved. The Austrians were on their way to Iraq to participate in an archeological dig and had entered Syria on a transit visa.

They met with the guards and demanded our belongings back and the return of our friend, Paul, explaining that they would otherwise contact authorities. The English speaking guard then stated that they were only trying to "help" us and that of course they would find Paul and bring him to us in the morning. The Austrians camped with us at the border post that night. We ate bread and cheese and drank cold soda, and I was able to enjoy a cigarette and relax around their campfire. We had no camping gear, so they formed a circle around us and we all simply fell asleep on the ground. I was relieved and exhausted but lay awake for quite some time viewing a beautiful night sky with a million stars to enjoy.

In the morning a couple of the guards drove off and returned a short while later with Paul. He had been held in the nearby village and was told he had illegally entered the country since he had no visa. He was told that his passport was sent to Aleppo to get the appropriate visa and that he should be patient. Our backpacks and passports were finally returned, but when I searched through my pack I realized my camera was gone. Now suddenly quite furious, I demanded my camera be returned! An hour later after another trip into the nearby village they returned my camera saying they had only wanted to "borrow" it.

The Austrians offered to drive us back to Turkey but the Syrian guards said if they left Syria, having already used their entrance visa, they would not be allowed back in. Since they were on their way to Iraq they could not give up their entrance visa. We asked them to just wait at the border to "protect our back" while we walked the mile or so across that open stretch of desert into Turkey.

And indeed, the Turkish border guards were happy to see us, albeit surprised and puzzled by our quick return. But since they spoke no English and we spoke no Turkish we had no way to explain what happened.

As we relaxed with our old smiling friends, we felt once again safe, while at the same time discussing our next route. I was genuinely excited to start a new adventure, exploring places I knew nothing about. And yes, I was sort of patting myself on the back saying, "Ruthann, you've come a long way from that little farm in Hortonville, Wisconsin!"

Turkish border guard with Paul, Judy and me

Even the three terrifying days in Syria did not alter my desire to keep going on to new and exotic places. Where did this deep passion come from? Good question, and I think the answer is: I was born this way. It must be in my genes from somewhere, inherited from ancestors. So to write this story I need to start back before I was even born.

CHAPTER 2

RULE # 2: Keep a Journal

A journal is not a simple diary, it includes major events in one's life, but more importantly, it is a time for self-reflection and goal-setting. Keep track of where you have been and what you are thinking, then plan ahead and stay focused, in order to get where you want to go. Too many people rarely "lead" their life, they mostly just let it happen.

MY ANCESTORS

I had always wanted to travel. I read of past adventurers like Sir Richard Burton and Gertrude Bell and Freya Stark. They were my idols and I worried that the earth would have no exotic places left for me to explore in my century. How easy it would have been, I thought, to have a real adventure in the 1800s and earlier. Back then every country visited would have been exotic. I imagined that the Dutch would still have worn wooden shoes, Hawaiians would have worn grass skirts and danced the hula for celebrations, the Swiss would have yodeled and the Japanese still would have had Samurai warriors. In my coming of age during the 1960s it seemed that much of the planet had become "Americanized." I had spent eight months backpacking around Europe and thought that although it was beautiful and enchanting, it was neither exotic nor entirely "authentic" anymore. For example, while walking down a country road above the Arctic Circle in Norway I passed a little farmhouse where I could clearly hear a recording of Johnny Cash singing "Ring of Fire." At a flea market in Barcelona, the hottest item turned out to be the American Levis I was wearing. All the teens wanted my jeans.

My parents were always amazed at my desire to see the world. My mom would laughingly ask, "Where did you come from?

We are farmers, not adventurers!" But I knew that given the opportunity, she would have loved to travel. And I also realized that my ancestors had to have been even more adventurous than me, after all they had left the country of their birth, everything they knew and loved, and moved to America knowing they would never see their homeland again.

I didn't get to know many of my grandparents or great grandparents on a personal level. Whatever understanding I have of them comes from stories told to me. I have no way to verify these stories since no one from their generation is still living. The lives of my ancestors have always been of interest to me, and I consider them part of my life, a part of who I am.

SCHULZ FAMILY

By the time I was born, my grandparents were all deceased except for my mother's father, William Schulz. He was seemingly easy going, and always upbeat. He would come out to our farm about once a week, usually on a Monday, and talk to Mom as she was doing laundry using the ringer washing machine. This was an all morning project so they had lots of time to talk. While there he would get worms for fishing. I liked helping him because I knew where the big ones were, and Grandpa was always complimentary about my worm finding abilities. Grandpa was a huge baseball fan. In his youth he played, and later coached his sons, Donald and Mert, in the "Cow Pasture Leagues." He loved the Milwaukee Braves and would drive to Milwaukee at least once each summer to watch a game. Before the Braves came to Wisconsin he was a Cubs fan and back in the 1930s he and my grandmother would go to Chicago on occasion to watch the Cubs play.

Sadie Amelia Raprager was my grandmother, my mother's mother. She was born on December 8, 1889 to Caroline Abraham Raprager and Fred Raprager in the township of Dale, Wisconsin. Caroline and Fred were both second generation German immigrants and German was the language spoken in their home. They owned a prosperous dairy farm, large enough to require

Fred and Caroline,
my great-grandparents

Sadie Amelia

hired help in the summers. Caroline was an excellent seamstress and at one time sewed dresses professionally. Sadie also was a good seamstress, but she much preferred to work outside in the fields, in the barn, or in the garden. The Rapragers were a serious, soft spoken, hardworking family. Sadie was the oldest child, followed by her brother Vernon who was one year younger. When Sadie was 21 years old she fell in love with my grandfather, William Schulz, who was a hired hand on her father's farm at the time. Will, as he was known, was one of eight children of Wilhelm Schulz and Hannah Korth Schulz.

The Schulz's were also German immigrants and German was the first language spoken in their home, but they were the opposite of the Rapragers in terms of lifestyle. The Schulz's were loud, fun-loving, and liked to joke around. It was a characteristic that Sadie really enjoyed in Will. They were married on April 28, 1910 in a little Lutheran church in Hortonville, Wisconsin. The ceremony was in German. Their first years together were spent on the Raprager farm, and they had two sons during this time, Donald and Merton. Also, during this time Will went to Madison to study cheese-making at the University. Upon completing the course, he moved with his family to Stanley, Wisconsin to operate a cheese factory. After a short period an opening became available at a cheese factory a few miles from the Raprager farm, so they moved there. The property contained a home and a cheese factory, and it was in that home that my mother, Anita, and her brother Arlyn were born. Shortly after World War I, cheese factories became fewer and fewer, replaced by "condensories." Higher prices were offered for condensed milk than for cheese. This trend caused the Wm. Schulz Cheese Factory to close. The phenomenon of the condensories did not remain widespread as they made demands on the farmers regarding milk temperatures, building milk houses, and so forth. Eventually farmers went back to selling their milk to the many cheese factories in each area. At that time, it was quite common to find a cheese factory as well as a schoolhouse every two or three miles in the rural areas.

Will and Sadie's wedding

A farm about one half mile north of the factory location was available and purchased by Will and Sadie. Sadie was not just a housewife, but a partner to Will with the farm work. She kept a large garden that the children helped with. Included in this were three acres of beans that were sold as a cash crop and ten acres of potatoes that were harvested and stored for family use in the winter. She never wore pants, only dresses, and never learned to drive, but she helped with all the manual labor on the farm including milking the cows. Once a cow kicked her in the breast, causing an injury that took months to heal. Some years later she was diagnosed with breast cancer, and she always insisted this was the result of the earlier injury. Mom and my dad moved in with her parents so she could take care of her mother at the time. It was a difficult time since Sadie was in a great deal of pain and there was not a lot my mother could do to help her. She died of breast cancer in 1940 at the age of fifty. It was a terrible loss to my mother, who was only twenty-three years old at the time and a new mother herself.

Grandpa Schulz, the prankster, on the right

ZIMMER FAMILY

Dad's mother died of the "war flu" in 1918 when he was only three years old so he never got to know her. Her name was Carrie Carpenter. She was twenty-five years old when she married Wilbur Zimmer, my grandfather. He owned and operated a silo building company at the time and was a man of some wealth. He bought his new wife a surrey with fringe on top, which was the

Wedding of Wilbur Zimmer and Carrie Carpenter, seated

subject of much talk in the village of Hortonville. They lived on a small farm, less than a mile from the Carpenter family farm where she had been born. They had two sons, my father, Floyd, and his brother Lavern. She was pregnant with her third child when she fell ill with the flu. Following her death, her sister Flavilla helped raise Floyd and Lavern. Wilbur mourned her death for many years while continuing to build silos around the state. When my father was fifteen years old, Wilbur married Flavilla and so Dad's aunt became his step-mother and the woman I knew as "Grandma." Flavilla and Wilbur had two children together, my aunts, Pearl and Grace.

Wilbur, my grandfather, was an interesting character. He liked to hunt and fish and didn't always follow the law. He was the oldest of eight children, a second generation German immigrant who learned to speak English only after he started school. His father, August Zimmer, emigrated from Stettin, Germany as a young man. He had grown up in a Jewish ghetto of Stettin and was working as a farm hand, picking apples. As a worker he was not allowed to eat any of the apples, not even those that fell on the ground since the farmer wanted those reserved to feed his pigs. When August had saved enough money, $40 , for the passage to America, he left the apple farm. He went down to the shipyards and the night before the ship left, while sleeping in a bunk bed with his money hidden under his mattress, he was stabbed by a would be robber. Fortunately, the wound was not serious and the robber was prevented from stealing his money. The next morning August sailed for America and landed at Ellis Island in the late 1870s. He worked in New York for some time, then Pennsylvania, before making his way to Wisconsin. He eventually was able to save enough money to bring his brothers, sisters, and parents to America. He married Anna Staedt, bought a farm in Appleton, Wisconsin and raised his eight children.

Since Wilbur was the oldest, he struck out on his own and got into the silo building business, eventually owning his own company and building silos all over the state of Wisconsin. It is with pride that I can still find some of these little cement silos

Silo Building

with the initials "WZ" written in the cement. Tragically, my grandfather eventually lost his business when a man on one of his work crews fell to his death from a silo under construction. He had no insurance and the lawsuit that followed put him out of business. In 1933 at the age of forty-five he was diagnosed with colon cancer. He lived another five years, some of it in a wheel chair with a chamber pot underneath since he could no longer control his bowel movements. In the first years following his diagnosis he went to different parts of the United States, including Hot Springs, Arkansas, seeking a cure. He died in January 1939, just two months after my parent's marriage.

MY PARENTS

In 1938, she was as happy as she had ever been. It was sunny and unseasonably warm. It was a perfect autumn, a true "Indian summer," and the day of her wedding, October 29th, was no exception. My mother, Anita June Schulz, was about to marry my father, Floyd Ethan Zimmer. Her family were fun loving, easy going folks who valued their recreational time as much as their farm work. They were Lutherans, but only somewhat serious about their religion. His family were of Jewish ancestry but practiced the various Christian religions they had married into. Dad was raised pretty much without religion, though his mother's side of the family was Baptist and they did go to church a few times a year. The Zimmers were more serious and valued hard work more than leisure time. Recreation for the Zimmer family involved practical things like hunting and fishing for food, and entering cattle in the local and State Fair to earn money and recognition. Recreation for the Schulz family involved music and dancing and summer

Dad and Mom, 1937

Dad and Mom on their wedding day

baseball leagues. Dad and his brother Lavern had a bit of "prankster" in them and it was a characteristic that Mom enjoyed. Dad could always make her laugh. Early on their wedding day he appeared at her parents' house, standing at the base of the stairs stomping and dragging his right foot like a bull ready to charge. It was a memory that continued to bring a smile to Mom's face throughout her life.

Mom and Dad's Wedding Picture, October 29, 1938

Floyd and Anita Zimmer welcomed me, their third daughter, into the world on August 22, 1943. Their first child, June, was born in 1939 and then Audrey, their second child, was born in 1941. Since my father was a dairy farmer, he really wanted a son. The story goes that old Doc Towne walked out the back door of the hospital the night I was born rather than face my dad with the news of another daughter. Fortunately for all of us, a year later my brother Gary was born. That should have been the end of it, but after five years mother gave birth to their fifth and last child, my sister Jane. They were very busy with the farm by the time Jane was born so there are no professional baby pictures with her. Mother once told me that she cried when she found out she was pregnant with Jane and cried again after Jane was born to think that she had ever regretted the pregnancy.

My father indulged in few leisure activities, and these became our main pleasures as children. He loved horses, and he liked to hunt, especially raccoon with his coon dogs. He also enjoyed the annual deer hunting ritual with his uncles and cousins. As soon as we were old enough, we joined in on the hunts. Coon hunting was my favorite. It gave me a chance to prove I was tough and had stamina. Coon hunting took place at night since raccoons are nocturnal animals. It meant piling into the pickup truck with the dogs, driving to some prospective good hunting spot, preferably to woods, near a cornfield. We would then turn the dogs loose and listen for their bark. Dad could tell the difference between each dog's bark. He knew the type of bark each had when they were on the trail of a raccoon. We all recognized the sound of that loud wolf-like howl when the dogs had treed a coon. At that point we would be running through the fields, over fences, into the woods and under branches and through brush until we reached the tree the dogs barked at. Most times we ran in the dark or the light of the moon. Dad carried a flashlight and a pistol. When spotted, the raccoon would be shot and bagged. The dogs were then off to find another raccoon. This procedure would be repeated, sometimes for hours. Audrey, Gary, Jane, and I were the ones who accompanied Dad on these coon hunts. I don't think Mom or June ever went along. Mom did have the task of roasting the coon meat and I remember it was a difficult job. All the fat had to be scraped off the meat before it was roasted. I do not know what spices mother used or the roasting process, but when done using her methods the raccoon meat was delicious.

Since Dad loved horses, they also became a major part of our entertainment. Besides pleasure riding, we participated in rodeo events, with Gary winning a number of trophies. Dad had buggies and fancy carriages and cutters and wagons and harnesses of varying types that he could use to hitch the horses up and participate in local parades or give a bride and groom a ride to the church, or just give people rides around the farm. I remember as an adult, one winter when I came home for a visit. I was living in Saudi Arabia at the time and was used to hot weather and desert scenery. I returned to temperatures below zero and fields and roads covered with snow. Dad and his friend, Melvin, were hitching horses to a sleigh Dad had acquired. They were so happy with their new "toy" and insisted on giving me a ride down country roads and over fields. It was a beautiful and romantic view of what Wisconsin must have been like a century before and I enjoyed every moment of it, even though I was so cold the feeling had crossed the line into one of pain.

My first birthday

An absolute joy of my father's was the county fair each summer. He had participated in the fairs throughout his childhood. His uncle, Charles Carpenter, was an avid dairyman. He raised purebred Holsteins and was a long time member and sometime officer in the Wisconsin Dairymen's Association. Together my dad and his uncle entered livestock in the judging competitions at the local

June, Audrey, me and Gary, 1945

fairs and the State Fair and prided themselves on the many blue ribbons they earned. Since Dad enjoyed it so much, from an early age each of us joined the local 4-H club and participated in the county fair. We each entered our Holstein calves, heifers, and cows at the fair and since Dad knew how to pick a winner, we expected and received many blue ribbons and even some grand championships.

Dad also took pleasure in playing cards, specifically the game of Sheepshead, with family and friends throughout his life. The game was played with pennies as "bets." Each player carried a bag of pennies to the card games. My Dad loved the game, but I think my mom loved it even more.

My mother was quite the opposite of my father. He was tall with thick dark curly hair and dark brown eyes. She was short with soft light brown hair and hazel eyes. She loved music, literature, movies, and dancing. And she loved to travel, though she didn't get to go far until her later years. Mom was a romantic and remained madly in love with my dad throughout her life. She kept a diary

Gary and Dad. coon hunting

Dad and his horses

in her teenage years and it was stored in the attic. I discovered it one day when I was about twelve, and read it many times in secret. I loved the description of her encounters with Dad, before they actually started dating. She would write an entire page about just seeing him from a distance, more if he actually saw her and waved or something. She plotted ways to see him, including dating his cousin! At the age of sixteen she fancied herself in love with him though they didn't actually start dating until she was eighteen. Dad was shy around women and admitted later in life that had she not "chased" after him, he would never have noticed her. He also stated he "got the better half of the deal" and could not imagine his life without her.

Mom was raised on a farm but had three brothers so she never did much of the actual farm chores. Instead, she helped her mother with the usual household chores of cooking, cleaning, and sewing. For pleasure, she played the piano and a mandolin,

Me and my holstein heifer, Ruby, ready for the fair

and she read. School was enjoyable to her and she had thought of becoming a teacher.

She was the calm one in our family, easy going and patient. I never really saw her angry. She was always able to control her emotions, unlike my father who was prone to emotional outbursts. Along with this, he was a worrier, she was not; he had high blood pressure, she did not; he had ulcers, she did not. I never really saw my mother cry, but I saw my father cry on a number of occasions, and each time it had a very long-lived effect on me. Once when I was around ten years old I walked into the barn to see my father sitting on the floor next to my cow, Star. When he saw me he just burst into tears, apologizing for being unable to save Star's newborn calf that he knew I had been anxiously awaiting. I tried to assure him that it was okay, but he continued to cry and berate himself. When I walked out of the barn that night I stood in the yard, staring up at a billion stars, and swore I would never again have feelings for an animal. At that moment I didn't care about Star or her stillborn calf, I only cared about my Dad.

Another story, one I often told whenever I wanted to describe my parents' characteristics to someone, was that of my maternal grandfather, Will Schulz's funeral. I was a freshman in college and returned home for the funeral. Grandpa had died of cancer at the age of seventy-four. My dad wept openly during the funeral service, my mom was dry eyed, and this was for her father, not his. Mother was not one to cry easily. The opposite was true for my father; he was very emotional. In this regard I take after my father, in most other ways I am more like my mother.

CHAPTER 3

RULE # 3: Practice Empathy

Practice empathy; every day, with everyone.

WISCONSIN CHILDHOOD

Mine was a happy childhood, confined to the small world of my parents' farm in rural Wisconsin. Though I was born in 1943, life really began for me in 1947, the time of my first significant memories. We lived in an old farm house along Highway 45 between the city of Appleton and the village of Greenville. We had electricity and a telephone, but no indoor plumbing. I remember the scary trips to the outhouse at night because there were sometimes stray dogs in the yard and I could see their eyes in the dark. Dad was renting the farm and raising some cash crops like peas and sweet corn, for the local canning factory. He also milked a few cows and worked part time at the Farmer's Co-op in Greenville.

My earliest memory was when my father's grandfather, August Zimmer, died in early spring of 1947. I was about three and a half years old. I remember him only as a "white" man —white hair, white clothes, white skin, lying in a bed of white sheets. My parents went to the funeral and left my sisters, brother, and me with a neighbor lady. As a "treat" I got to take a nap in my parents' bed that afternoon. At some point I must have fallen out of bed knocking over a water glass on the side table and cutting my left leg in a deep semi-circular gash. I remember riding to the hospital with Dr. Towne, his black bag beside him; being wheeled around on a table covered with colored "wrapping paper," seeing large bottles filled with orange liquid, smelling odors of "medicine," and having a funnel placed on my face. I felt sick and "saw" my vomit going down into that funnel, deeper and deeper. When I awoke, my parents were there and my dad carried me out of the room. At home my sisters, June and Audrey, wheeled me around in a big baby buggy. When the twenty-eight stitches were finally removed and I could walk again, I had a large semicircular scar on my leg, with little dots along the sides where the stitches had been. It is still very much visible today.

My dad's sisters, Pearl and Grace, would babysit us sometimes when my parents went out for the evening. Pearl was tall, thin, and beautiful, with long dark hair and big dark eyes. When she babysat she paid little attention to us. She liked to read and listen to baseball games on the radio. She would sit right next to the radio, with her ear close to it so as not to miss a word. Grace was a year younger than Pearl and they were opposites in every way. Grace had short curly hair and a round, plump face and wore thick glasses. She was shy and fearful, yet had a wonderful sense of humor and was very playful. We loved it when she would come because she would spend the evening playing games with us. She was terrified of storms, so whenever there was thunder and lightning she would make us all climb in bed together, with her in the middle, and we would cover up and hide. We followed this same routine whenever she heard any unfamiliar noises in the yard.

Aunt Pearl graduated from Hortonville High School in May of 1947. She was the salutatorian of her class, bright and beautiful and ready to take on the world. A week later she was dead. I was not yet four years old but I clearly remember the day she died. A car drove into our driveway and a man got out and spoke softly to my mom and dad. They hurried us into the family car and we drove down the road to a place where the railroad track crossed the road. Dad stopped the car, and leaving us there, walked down the train tracks toward some people gathered next to a big white sheet on the ground. He didn't come back and after a while Mom drove us over to Grandma's house. There were a lot of people there and we overheard them saying that Pearl was dead. My brother Gary and I did not understand what "dead" meant.

When Dad finally arrived to drive us all home, Gary and I started singing a song we made up about "Pearl is Dead, Pearl is Dead." Dad stopped the car, and got out and spanked us! We were totally shocked, this was the one and only spanking I ever received and I knew then that there was something bad about "dead." Pearl had been driving the family tractor from one field to another and when she crossed the railroad tracks she had been hit by a train. The funeral took place in the living room of Grandma's house. The shades were all pulled and people sat in silence except for the sobbing around the closed casket.

There are some memories that seem to have been "always there." I can't remember life without them. I loved the color yellow and three was my favorite number. I preferred odd numbers not even, left not right, west not east, autumn not spring, water not milk, brown not black, bugs and birds not bunnies and squirrels, sheep not cows, early mornings not late nights, and hot not cold. I don't know why, I think I was just born this way. These preferences remain with me to this day.

Another ever-present childhood memory is of my mother encouraging me to "talk slower." "Don't talk so fast, slow down so we can understand," she would say. I tried, but was probably not very successful since I've always been overly excitable and enthusiastic about life. Besides, it seemed to me that everyone in my family talked fast — and loud.

In the summer of 1947 Mom and Dad bought their own farm and we moved into a house with indoor plumbing! Mom said she thought she had "died and gone to heaven," having such a spacious, "modern" home. This farm became my whole childhood world. It was about one hundred acres of rich farmland with fifteen acres of wonderful hardwood forest. The big old farmhouse was made of sand colored bricks and had a green, shingled roof. There was a large open front porch and a closed in back porch where my mother did the laundry with her ringer washing machine. We always entered the house through the back porch which opened into the kitchen. The refrigerator, a large kitchen sink and cupboards were on the left. In the middle was a yellow and chrome kitchen table and chairs. On the right was a combination wood burning and gas stove, and a door leading down to the cellar which housed the coal burning furnace and stoker. I hated the cellar because it was cold and dark, with the occasional mouse running around. On the main floor was a formal living room, a combination family / dining room, a "play room" (which later became the master bedroom), a "sewing room" (later the T.V. room), and a bathroom. Narrow steep stairs led to the upper level with four bedrooms and a big attic.

When we first moved into the house we all slept upstairs. I had my own bedroom but I was afraid of the dark so when I went to bed Mother would leave the hall light on for me. I kept my door open and the light from the hall was enough to chase all fears away. One time however, I awoke in the night and found it was completely dark. I realized that Mother had turned the hall light off when she went to bed. I lay there in the dark and told myself that since this had probably always been the case there was nothing to worry about. After that night, I no longer needed the hall light on. Sometimes, in bed, I would close my eyes and "look" deep into the darkness until I could see millions of what looked like little "green marbles." The further in I "looked," the more of these "green marbles" there were, the path and the supply were endless. Eventually this exercise led me to a glimpse of "eternity." The feeling would sometimes terrify me, and I would then quickly open my eyes and try not to think about it. The realization that came to me was how long I would be dead, once I died. Throughout my childhood I returned to this exercise to try to understand "eternity," the scary sense of no beginning and no end. I can no longer see these "green marbles" but in the dark of night I still sometimes conjure up the realization of how long my body will be "dead." Only now I'm not sure that "I" am my body, maybe "I" am currently residing in this body, but am free to go, and one day I will.

Growing up on the farm was stereotypically Midwest, 1950s. Dad was a dairyman in every sense of the word. He loved his cows. They all had names and a family history. The size of the herd grew each year and the farm prospered. We also had pigs, chickens, sheep, cats, dogs, and horses. The animals were kept because each had a job to do. Of course we made "pets" of some of them, but we always knew they were animals serving our needs. None were ever allowed in the house.

Mom was a housewife and homemaker. She cooked big meals, all from scratch. In the summers she always had a large garden and we ate as much as we could fresh from the ground; the rest she canned or stored in the root cellar for the winter months. Grocery shopping meant buying sugar, flour, coffee and not much else. Mom was a wonderful seamstress and she made many of our clothes, but she always complained about her sewing ability and would talk about the skills of her grandmother, the professional seamstress.

Most of my memories from the farm are from the summer months. The summers were always so busy and full of life. It seemed like a new baby animal was born every day. The fields were alive with insects and birds and flowering plants. I was fascinated with insects from a very young age. I would spend my summers collecting insects and putting them in old canning jars. I would pound holes in the lids with hammer and nail so they could breathe. Mom was not a fan of insects but was very tolerant of my desire to collect as many different kinds as I could. I think that I must be one of a very few people on the planet who discovered for herself that butterflies come from caterpillars. It was a discovery made when I was about five years old and the thrill of watching that butterfly emerge from a cocoon was enough to keep me collecting and watching insects for years to come. I also was interested in all the birds that came to the farm. Dad built a purple martin house and put it on top of our windmill. He said they were great for reducing the mosquito population.

In the spring I learned where to find bird nests and I would watch over them dutifully to see the newly laid eggs, the baby birds when first hatched, and to follow their growth until they flew away. The bluebirds nested in hollow fence posts, robins in the thick Bridal's Wreath bushes by the house, cedar waxwings in the mulberry tree, and so on. Our little forest, about a quarter mile down the lane from the house, was my favorite summer retreat. My brother, Gary, and I went there often. We knew where the rabbits and squirrels were; how to find the best Mayflowers like the patches of trilliums in the shaded, damp areas; the coolest spot in the summer, the small cedar grove; and the biggest tree in the forest, a beech tree, where we carved our names in the bark.

My sisters and brother and I had daily farm chores which we had to complete each morning before school started. This involved feeding and watering the calves, sheep, chickens and pigs. Dad took care of the cows himself. In the summer the work was harder, as we helped cut, rake, and bale hay. Dad wanted me to drive the tractor during these times but I was afraid of big machinery and finally convinced him that I was strong enough to lift bales of hay. Stacking hay bales in the mow was a hot, dusty job but I preferred it to the responsibility of handling a tractor. Besides, Audrey and Gary were much better at driving tractors than I was.

June, Audrey, me, Jane and Gary
at the new farm, 1952

One of our most hated jobs was picking up stones. This involved walking behind a tractor pulled wagon, picking stones out of the field and loading them onto the wagon. We did this every year, in the same fields, and yet the following year there were always more stones to pick up! We never really took vacations since Dad had cows to milk morning and night, seven days a week. However, each summer we would spend one day at Dad's uncle's cottage on Pickerel Lake. This meant Dad would milk the cows at 4 a.m. so we could leave early for the two-hour drive to the lake. After a picnic lunch by the lake, a dip in the water, and a fishing trip in Uncle Hank's boat we would pile back in the car for the ride back to the farm for the evening milking. I loved this little adventure so much that my excitement always led to car sickness on the drive there. One year Mom and Dad decided not to tell me where we were going. That year I did not get sick until we were almost at the lake house and I recognized where we were. I had to have Dad stop the car, and I threw up as we entered the cottage driveway!

My best friend was Karen. She lived on a dairy farm about a mile and a half from us. We both started first grade at Cedar Grove School, a one-room country school for grades 1-8. There were only three students in my grade: Karen, Sonny and me. Karen and I did everything together. Sonny was a shy boy who didn't do much talking but was an important part of our little class. The three of us worked well together, we learned at the same pace and our friendly competition kept us moving ahead of expectations.

I could already read when I started school because my sisters had played school with me every night. They were the teachers and I was the student. They taught me what they learned in school so, in no time, I was reading. Dad would sit me on his lap and ask me to read parts of his newspaper and then he would compliment me on how smart I was. This was all the motivation I needed to continue my reading lessons from my sisters. When I eventually entered school, I was very excited to finally have a "real teacher." The excitement was short lived, however, when the teacher started out with the letter "A" and I realized that she would proceed at this slow pace, covering the alphabet one letter at a time. I was bored! Even the coloring assignments were uninteresting. She would hectograph a picture of a very large circle with the letters r-e-d inside and ask us to color it using the correct color. The circle was huge and the nice point on my new, red crayon was quite flattened by the time I was done. I thought that the finished product was also quite boring.

After first grade, I was never bored in school again and I have wonderful memories of the years I spent in that little schoolhouse. My desk contained my school supplies, which included a box of crayons, a few pencils, an eraser, one fountain pen, and a bottle of ink. The teacher distributed our books, paper, and one weekly "goiter pill." I hated the taste of those pills so I hid them in my unused ink well and at recess I would throw them out. Sometimes I gave my pill to Ellen. She was older than me and she loved them, she thought they tasted like chocolate. Years later I heard that these goiter pills contained large amounts of iodine and were believed to cause severe acne. Ellen had moved away by then and I wondered if it ever had that effect on her.

School started each morning with music. The teacher would play piano and we would all sing songs from The Golden Book of Songs: songs like "My Country Tis of Thee," "My Darling Clementine," "Swanee River, "Oh Shenandoah," and "Oh Suzanna." Sometimes we were taught to sing songs in harmony, like "Whispering Hope" and sometimes in rounds, like "Three Blind Mice." We would sing these songs over and over until we knew them by heart. Then we would perform them at one of the monthly PTA meetings.

The monthly PTA meetings were a major source of entertainment in our rural community. Students would make "invitations" and then children in the older grades would hand deliver them to all the residents on their walks home from school. The invitations were seasonally decorated and included a request to "bring a dish to pass." The night would start with a meeting of the adults and the teacher. We students would play outside if the weather was nice or, if not, in the basement of the school. This was followed by some "entertainment" usually planned by the teacher and performed by the students. For example, square dancing was popular. Karen's father did the calling and we did the dosey doeing! And finally, came the "potluck" supper which

Cedar Grove Elementary School: My friend, Karen, is holding the sign and I am standing to her left. We are in 1st grade. My sister, June is in the top row, 4th student in. My sister, Audrey, is in the second row, 2nd student in.

featured items like cold sandwiches, Jello salads and cookies. Erna Culbertson always brought her homemade dill pickles and everyone raved about them.

About twice a year the County Superintendent, Mr. Steffen, would visit our school. When he came he usually brought a movie projector and a movie for all of us to watch. Looking back, I can truthfully say that these movies were, at best, poorly made propaganda. Sometimes after watching them I would have nightmares for days. One was about kidnapping and it was meant to teach us not to accept rides from "strangers." I wasn't even sure what a "stranger" was; we knew all our neighbors and whenever a car drove by it would have been impolite not to wave. Another film warned of the dangers of using "dope." In this film there was a scene in which some "doper" tried to get children hooked by using needles to inject it into gum or candy and then giving these to children. I didn't understand what this "dope" was, but for years it caused me to carefully inspect all my candy and gum for little holes.

Surprisingly, the presidential election of 1952 was another school topic that was aimed at creating bias in our minds. My parents were very much pro-Taft and anti-Eisenhower, so I became accustomed to thinking of Eisenhower as the "bad guy." When our school held a mock election that fall and we all got to vote for the candidate of our choice, I could not find Taft on the ballot. The names there were Eisenhower and Stevenson. I recognized Eisenhower as the "bad guy" so I cast my vote for Stevenson. The next day the vote was counted and the teacher was shocked and seemed upset to see that Stevenson had received a vote. She wanted to know who had voted for him. I was so embarrassed, I knew I had made a terrible mistake, and I never told anyone that it was I who had cast the misbegotten ballot. As I grew older, I came to realize that mine was indeed a very Republican community. The John Birch Society originated in my county and Senator Joe McCarthy was born in the same hospital as I.

Cedar Grove was a small white school house in the country, set on about two acres of land with a grove of cedar trees on one end. Placed among the trees was a swing set. Between the cedar trees and the schoolhouse was a baseball diamond with a merry-go-round off to one side. We played many games and took full advantage of our available resources. In the fall and spring we played softball, and even had competing games with neighboring one-room country schools. Every student participated since we only had about twenty to twenty-four students in 1st through 8th grade. (There was no kindergarten.) A home run was a ball hit over the swing set into the cedar trees. We also played "ante ante over," each team trying to throw a ball up and over the schoolhouse to the team on the other side.

In the winter we would ice skate on Melvin Loudon's farm which was across the road from the school. He would shovel the snow off the natural pond that formed there and we would skate during recess and play games like "crack the whip." The other favorite winter game was "fox and goose." We would make a big circular track with spokes, like a wheel, in the snow and someone would be the "fox" and the rest the "geese." The fox would chase the geese around the track, and when caught, that goose would have to become the fox and begin the chase. We also would slide down the deep ditches along the school property, on our butts in the snow. Once my underclothes turned blue because my snowsuit got so wet that the dye ran.

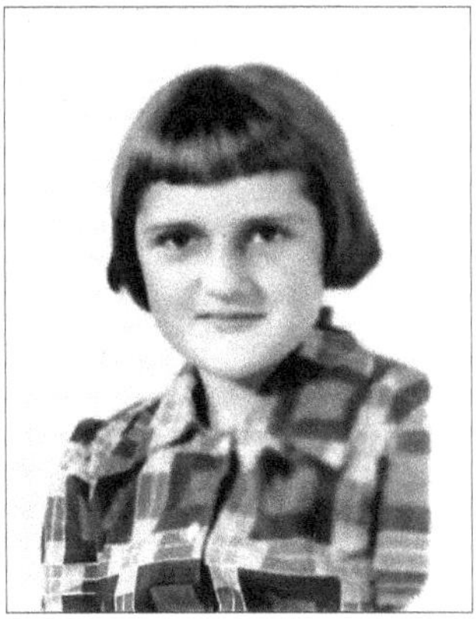

Me, 11 years old

I had six different teachers in those eight years of school, and I remember them all. I remember the last three best, probably because I was older by then. Mrs. BF was my 5th grade teacher. She was a pretty, rather large woman, with a great smile. She had black hair and blue eyes and a smooth, white complexion. She was very strict, but I liked her. I liked order in my life and she was very good at maintaining an organized and quiet learning environment. Some of her disciplinary methods were certainly unique: if she caught a student chewing gum she would make the culprit stand over a waste basket, stick out his or her tongue with the gum attached, and then, using a ruler, she would swat the gum off the tongue and into the waste basket! I never chewed gum in school and to this day I really don't care much for it. If a student got out of his or her seat without permission, the offender would be tied to the desk with crepe paper streamers, finished off with a great big bow. I never disobeyed Mrs. BF, neither did any of my siblings or my friend Karen.

My dad was on the school board, as was Karen's dad. Their job was to interview and hire teachers, and fire them if necessary. They both really liked Mrs. BF and her ability to keep order in the school. Nobody seemed to mind her unusual discipline strategies. At the end of the year she left, pregnant with her first child. I think this was the year I started wondering about how babies were made. On the farm I saw many animals give birth, saw cows and dogs and cats mate but never transferred that information to humans. I decided to ask my friend Karen since she was very smart and knew so much. She told me that a boy pinches a girl on the butt and that's how they get pregnant. I didn't want to appear ignorant so I told her, "Yes, that's what I thought." A few months later my cute sister Audrey was helping to decorate the school Christmas tree by standing on top a ladder. One of the boys came up and pinched her on the butt! I was shocked but my sister didn't seem concerned, only angry with the boy, so I thought it must be okay.

The next year, in 6th grade, I had old Miss K and she was a crank! None of the students liked her. She was always grumpy and scowling. She would yell and kick things over to maintain order, but the louder and angrier she was, the more unruly we all became. She was fired at the end of the year, and died two months later of a brain tumor. We all felt bad then.

In 7th and 8th grade we had Mrs. AT as our teacher. She was young, probably only twenty years old and right out of County Normal School, a two-year teacher education program. She was pretty and lively and we all really liked her. Our parents feared she was too interested in the arts, not strict enough and not teaching us enough, but all twenty-four students in grades 1-8 loved her. She played ball with us at recess and sometimes, on nice warm days, our recess periods stretched a bit longer than they were supposed to. She taught us to jitterbug to Elvis Presley's "Blue Suede Shoes," and once, for the PTA, she performed a dance in the dark to "Glow Little Glow Worm," dressed in a tight leotard jump suit with fluorescent caterpillar-like painted stripes! We all loved it; the parents were shocked!

For science class we went on nature hikes and in the winter we tracked animals, learning their track marks, and we found field mice and their underground homes. We took old telephones apart to see how they worked. We learned to identify birds by their songs. We studied constellations and the night skies of the seasons. When Karen and Sonny and I graduated from 8th grade Mrs. AT gave us each a dictionary. I still have mine.

I loved reading and was always very excited when the book mobile visited our school. I made my choices carefully, trying to pick books from different categories and subject matter. When I learned that "fiction" meant they weren't "true," that these were stories that people just "made up," I switched entirely to non-fiction. Science, history, and the geography of people and places became my reading genre. Early on I dreamed of seeing the world. From the stories I read I wanted to live like "Pedro" on the Amazon River, with his pet parrot and monkey, or like Hassan, traveling by camel from village to village across vast stretches of desert. Sometimes I imagined myself a doctor in Africa, able to cure dreaded illnesses.

One day Dad came home with a Sylvania television. He had traded in his old Buick for the TV, and it was the first one in our area. It was a large, blonde console model that nearly filled the little sewing room at the open end of our family room. This purchase was a real hit with the neighbors and relatives who would regularly fill the TV viewing area on Saturday nights. There was only one channel and it carried programming from Green Bay. A test pattern would be visible until 4 p.m. and then Cowboy Theater came on. My siblings and I loved to watch this when we came home from school and we soon became familiar with many of the famous cowboys: Roy Rogers, Gene Autry, Hopalong Cassidy, and the Lone Ranger. Week night programming ended at 8 p.m. when the station signed off with a solemn and martial rendition of the National Anthem. On weekends there was always a feature movie on "The Late Show," which started at 8 p.m. This was past our bedtime but, on occasion, we were allowed to stay up and watch it together with the small crowd of whichever neighbors had come over for that evening's entertainment. About twice a year the TV would quit working and Mom would have to call "the TV man" to come out and replace some of the tubes in the back. Within a few years, programming had greatly expanded and most of our friends and family then purchased their own televisions, and so the social weekend gatherings came to an end.

My sister, Jane, was born when I was six years old and this

event changed my childhood more than any other. I cared for her, worried about her, played with her, and told her endless bedtime stories. Mother was busy helping Dad with the farm work and so, in many ways, Jane became my "charge." We played with Jane's many dolls, each with names and individual characters that we gave them. We played with baby kittens, carrying them around in a bushel basket. I tried to get Jane to love insects as I did, but was never successful, not even with butterflies. We played "spying games" and I taught her to speak Pig Latin so we could have a secret language. I also taught her to read and when she was three years old she would sometimes accompany me to school. I loved those days. The teacher would put a little chair next to my desk and Jane would stay there by my side. She quickly became the "teacher's pet." Jane had a beautiful singing voice, like my older sister June, so from an early age Jane would often sing for everyone at the PTA meetings. Her rendition of "I Saw Mommy Kissing Santa Claus" was the smash hit at the Christmas Program one year.

I have always loved music but had no musical talent. We had an old player piano that my siblings and I liked. We had many rolls of player piano music that were inserted into the piano and then we would pump away with our feet while the piano played "The Tennessee Waltz" or "Pittsburgh, Pennsylvania." When I was about nine years old I asked my mother to teach me how to play the piano, but instead, I was given a red piano accordion and lessons from some old man in Hortonville. Because Dad loved piano accordion music, off I went to learn this instrument. June always came along and would sit in the back of the room while I had my lesson. In no time at all she had learned how to play. I, on the other hand, struggled with this instrument that I didn't care for. It was heavy and cumbersome and the straps were painful on my summer sunburned shoulders. Yet somehow, by the middle of the next school year I had learned to play the "Julida Polka" and made my father proud by playing it for the parents at one of those PTA meetings.

One summer Mom drove June, Audrey, Gary, and me to

Appleton's Erb Park for swim lessons. This was a huge event for us. I didn't know anyone who knew how to swim, so the idea of swimming lessons was both exciting and scary. Unfortunately, the summer lessons were only three weeks long and in that time none of us learned to swim. The following summer the pool was closed due to the nation-wide polio outbreak. I did not learn to swim until my college years when it was a requirement for graduation.

Birthdays were a big deal in my family. Mom baked a cake from scratch and decorated it. "Company" always came in the evening after milking time, around 7 p.m. The company was usually Dad's aunt and uncle, or some of his cousins and their families. The adults played Sheepshead for pennies, and the children watched. Cake and ice cream followed. Holidays were also ritually celebrated. For Halloween we would dress in Mom-made costumes, and trick-or-treated at the neighbors' farms along our country road. The Thanksgiving feast rotated among our house, Uncle Lavern's house, and Grandma and Grace's house. It was always roasted turkey with all the fixings and pumpkin pies. This was also the week of deer hunting so the men would hunt from daybreak until sundown, except for Thanksgiving Day when they spent the afternoon eating. Christmas involved decorating a tree that Dad had cut from our woods. On Christmas morning we would wake up early to run downstairs to see what gifts we got. The presents were all there under the tree, unwrapped, and located in individual places so that we each knew which gifts belonged to whom. As we laughed and shouted and marveled at what each of us got, Mom and Dad would be out in the barn milking cows. They had stayed up late, assembling the toys and organizing the presents, but they never got the pleasure of seeing our initial reactions. There are a few gifts I remember most from my childhood: a little wooden cupboard that Dad made for me (I still have it), the matching pajamas that Mom sewed for me and my doll, and my parakeet, Pretty Bert. This parakeet brought me great joy. I taught it to sit on my head, eat seeds from my hand, and go back in its cage when I held out its perch.

Easter was a time for new clothes, pretty dresses and Easter bonnets, and also the knowledge that spring was imminent. On May Day we would pick wild flowers from our woods and secretly place a basket on some neighbor's porch. Memorial Day marked the end of the school year and was celebrated with a picnic, always a much anticipated event. The parents would play softball with the children, hot dogs and hamburgers were grilled, and soda pop was served. This was my only bottle of soda each year, so I always had a hard time choosing which flavor to take. One year it snowed on Memorial Day and we had to bring our picnic indoors. I remember being terribly disappointed and telling myself that when I grew up I was going to live someplace where it never snowed.

Our family did not customarily visit doctors or dentists unless there was a serious problem. When it did become necessary to go to the dentist we went to Dr. Grimes in the village of Dale. These were painful visits of old-fashioned slow drills and no novocaine. Consequently we much preferred to deal with toothaches by putting a dab of vanilla on a small cotton swab, stuffing it in the painful cavity and hoping that by numbing the pain, we would resolve the problem. Cuts and scrapes were treated by Mom with iodine and a gauze bandage, and stomach aches with a variety of home remedies such as warm water with ginger or blackberry juice. In later years we were given Pepto-Bismol. For colds and sore throats we drank a concoction of hot lemon juice and honey, and of course there was ample use of Vick's Vapor Rub.

One summer while playing on our swing, which Dad had hung from a big maple tree in the yard, Audrey broke her arm. She broke the humerus bone which required a complicated cast and an extended hospital stay. The hospital was in New London, about eight miles from the farm. June stayed at the hospital with Audrey to keep her company. June was ten years old at the time, and Audrey was eight. Mother tried to visit every day, but with three other children at home, including a three month old baby, and all the summer farm work to do, this was not always possible. Audrey remained in the hospital for over a month. There was no health insurance; the bill was simply paid off in small monthly payments over the course of many years.

We belonged to the Emmanual Lutheran Church of Greenville. It was a small brown brick church, just a few miles from our farm. We, that is Mom and us children, attended this church on a fairly regular basis. Dad came only for the Christmas Eve service or for special events like weddings and funerals. The Christmas Eve service was my favorite; we got to sing beautiful songs and recite our verses in front of the whole congregation, for which we were each rewarded with a large brown paper bag filled with peanuts, some candy, one orange and one apple.

I remember the church well: the scenes in the stained glass windows of Jesus and the disciples and the Virgin Mary; the high peach colored ceiling; the balcony where, as we got older, I sat together with my classmates and where the organ was located; the well-worn hymnals (with the most musically displeasing songs imaginable,) and the Rev. S who conducted the weekly service in a repetitive format filled with memorized creeds and dispassionate clichés. After a few years of attending these weekly services, I believed that any member of the congregation could have taken over for Rev. S and carried it on, word for word. Almost nothing in those messages seemed acceptable to me.

The Lutheran Church of the 1950s was exclusionary and seemed to me to be filled with fear and hatred. God the Father, was nothing like my father. Punishment for a wrongdoing was not a scolding, or even a spanking, but a threat of eternal fire in hell. To me, this God the Father sounded very mean and very angry. Jesus the Son, was much kinder and I tried to take his message of love and compassion and empathy to heart. The fact that it was God the Father's "will" that Jesus the Son be crucified, disgusted me further. This was certainly no loving father! And finally, there was this Holy Ghost, who never made any sense to me, but Rev. S never talked about him much anyway.

At the age of fourteen I was confirmed into this faith. I memorized all the required oaths, passages, and creeds with little or no understanding and less interest. By the age of sixteen my disinterest turned to disapproval. I did not like most of what I heard from the pulpit week after week: constant reminders of death, sin and hell, along with the idea that we, as Wisconsin Synod Lutherans, would be saved while all others, Catholics, Baptists, other Lutherans, nonbelievers, and of course Jews, would be condemned to hell. I knew that my father was in this category along with my best friend Karen (a Baptist) and my many aunts, uncles and friends who were Catholic. Rev. S never mentioned Muslims, Buddhists, or any other major world religions. About once a month he would ask for a special collection to support the work of the missionaries who were converting the heathens of Africa to Lutheranism.

In my freshman year of college, at the age of eighteen, I wrote Rev. S a letter asking him how it could be possible that all these other people of the world, from China to Arabia, could be condemned by God if they had never in their life even heard of Lutheranism. Essentially, I told him I was sure that what he had been preaching simply could not be the truth. He did not respond to my letter, and years later, at the celebration of the 150th birthday of that little brown church, I discovered that my name had been removed from the books, as though I had never been a member.

I started high school in the fall of 1957. From this year and for the following twenty years, music would define and underscore my life. "Wake up Little Suzie" by the Everly Brothers and "Peggy Sue" by Buddy Holly were among my favorite songs that fall. It was also the year that American Bandstand began as a daily TV show hosted by Dick Clark. I discovered that I really liked to dance, and I learned the steps by watching this show. I loved high school and, as in elementary school, I got good grades. My parents had convinced me that I was definitely a "smart girl," so I expected to get A's, and usually I did. Science and history were my favorite subjects. I played drums in the band, joined a number of clubs, and attended every athletic event that I could. Karen was still my best friend, but now I made more friends. There were a hundred students in our class and, in time, I got to know them all. During freshman year the best athlete was a senior named Denny; of course I had a crush on him, but my real favorite boy in the school was my cousin, Galyn Schulz. He had a great and optimistic sense of humor and could always make me laugh. He was a member of my class so I had the pleasure of enjoying his optimism during all our four years of high school.

Near the end of my freshman year, our English teacher brought in a tape recorder and recorded each of us as we read a passage from a book. This day shocked my being to its core. Within moments of hearing my recorded voice my mind was racing and a sudden understanding flooded in. I was stunned. I could not understand my own words. The sounds and pronunciations were all wrong. At that moment I understood what it meant to have been born with a cleft palate. I always knew I had that 'hole' in the back of my mouth, but heretofore I had considered it only a hindrance to eating certain foods. Gradually the memories and clues came forward: my mother asking me to speak slower; a peddler, who had once stopped at the farm, asking me if I was "tongue-tied;" (I then angrily stuck my tongue out at him!), the adults at a baseball game who kept turning around and looking at me whenever I spoke; the older neighborhood boy who once said he couldn't understand me; the grade school teacher who asked me to sing more softly than the others in our choral group; and the high school teacher who never called on me in class.

For the next few days I walked around in a daze, unable to decide what to do with these new feelings and questions. How was it possible that I could not hear myself accurately? The voice I "heard" inside my head sounded perfectly normal. I said nothing to my family or friends, but wondered how it was that they were able to understand me. I began to pay close attention to my conversations with them. Did they ask me to repeat myself? No. Did they say "what" more often when listening to me? No. Were they seemingly more attentive when listening to me as compared to others? No.

Then I remembered the brochures on a "Cleft of the Soft Palate" that my mother had given me years ago. I guess she had received these from the hospital when I was born. I dug through the bottom drawer of the kitchen cupboard, where all important papers were kept, and found them. I read them over and over and realized how well it described my speech. The brochure explained that an "L" is normally pronounced by placing the tip of the tongue behind the front teeth, but that those with a cleft of the soft palate move their tongue back in the mouth and place the tip on the floor of the mouth. Yes, that is exactly what I did. I tried saying an "L" like the brochure explained but it felt awkward and uncomfortable.

After a while I grew more accustomed to the realization of what having a cleft palate means. Since I still sounded "normal" to myself, and since my friends and family appeared to be oblivious to my discovery, my anxiety soon calmed and I returned to my old optimistic self. I simply followed Cicero's advice and continued to "live joyfully."

The remainder of my high school memories are of good times with great friends: sporting events, music concerts, street dances in the summer, sock hops in the winter, pep rallies, school plays, slumber parties, and beer parties. Beer was of course illegal since we were under the age of 18, but it was almost always present at our teenage parties. I think most parents knew about it, but didn't think much about it since they had done the same thing when they were teenagers. Occasionally a group of us would meet up late on a weekend night to steal watermelons from some local farmer. I don't know why this was so popular in my hometown, but it was accepted as a time-honored tradition. I know my father and his friends had done it when he was young. I certainly loved the thrill of it: sneaking onto someone's property at night, avoiding the barking dogs, finding the ripe melons in the dark and then escaping to our waiting "get away" cars. We usually went out in a group of eight to ten; two or three would wait quietly in their cars or pick-up trucks and when we scampered up with the stolen goods, they would drive us off to an empty quarry where we enjoyed our prized melons, spiked with cheap vodka, which was sometimes purchased by an "older" brother, but more often at a local bar where the owner was known to sell to minors. I was especially happy when my cousin Galyn came with me. He could make me laugh even in the scariest of situations, like the night a farmer heard us in his fields and began yelling and firing his rifle in the air. As we all ran like crazy, Galyn made jokes about the rip in someone's pants earned while jumping over a barbed wire fence!

Most of my girlfriends had curfews but I never did. Early on, Mom and Dad had explained to us that as farmers their bedtime came early since they had to wake up so early. They knew they could not enforce a curfew since they would be deep asleep and would not hear us come home. They said that they trusted us to just "be responsible," and not get in any "trouble." Since most of my friends had curfews I was usually home at a reasonable hour, but my friend Susie liked being out late as much as I did, and she would sneak out her bedroom window after her parents had gone to sleep. She and I had some great times sneaking out the window to a waiting car full of friends and driving down the road to a late night "party" —rock 'n roll music from the car radio, a bit of beer and dancing or going to someone's house whose parents weren't home. Often she and I were the only girls there because all the others were home on curfew.

I don't know why I never gave much thought to my future during those high school years. I took some business education classes but only because my father insisted; I knew I did not want to work in an office. I intended to go on to college even though Dad said it would be a waste of my time; he believed that girls just got married and had babies and didn't need a college education. But his uncle, Charles Carpenter (who we referred to as simply "Uncle"), was always one of my favorite people, and he had told me repeatedly that one day I would go to college. When he passed away in 1957 he

"Uncle"

left me $1000 in his will and I knew this was intended for my education.

Following my high school graduation in 1961, I went to see Dr. Russell, an Ear, Nose, and Throat specialist, recommended by Dr. Towne who had become a "friend" of mine. During my high school years I would sometimes walk to his office, which was only a few blocks from school, just to talk to him about all sorts of things, and sometimes about my cleft palate. He told me that he wanted me to have the corrective surgery when I was a baby, but my father would not give his consent. After Dr. Russell examined me, we spoke and I decided to have corrective surgery on my cleft palate. I was old enough to make this decision on my own, and although Mom was supportive, Dad was still not in favor of it. Reading all the consent disclaimers, including the possibility of death due to "complications" still frightened him. But I knew that the risk was small, and my ever present optimism didn't allow me to seriously consider worst-case scenarios. I stayed "on the sunny side" and we scheduled the surgery for July. I looked forward to the day and dreaded it at the same time. The thought of someone cutting inside my mouth repulsed me. I kept thinking "it is too close to my very being; this is my head, after all, and I 'live' in here." On the other hand, I was excited about the prospect of having a "roof" in my mouth. I wondered how different it might feel to eat, to drink, to swallow, and to talk.

The surgery went fairly well, considering that it is meant to be performed on babies, not eighteen-year-olds. I now had a complete soft palate. During healing I was told not to touch it with my tongue, but this proved very difficult since even in my sleep my tongue went automatically to the sutures and the strange new closure. Within a day a small hole formed between my hard palate and soft palate. Dr. Russell tried unsuccessfully to re-close this with additional surgery, so I still have this little hole in the roof of my mouth. I have come to love it. It is a constant reminder of my uniqueness and it helps me to realize that each one of us is unique in our own way. I spent five days in the hospital and then came home to recuperate on a strictly liquid diet, which included banana flavored penicillin. The amazing thing was that, afterwards, nothing really changed; eating, swallowing and speaking all felt and sounded pretty much the same as before the surgery.

While I was in the hospital Mom informed me that she had filled out the entrance application for college and had sent it in to the University of Wisconsin at Oshkosh, about twenty-five miles from our home. I was elated! I didn't know anything about this school and I had no idea what I would study once I got there, but I knew that I was going to college!

CHAPTER 4

RULE # 4: Live Joyfully

Remember Cicero's advice. "live joyfully." I've always been an optimist, and feel sorry for the pessimists of the world. I often say, "If you can't see the world through rose colored glasses, I think you should buy some!"

ON MY OWN: COLLEGE, NEW ORLEANS, AND HAWAII

Moving into my freshman dorm room at Oshkosh was an exhilarating experience. I had never been away from home before. I had always lived around people I knew, so moving to a place where I knew no one was a big first step for me. Mom drove me to the campus with one suitcase, my record player and records, and the little transistor radio that I had gotten as a graduation present from my sister Audrey. The room was small, but it fit two twin beds, two student desks, two dressers, and a closet. The bathroom and the showers were down the hall. The dormitory building was rather new, two stories high, with about fifty dorm rooms full of freshmen girls. In 1961 dorms were not coed, and the women's dorms had much stricter rules than the men's dorms. We had curfew seven nights a week, the boys had no curfew. On week nights we had to be in the dorm by 8 p.m., and on weekends by 10 p.m. We were allowed two "late nights" per semester and this meant we could stay out until midnight on a weekend night.

Mom helped me unpack and settle in, we walked around the campus and then said good-bye. I told her I would be home for Thanksgiving. I was very excited to start my new life as a college student and was sure I would not get homesick. Seven days later I called Mom and asked if she could come and pick me up. I decided I wanted to come home for the weekend. Really it was not so much that I was homesick, I just had so much news I wanted to share with the family. I realized that as a family we had always had dinner together and each of us would talk about our day. I now had seven days to catch them up on! I had a wonderful weekend and when Mom drove me back to the dorm on Sunday night I could tell that she was as pleased as I was with the start of my college life.

I was very happy with life on a college campus. My roommate was Joanne (I called her Josie) and I liked her from the moment we met. Over the next four years she was my best friend, and confidante. I found my classes interesting, for the most part, and I loved being introduced to new and challenging ideas every day. My psychology professor asked us to contemplate what it would feel like to be a pea in a can. My Western Civilization professor went off on a tirade about the evils of "Red China." My History of Education professor convinced me to do some volunteer work at a local orphanage where I met and enjoyed the company of some wonderful young children.

I started out as a physical education major (not sure how or why!) so I took classes in individual and team sports. I learned how to play badminton, golf, and field hockey which was my favorite. In team sports like field hockey, we competed with other colleges in the state and also with the women's prison at Taychedah. At the prison we were each made to "buddy up" with one of the inmates. My "buddy" handed me a letter and asked me to smuggle it out and mail it for her. I took the letter and hid it in my belongings, but it was a moral dilemma for me. I wondered if I should mail it, or not. Finally I decided to read it and see if it contained any "criminal" intent, it did not. It was simply a love letter to a man who was not on her approved mailing list. I mailed the letter.

Field hockey is a very physical game and the position I played was halfback, which meant I played both offense and defense. As halfback, I ran the length of the field, back and forth, for the duration of the game. It was great exercise and by the end of the fall semester I felt I was in excellent physical shape.

Socially the majority of the students were much like Josie and me: middle class, white, and from small towns and rural areas nearby. Many of the students went home every weekend, but not Josie and me. We discovered and frequented bars where there would be a live band and a dance floor. We went to movies, a real treat for me. (The only movie I remember seeing as a child was when Mom and Dad took us to an outdoor theater to see "Ma and Pa Kettle on the Farm"). Sometimes, on weekends, the university held seminars or panel discussions and we would attend these. I remember one in particular which featured a heated discussion involving foreign students from the Tanganyika Territory. Tanganyika had declared its independence from British military rule, and had become a constitutional monarchy, later to be named Tanzania. The students were divided in their opinions on this event. A few months earlier, Dag Hammarskjeld, Secretary of the United Nations, had died in a mysterious plane crash over Rhodesia (Zimbabwe today), and that too had become a controversial topic of much interest to the African students on campus. I knew nothing of Africa at that time in my life, but I loved listening to these students with their strange accents and wealth of political knowledge. I tried to visualize what their lives were like in their homeland, and added Tanzania to my list of countries I wanted to visit one day.

Josie

Josie and I made friends with nearly everyone in our dorm and had some great "slumber parties." We would have pizza delivered and stay up late and talk about every topic imaginable. We discussed our reasons for going to college and our future goals. I was surprised to hear that a number of the young women were there to "find a husband." Josie and I planned to graduate and move to New York City! We plastered our dorm room walls with posters of New York, and repeatedly listened to Ray Charles sing "New York's My Home."

I loved music. I played drums in high school and college so rhythm and dancing were a constant pleasure, but the words of the songs had the most influence on me. My favorites were songs about traveling or more specifically "rambling," and about enticing places like New Orleans, New York, and "Surf City." I especially liked songs about trains and planes, about "Spanish boots of Spanish leather," about the "redwood forests and the gulf stream waters," about "going away with no words of farewell" and being "five hundred miles away from home." These songs powerfully influenced my desire to travel, to one day move away from Wisconsin and see the world.

Josie became my mentor of sorts. She would come up with great ideas — sneaking out of the dorm after hours, peroxiding our hair, finding rides to 'The Loft' where there was always a live band and boys to dance with — and I was always game to go along. Her best idea was to transfer to UW-Madison, and so we did.

The University of Wisconsin in Madison was another whole world away from my previous experiences. The campus was huge, over 150 buildings stretching over three miles in length, and an enrollment of about 30,000 students. These students were not mostly from small rural towns in Wisconsin, but rather from all over the U.S. and the world. I definitely felt myself to be the naive country girl with a whole lot to learn, and not just inside the classroom.

My first surprise was figuring out how buses worked. One rainy day I was on the far end of the campus from my apartment and I could see people getting on buses at covered bus stops. The only bus I had ever ridden was my home town school bus that had picked me up at my house and brought me to school in town. The bus driver was a neighbor who knew where we each one lived. I could not imagine how bus drivers in Madison would know where everyone lived and how to take them to their homes. I decided to get on a bus and see what happened. I rode the bus until I was the last person still on board. The driver stopped and said, "This is the end of the route, where did you want to get off?" I answered that I wanted to get off at my apartment but that he hadn't gone anywhere near it! He then explained city bus "routes" to me and we both had a good laugh. He took me back to campus and following his advice, I got on the correct bus this time.

Josie and I rented a small apartment on Lake Street, a few blocks from the main library and the student union with its famous 'Ratskeller'. The 'Ratskeller' became my second home. It certainly didn't contribute much to my GPA, but I learned a great deal from my fellow students in the many hours I spent there. I was especially drawn to the New Yorkers. Many of them had already traveled to Europe over the summers and had tales to share of backpacking and youth hostels and trains and museums. They introduced me to books like John Knowles' *A Separate Peace*," and magazines like *The New Yorker* and The Book Review section in *The New York Times*. Through them, I became politically active and participated in Civil Rights rallies on campus, holding hands, singing "We Shall Overcome," and getting to know my first African Americans. It was 1962 and I was nineteen years old.

One young New Yorker, Dee, became my good friend. She loved to come to the farm with me, milk cows with my dad, and ride our horses. Everyone in my family was amazed by her; this "city girl" from New York who loved the farm. She was very good with horses and in just a few short visits she managed to train our stallion, Flash, to jump. She rode him bareback and had him leaping over fences much to the amazement of my father, who had thought it impossible. Dee invited me to come to New York City with her for Spring Break, and I was absolutely thrilled at the prospect. I begged my parents to let me go and since they knew Dee and liked her, they said "yes."

I thought hard and long over what to pack, how much money

it might cost, and how I would fit in with Dee's family. I never felt as completely comfortable with Dee, as I did with Josie. Dee seemed so much more self-confident and independent; I was sure she hadn't spent time worrying about what to wear when visiting my family. I ended up packing the only dressy clothes I owned, some pants and sweaters along with a suede jacket. We flew out of Madison direct to New York City on a charter flight full of UW-Madison students. It was my first flight! It was crowded, students sat in the aisles to be near friends, many had guitars and they played while we all sang, and we laughed and talked and sang all the way to New York. I don't remember flight attendants or seat belts. Upon arrival in New York we were met with a large banner reading "Welcome UW-Madison Students!" There were so many students from New York attending UW-Madison that the airport provided a separate gate and baggage claim for all returning students!

Dee's father, Dave, drove us to their home in West Nyack, along the Hudson River. Their home in a high rise apartment building occupied an entire floor with a private elevator entrance. Upon exiting the elevator I was astonished to see a huge suit of armor, authentic, the kind one finds in a museum. Dee's father had served in Europe in World War II and their home contained many art pieces he had collected while there. He was an artist, the creator of the cartoon character, 'GI Joe', and, hence, a man of some wealth. Dee's home and lifestyle were worlds apart from my own. We had no works of art, while every wall in her home was covered with paintings from Baroque to Modern. My father wore black framed glasses and hickory striped overalls. Her father wore light blue framed glasses and a suit. My father had a wood shed with a circular saw where he made bird houses and lawn ornaments. Her father had an in-home studio with a large easel and drawing table where he worked on his art.

Dinner was a formal affair; Dee explained that I should dress for the occasion. She loaned me a skirt and I wore it with one of my sweaters. The meal was prepared and presented in the formal dining room by a servant; Dee, her parents, her sister, and brother, and I ate and conversed quietly. At home Mom would have cooked and we, in our blue jeans, would have eaten around the large chrome-legged kitchen table with lots of loud talking and laughter.

The following morning Dee and her father took me to the subway station at the end of the George Washington Bridge and gave me some tips on where to go in 'the city' including the location of the Hudson River Circle Line where I might want to take a cruise with great views of the skyline. We arranged to meet around 5 p.m. at an art gallery in Manhattan where Dee's father was hosting an event. The day was full of mixed emotions; I was continually fearful that I wouldn't be able to navigate such a huge and unfamiliar city on my own, but then I was totally captivated by the sights and sounds around me. I just kept saying to myself: "I am in New York City!" I followed the directions, rode the subways, and enjoyed the thrill of accomplishment when I found each location. I even got off at the East 125th St. station to get a look at Harlem. I had read about it and wanted to see what it looked like. A short walk and a quick look around was all I could manage. I was too uncomfortable to spend more than a few minutes above ground here: young men were sitting and lying about on the sidewalks, there was unpleasant graffiti on the buildings, and seemingly no trash pick-up, ever...

After a full day of walking and gawking, I met Dee and her family at the art gallery. It was an opening event honoring some artist. I don't remember who, but everyone there knew Dee's father and greeted him with much respect and even reverence. From the gallery we went to Chinatown for dinner. It became my favorite part of New York City because it was so unique and exotic: the little shops, the lanterns, the colored lights strung across the street, and the herbal shops with strange looking powders and animal parts pickled in jars. We entered an obscure little restaurant, below street level and, again, everyone there seemed to know Dee's father. After many friendly greetings and introductions, we were seated around a large table and given a multiple page menu, nothing was familiar to me other than "rice" and "tea." Dee's father recognized my consternation and said he would order for me. I was served sweet and sour chicken and marveled at how wonderful it tasted, like nothing I had ever eaten before. That night I learned how to use chopsticks, a skill I still enjoy, although my love of Chinese food now goes way beyond sweet and sour chicken.

The following day Dee and I went to Greenwich Village and I loved everything about it. There were sidewalk vendors and outdoor cafes, underground coffee houses and street musicians. I bought a shoulder purse, the first I ever owned. It was large, made of brown leather with an adjustable shoulder strap, and I loved it. In Wisconsin at that time shoulder purses were unavailable, the style was considered "Bohemian;" it would take years before such fashion reached the small towns of the Midwest. To this day I have never carried a handbag again, I only use shoulder purses.

Upon my return to Madison I realized that my opinion of myself had changed, I now had bigger dreams. Maybe I wouldn't live in New York City, maybe I would learn French and live in Paris, and then I would do my own backpacking trip around Europe. I realized that if I could make my way around New York, I could do it in other places. I saw how much pleasure I had taken from the experience, and how little fear I had actually felt.

During the summer months of my college years I moved home and worked to make money for school. The jobs were pretty awful and I understood how lucky I was and how much I enjoyed my life at the university. One summer I worked as a car-hop at a root beer stand. Another summer, Josie came home with me and we worked together at the local canning factory. Having a friend there made it almost fun. We would do crazy things to get a rise out of the old ladies who worked there, like bring a lunch pail packed with just one dill pickle and a cigar to smoke! Another summer I worked in the Knitting Mill in Appleton. My job was to inspect mittens as they came by on a conveyor belt to make sure they had no holes in them. I was terrible at this job! It was so boring and I just couldn't stay focused. The supervisor kept telling me I had to work faster, but when I did I made numerous mistakes and many mittens passed me by with holes in them. The mill was extremely dusty. I am sure OSHA was not a factor back then. The air was filled with particles of wool and my eyes burned constantly. I even developed an uncontrollable twitch in one eye. I went to see Dr. Towne and he told me to quit that job and get out of that mill. Mom and Dad agreed, and I left there with three weeks still left in the summer, and a supervisor who probably would have fired me anyway.

In my senior year five friends, Char, Mary Lou, Helen, Molly, Josie and I moved into two adjoining apartments on Langdon St. We converted one of the apartments into an all-bedroom space where we slept, studied, and showered. The other apartment we used for entertainment, cooking meals, listening to music, having friends over, and hosting parties. This arrangement worked out wonderfully and with six of us sharing the rent it was affordable. Langdon St. in Madison is "Greek Street," housing all the fraternities and sororities. Of the five of us, only Helen (known as Herbie) was in a sorority but all of us enjoyed the weekend parties that took place up and down the street.

In the winter of that year I met a boy named Woody. He was not my first boyfriend, but he was the first I was "in love" with. He was good-looking, tall, with dark hair and he wore 'Buddy Holly-style' dark rimmed glasses. He had been attending some private college in Kansas but had dropped out and was visiting Madison when I met him. He was a soft spoken and gentle man. He loved music and was a great dancer. He liked the Beatles and I liked Bob Dylan, but we both liked to dance to rock music. He was a good skier and one weekend we drove to the UP (Upper Peninsula of Michigan) to ski at Iron Mountain. It was about a five hour drive from Madison so we left at 3 a.m. together with Tom, a friend of Woody's, and my roommate Char. Char volunteered to drive; it was snowing, the roads were icy, and we were all tired. Suddenly, around dawn, we were jolted awake; Char had fallen asleep at the wheel and we found ourselves off the road, in a farmer's field! In his calm, quiet way, Woody got behind the wheel and drove back over the icy ditch and onto the road... no harm done.

I had never really skied before, except when I had used clamp-on skis for going down the barn hill as a child. Iron Mountain, though not exactly the Rockies, was a few thousand feet high and required riding a chair lift. I considered myself reasonably athletic, but putting on those boots and skis and trying to follow Woody down that mountain exceeded my ability to stay upright, much less turn. After a few major spills, Char and I went back to the "Bunny Hill" while Woody and Tom skied the more challenging mountain runs. I didn't try skiing again until I was thirty-five, but now I really enjoy the sport and ski in the Rockies every winter.

Woody had a motorcycle, a Honda 450, and he took me on some wonderful rides. I loved motorcycles and really wanted one of my own, but I had no money so such dreams were out of the question at that time. The next best thing was a boyfriend who owned one! Once we rode all the way down to the small town in Kansas where Woody had recently been a student. We stayed at his old fraternity house, and partied away the whole weekend. I knew I should be putting more work into my classes, but I was not willing to give up my personal fun time. This led to many all-night cram-sessions and a growing reliance on cigarettes to keep me awake. Woody lived and worked about two hours from Madison, so I did not see him very often, other than weekends, which was probably a good thing since it at least allowed me to concentrate on my studies during the week.

I was enjoying my life as an undergraduate student, but I struggled with choosing a major field of study. I had always loved insects so I thought, perhaps, I would be an entomologist. In the first entomology class I took, I was the only female among a few hundred students. One day after class the professor made a point to seek me out and ask me what I was doing in his class. When I told him I wanted to be an entomologist, he said, scornfully, "You are a girl and you will never get a job in this field." Oddly, my immediate reaction was not one of anger, but embarrassment. I thought: *Well, of course, he's right.* What WAS I thinking! So I started considering other options, but only in science. It was the only field I felt comfortable in. I enjoyed history and literature on a personal level, but I did not like the subjective nature of the exams, and I was too left-brained to be able to deal with symbolism and varying opinions. In science an answer was right or wrong. I decided to study biology and perhaps become a teacher.

The following semester I registered for classes which would take me in this direction and one of these classes was "Speech 101." My speech professor suggested I would benefit from "speech therapy." I had never heard of this but agreed to give it a try. These sessions took place in the basement of Bascom Hall, the main building on campus. They were conducted by graduate students and each session lasted about thirty minutes. I went twice a week and learned more than I wanted to know about my speech patterns. They used special headphones that allowed me to hear my own voice. We started by practicing vowel sounds, but I noticed the biggest difference when I learned how to vocalize "S" and "Z." I had always been pronouncing these from the back of my throat, as guttural sounds, rather than pushing air through my teeth. It made a huge difference and I very quickly learned how to do it. Incorporating it into my daily speech was another matter. I had to speak more slowly and consciously think about each word, but in time the new speech pattern took over.

Although I continued speech therapy sessions for two full semesters, I did not stick with the idea of being a teacher. I couldn't imagine working with teenagers, and I was becoming more and more interested in cellular biology, genetics, and microbes, and their impact on disease. At the beginning of my senior year I went to the Dean's Office in the College of Liberal Arts to ask for advice on choosing a major so that I could graduate within a year. I had over seventy-five credits in science but in a wide range of courses, so I was informed that nothing matched their requirements for Liberal Arts and they sent me to the College of Agriculture. Fortunately, there was a major field of study offered there called "Natural Science" and as long as I took five credits in the College of Agriculture plus ten credits of physics and another five credits in chemistry I could graduate within a year. So I switched.

I particularly enjoyed the Plant Pathology course in the College of Agriculture; it allowed me to focus on genetics, microbes, and diseases — in plants. I did not enjoy the physics classes, they were too abstract and involved too much mathematics. The additional chemistry class I needed was Quantitative Analysis and I found this the most challenging. The laboratory portion of the class required weighing tiny amounts of chemical compounds before and after reactions in order to accurately determine the results. We were told that even small amounts of oils from our fingers could sway the results so we were not to touch any of the tiny plates for weighing, these had to be handled with tweezers. I had no patience for this kind of work, but fortunately I met Tom who became my lab partner and seemed to actually enjoy this meticulous level of lab work.

One day after class as I was walking past an area where motorcycles were parked I got a sudden urge to ride one, so I looked them over, picked the nicest one (a Triumph 700cc) and waited for its owner to show up so I could ask for a ride. Fifteen minutes later who should approach the bike but Tom, my lab partner! Tom was good looking, blondish hair, greenish eyes, tall and thin. In lab he was not much of a talker and frankly I had paid little attention to him. The motorcycle changed all that. We started dating and our "on again-off again" relationship lasted about fifteen years. For a few months I dated Woody on the weekends, and Tom during the week, but by the end of the school year I was dating Tom pretty much exclusively. Tom was in pre-med, he liked science and motorcycles, but that's about all we had in common. Still, I enjoyed his company, even more so than Woody's. We would go out to eat often and I learned a great deal about foods I had never tried before.

I remember the first time we went out for steak and the meal came with a "dinner salad." I had never seen a salad like this before. At home "salads" were served on the plate with the meal and they consisted of fruit with Jello or potatoes with mayonnaise or maybe cucumbers in sweetened vinegar. A bowl with greens and tomatoes and other vegetables served on the side with a dressing was completely new to me. Sophisticated I was not, and

I think, secretly, Tom was a bit shocked by my naiveté, though he never said anything to me. He had much more money than I did; his family was more educated than mine, and they vacationed on Lakeshore Drive in Chicago. His father and grandfather were both ophthalmologists and he intended to follow in their footsteps. He was less adventurous than me. While I liked to try all kinds of different food, he stuck with his favorites. I loved to dance to loud rock music, he liked to listen to soft folk music. I had many friends, he had few. While I dreamed of seeing the world, his idea of travel was staying in a five star hotel not far from home. We liked each other, but we were definitely not 'well matched'.

When school finished that May I still needed two courses to graduate, one in physics and the other in genetics, so I decided to go to summer school and finish in August. Happily, all of my roommates also stayed for summer school. By this time Josie had met and fallen in love with a guy also named Tom. I referred to our boyfriends as "her Tom" and "my Tom." My Tom went home for the summer and did not come back until the end of August. Her Tom did not live too far away and visited often. I also saw Woody a few times before he got drafted and left for the army. Of all the boys I knew back then he seemed the least suited to army life, but in his quiet resolved way he accepted the situation without complaint.

I had a great summer and very much enjoyed the slower pace of campus with just a few thousand students in attendance. Our Langdon Street apartments were only a block from Lake Mendota. We would often go down to the pier across the street and sunbathe. We would look for cute guys with motor boats who would stop and give us rides or ask us if we wanted to water ski. I learned that sport by the end of the summer even though I couldn't swim and was afraid of the water! I had taken a swimming class at UW and I learned how to float on my back and do a side stroke, but it was the life jacket that gave me the confidence to try water skiing.

One of my roommates, Molly, was an artist, a musician, and a "flower child" before the term was popularly used. She liked to sketch objects, scenery and people and always carried charcoal and chalk in her book bag. I admired her drawings and one day she did a sketch of me which I still have. I also admired her style, the clothes she wore and the colorful dangly earrings she had. She offered to pierce my ears and so with a cork, an ice cube, alcohol and a needle I soon had pierced ears. She played guitar and we would sit at the end of the pier on Lake Mendota and sing songs to her accompaniment. Her favorite song that summer of 1965 was "Mr. Tambourine Man"; she knew all the words to this long, story-telling song. Sometimes we stayed out there half the night, talking and singing softly. She wanted to be "in love" and bemoaned the fact that she had recently broken up with her latest boyfriend. She told me that she intended to "fall in love" and get married before the year was out— and she did!

By the end of the summer she had taught me to play a number of chords on the guitar, and I wrote a song. I played it often over the next couple of years and continued to add verses:

MY SONG: "110 POUNDS OF WOMAN"

(Roughly to the tune of Yellow Rose of Texas)

A hundred 'n ten pounds of woman
Twenty-one years of age
a long long way from no where
just lookin' for a place.

Maybe I'll never find it,
maybe I really don't care,
but I'll keep right on a looking
just in case it's really there.

Hundred 'n ten pounds of woman
twenty-two years of age
a long long way from no where
just lookin' for a place.

Went out west to L.A.
but I couldn't find it there
so I headed east to New York
and hit New Orleans on the way.

Hundred 'n ten pounds of woman
twenty-three years of age
a long long way from no where
just lookin' for a place

Bought a big new cycle
strapped a suitcase on the rack
then I took off for that someplace
said I'm never comin' back.

The U.S. fell behind me
but that highway stretched ahead
still looking for that some place
across the border then I fled.

Hundred n' ten pounds of woman
twenty-four years of age
a long long way from nowhere
still a looking for that place.

Maybe I'll never find it
maybe I really don't care
but I'll keep right on a looking
just in case it's really there."

I graduated from the University at the end of August, 1965, and received my B.S. Degree in Natural Science with little or no fanfare. There was no celebration, no gifts, or congratulations from back home, even though I was the first in my family to graduate from college. The week I graduated was the week my parents sold our family farm. The decision was made when my brother Gary chose to leave the farm and go to college. By this time my oldest sister June was married to Gene, and they had two children, Tammy and Kurt. My next oldest sister, Audrey, had recently married Marly, and the youngest, Jane, was still in high school. Audrey and Marly were farming at the time, and probably would have been happy to farm with Dad, but because she was a daughter, not a son, I don't think the idea ever occurred to Dad.

Gary and I had long discussions about his future and what he wanted to do. He knew that if he decided against taking over the farm it would be very difficult for Dad to deal with. I told him that everybody gets one life to lead, their own, and it should be his choice what he wanted to do with his life, and not Dad's. I added that Dad himself had chosen to farm rather than go into his father's silo building business. Still, we both knew that Dad had expanded the farm and built it into a business that he very much wanted to pass on to his only son, so there was sadness in the whole situation.

Other than my discussions with Gary, I was pretty much disengaged from the process. I was, by now, deeply involved in my own life, wondering about my own future, and not thinking about what a huge decision this was for my parents. In hindsight I realize how difficult this must have been for them. Dad's health was not the best, he had high blood pressure and did not handle stress well. He was probably also experiencing a midlife crisis since he was one month shy of his 50th birthday. Dad was a product of the Great Depression and therefore not inclined to be a risk taker. The realization that he would sell the farm without knowing what he would do next totally amazes me.

I arrived home a few days before the auction to find everything organized for the big sale. All the farm machinery was parked in the field next to the barn, conveniently located for prospective buyers to view. Livestock were divided among barns, separated according to when and whether they were to be sold. Some of the horses were up for auction, while some my father intended to keep. Our stallion, Flash, was to be sold so I decided to take him out for one last ride.

Audrey came with me. She saddled up her horse, Sorrell, and we rode around a "country block," roughly four miles. It was a wonderful ride and I began to feel sad about losing the animals I had grown up with. It was the first time it hit me that we were really selling our farm, our home. Near the end of our ride it started to rain so we galloped the horses the last few hundred yards. As we were turning onto the driveway Flash lost his footing and fell. The road in front of the farm had been recently resurfaced and the rain had made it slippery. I landed on my left arm and knew right away that all was not well. Flash was startled and unhurt, but I felt nauseous and faint and my arm seemed numb. A trip to the emergency room revealed I had broken my elbow.

The day of the auction I was in pain. My arm was in a cast and any sudden movement caused a shooting pain. Sleeping was almost impossible since I could not even lean back without experiencing pain. I spent the night dozing off while sitting upright in a chair. The next day I returned to Madison to prepare for my final exams, the last hurdle before graduation. Woody came to visit me on his way to basic training and he painted my cast black. In the '60s white was not a cool fashion statement — black was — and I had to admit I liked the uniqueness of it. It was definitely a conversation piece since no one had seen a black full arm cast before. He had his motorcycle and he gave me a ride to the physics department so I could meet with the professor. I felt ill prepared to take a final exam and wanted to ask if I could take an incomplete and finish the exam later. The professor was very understanding. He said his wife had recently broken her elbow and he knew how painful it was. He said he could not give me an incomplete since he was a visiting professor from Tennessee and was leaving soon, but he said he would just average my other exam grades and that I did not need to take the final. It was a huge relief! The following weekend was my graduation but I did not participate in the ceremony. I did not go home either. I knew my parents would be in transition and feeling emotional about the new direction in their life. A neighbor had bought our farm to expand his own operation, and my parents were going to rent a nearby farm house from another neighbor while they looked for a place to buy.

Woody stayed for a few more days and drove me around to employment centers on campus so I could fill out applications for some of the numerous job listings available at that time. These were research jobs at the university, requiring only a Bachelor's Degree and no work experience. There was basically no competition for these jobs so I could just take my pick. I chose a position at the McCardle Cancer Research Laboratory, working for a professor who was trying to find the allusive "virus" assumed to cause cancer. This job involved a great deal of routine lab work, preparing petri dish cultures and mixing various chemical solutions.

The day after Woody left, Tom returned to start classes in the fall. He was younger than me and still had two years of undergraduate study left. The fall semester went by quickly. I missed taking classes and wasn't enjoying my job much. I just wasn't ready to be out in the "work world." Char planned to graduate in January and she and I talked about moving somewhere together. She wanted to go to Alaska and I wanted to go somewhere warm. I was really tired of Wisconsin winters and could not imagine going even further north. Still...Alaska did sound exotic. As it turned out Char and I had a falling out when I found out she had gone out with My Tom one weekend while I was visiting my family. In January she graduated and got a job in Houston. I quit my job and decided to move to New Orleans, just in time for Mardi Gras.

NEW ORLEANS

I moved my belongings out of the apartment in Madison and into my parent's new home near Hortonville. They had bought a small farmette of about forty acres and moved into the house on the property. Dad bought a trucking route and began to haul cattle to market for the local farmers. They were busy settling into their new lives and said little about my planned move to New Orleans. If they were surprised or in any way disapproved they did not share their feelings with me. I had an enjoyable visit with them, as always. I left most of my belongings there and packed one suitcase for the trip. I took the bus back to Madison where I spent a few days saying good bye to my friends. Molly had met and fallen in love with a recent graduate in engineering. He had been offered a job in Columbia and planned to leave within the month. They decided to get married so she could go with him. As a good bye gift she gave me her guitar which I truly cherished and took with me to New Orleans.

On February 15, 1966, Tom drove me to the train station and I left for Chicago. I spent a night with a college friend and her family in the suburbs, and the next day I left on the train they call "The City of New Orleans." Standing on the train platform that cold day is one of those powerful memories forever imprinted in my brain. I was singing the words to the Simon and Garfunkel song, "Sound of Silence" to myself: "I turn my collar to the cold and damp......" I felt so completely strong, independent and free! When it was time to board, a tall black conductor in uniform asked me where I was going; I replied, "New Or-LEENS." He looked smilingly at me and said, "You mean New AW-lins!" He directed me to the end of the train and told me to get on the last car. This was the only car going all the way to New Orleans. It would be decoupled in Memphis, Tennessee and attached to a separate train for the remainder of the trip. I was the only white passenger in the car; sitting there among all those black faces gave me such pleasure. I knew that I had made the right choice. New Orleans would be a lot different from anything I had known in Wisconsin. I would get to experience different people, customs, music, and food; with warm weather and a whole new city to explore. It would be a real adventure.

I arrived in New Orleans the next day at about four o'clock in the afternoon. I didn't know a soul there, in fact, I knew no-one anywhere south of the Mason-Dixon Line, and I had no idea where I was going to spend the night. I had about $200 in cash that I had saved while working in Madison. If credit cards existed back then, I didn't know about them. I put my guitar and my suitcase in a locker in the train station and walked to the French Quarter. It was the beginning of Mardi Gras and the city was one huge celebration. It was so crowded that I had to inch my way along, but, eventually, I found my way to Bourbon Street. Amazingly, there were liquor stands everywhere on the sidewalks and they were serving drinks to anyone tall enough to hand them the money. I was trying politely, Midwestern style, to make my way close enough to buy a drink when a young woman who simply pushed her way to the front, asked me what I wanted. I guess I was expecting a drink menu or something, and I didn't respond right away, so she said, "Never mind, I'll order for you." I ended up with a bourbon and water which tasted awful to me, but I drank it anyway. She told me she was from New Orleans and had an apartment on Bourbon Street, above one of the bars. She gave me her address and said I was welcome to spend the night there if I wanted to 'crash' on her floor. For the next nine hours I walked around the French Quarter meeting young people from all over America. I started a contest with myself to see if I could meet someone from each of the fifty States. (When Mardi Gras ended five days later I had nearly met my goal, with only Hawaii not represented.) That first evening I spent a lot of time just watching and listening and marveling at all the excessively drinking party-people, their costumes, the parade floats, the musicians on every corner, and the seemingly endless supply of alcohol and Mardi Gras beads. At about three in the morning, the party on the street was still going strong, but I was tired, and certainly had more than enough to drink, so I made my way to the young woman's apartment on Bourbon Street. The door was open and when I walked in I was amazed to see that the place was already crowded with many young people who had crashed on the floor! I found myself a spot in a corner and fell asleep immediately.

The next day I bought a newspaper and, fortified with a few welcome cups of black, chicory coffee, I went through the classified ads to find a room to rent. There was one available on

St. Charles Avenue in the Garden District. It was on the trolley line so I went over to check it out. It was a beautiful old home full of senior citizens. They certainly seemed safe enough and the rooms rented for $10 per night, so I paid in cash and took one. I then retrieved my suitcase and guitar from the train station and moved in to a slightly shabby, old-fashioned wallpapered room with a large private bath. At $10 per night I knew I couldn't afford to stay there very long without finding a job, but I decided not to worry about it until after Mardi Gras. After all, it was nearly noon and the city was already coming alive with food and drink and MUSIC!

The remainder of my experiences during Mardi Gras were much like the first day, except I did more drinking and a lot more dancing. I spent most of my time on the streets of the French Quarter and very little time sleeping in my rented room. When Mardi Gras finally ended I slept without moving for about twenty-four hours!

I liked walking around my new neighborhood. It was February and still mid-winter in Wisconsin where it was below zero. Here it was warm and flowers were in bloom; trees were leafing out, and a light sweater was all I needed. I found a furnished studio apartment to rent for $80 /month. It was just a few blocks from where I was, with easy access to the trolley. Moving in was simple, no deposit was required, and I paid the landlord in cash. The studio was on the second floor of an old house; down an outside hallway was one other apartment which was occupied by two young women from Monroe, Louisiana. They had heavy southern accents which were sometimes hard for me to understand, but I enjoyed their company and, occasionally I spent time with them watching their little black and white TV.

Renting the studio apartment and knowing I had a place to live for an entire month was a great relief. Now I would have time to focus on finding a job. I started my search by going to the Tulane University Medical School. I knew of Tulane through my work in cancer research at UW Madison and I was still contemplating a career in medicine. Being a doctor still appealed to my ego more than any other career idea. I filled out a job application at the Tulane placement office but was told there were no openings at the time; they said that they would keep my records on file. The classifieds had nothing that appealed to me, most were ads for door to door magazine salesmen and such, and I knew I would never want to do that.

Next I tried an employment agency. They gave me some sort of timed quiz with questions that were like solving a riddle. I only got half correct; the agent went over each of the items with me, one by one, to explain what I got wrong and what the correct answer was. She said she would call me when she found a suitable position. I then tried a second agency and, much to my surprise, they gave me the exact same quiz! I finished ahead of time and got all the answers correct; the staff was greatly impressed. They set up an interview for me the next day with the Shell Oil Company. The interview went well and I was offered a job. I can't remember exactly what it was that I would have been doing for Shell Oil, but I turned down the job after reading the employment requirements: my hair had to be short enough not to touch my shoulders, and I needed to wear nylons, heels, skirts below the knee, and red lipstick! I was completely put off by this dress code for women employees, and, besides, it was completely unfashionable — at least in my world. My hair was waist length, long and straight; I wore almost no make-up and certainly not red lipstick that I associated with corny Doris Day movies from the 1950s!

Two days later I awoke to a phone call from the placement center at Tulane's Medical School, asking me if I would be interested in working for the Infectious Disease Laboratory. I could hardly believe my luck, and I started work there the next day. The lab was run by Dr. Mo, and to say he was an unfriendly character is an understatement! He was a man of few words; when he did speak his voice was deep and loud and his words were blunt. He almost never looked you in the eye, nor did he speak directly to you, only at you. His physical being was also gruff. He was a large man, often unshaven, with unruly grey hair and a ruddy complexion. Dr. Mo was a researcher developing a measles vaccine. He was quite famous in the medical school for his work on viruses that cause human disease. Perhaps for that reason he came across as egotistical. I worked for him for nearly one year and I don't think he ever knew my name.

I was the fourth member of his laboratory team. The head technician was named Barbara. She was petite and soft spoken with a wonderful smile and an easy laugh. Bea, the second technician, was a heavy-set redhead from Dallas with a sassy personality and a need to boast about herself. She spoke about boyfriends we never met, the wealth of her parents, and of sailing her little Sunfish on Lake Pontchartrain. June, the third technician was a beautiful tall, thin African American from Mississippi. She loved music and her favorite artist was Nat King Cole. She would sometimes hum his music while doing routine work in the lab. Her parents were both teachers and she said she was thinking that maybe one day she would go into teaching as well. All three of them were older than me and still single, though June was engaged. Bea and June were in their late twenties and Barb was in her early forties, and I do remember thinking how 'old' they all were not to be married yet. Of course I assumed that I would be married before I was that old.

Every day we prepared and analyzed hundreds of blood samples in test tubes and tissue cultures in petri dishes. Barbara really ran the lab. It was she who set our schedules and assigned each of us our tasks for the day. She was the one who communicated with Dr. Mo, starting each day in his office down the hall. She would then return to the lab and explain what he wanted done that day. He rarely came into the lab and I preferred that since I never felt at ease in his presence. Sometimes, in anger, he would burst into the lab, find Barbara, and say in his loud, gruff voice, pointing at Bea or June or me, "Tell that 'thing' over there I need more racks of antiserum today." Sometimes Bea would snap back at him and he would grumble under his breath to Barbara and leave the room. June and I never spoke back to him, we coped by just being quiet and doing our job.

A month after I started working at Tulane I was asked by

another doctor (Roy) if I wanted to work on his acute lymphocytic leukemia project. This work took me out of Dr. Mo's lab about two days every week and this was perfect for me. I liked genetics and this project involved doing chromosome analysis on children with leukemia. At Dr. Roy's request and expense, I enrolled in a Cytogenetics class at the medical school and learned the art of doing chromosome studies on human cells. This was a lengthy and intricate process which had only been perfected by the science community a few years earlier. Students of biology in the 1950s were taught that human beings had forty-eight chromosomes in each cell since the technique to separate the chromosomes in order to get an accurate count had not yet been developed. In the early 1960s, using this new technique, the number was determined to be forty-six.

Completing a chromosome analysis was complex and time consuming. It began with the collection of human cells, usually from a blood sample, but sometimes also including specific tissues such as skin, gonadal, tumor, or bone marrow. Once the cells were collected they were grown in an incubator for three days to promote mitosis. Specific chemicals, such as colchicine, were added to stop mitosis at metaphase when chromosomes were in their most identifiable state: shortened, thick, doubled and attached at a centromere. They were then placed on a slide in a hypotonic solution so the nuclei of each cell would burst, and the chromosomes would spread sufficiently to be seen individually with no overlaps. Dye was added to make the chromosomes more visible, and they were then photographed using a camera placed on top of a microscope. A number of individual chromosome smears would be photographed, prints developed, and then chromosomes from each smear would be cut out and arranged in matching pairs in a pattern called a karyotype. Becoming proficient at this technique gave me a marketable skill for years to come.

Dr. Roy's lab was working to find an abnormal chromosome called the Philadelphia (Ph-1) chromosome which had been identified as being present in patients with some types of leukemia. At the time, Dr. Roy and most others involved in cancer research, believed that cancer was caused by a virus yet to be discovered. The hypothesis that a chromosome defect could be connected with leukemia, a cancer of the blood, was very intriguing. The role of genes in relation to cancer led me to think that cancer might be an inherited disease. I began to spend time in the Tulane Medical School library to read as much as I could on cancer research. The virus theory soon seemed improbable to me. Researchers had been looking for this elusive virus for decades with no results. In the weeks that followed I conducted chromosome studies on dozens of different tissue samples. I did not find the Ph-1 chromosome, but grew very fascinated with chromosome patterns in cancerous tumors.

These cells typically did not have a normal forty-six chromosomes, but rather varying numbers from around forty to fifty. These tumors were growing fast and with very abnormal cell divisions. In the fall of 1966, at one of our department meetings I mentioned to Dr. Roy and his staff that I thought cancer was 'caused' by our own genetic make-up. That maybe something in the environment triggered one's cells to go haywire and begin to multiply and divide in an abnormal fashion resulting in cancer. I reasoned that individuals inherit a susceptibility to whatever triggers cancer for them; for one person it might be cigarette smoke, for someone else it might be peanut butter, or whatever. I also thought that perhaps the trigger might be a biological clock that we were born with; when the clock 'goes off' it could trigger abnormal cell division and subsequently, cancer. Again, the timing could be different for each individual.

The reaction to this by Dr. Roy and my lab partners was, pretty much, laughter. I was told how viruses causing cancer in chickens had already been identified, and that it was just a matter of time before viruses causing human cancer would be found. Since viruses are simply pieces of DNA with a protein coat, (making them identical to small pieces of chromosomes,) most researchers were convinced that it was a virus causing the abnormality in chromosome replication and cell division in cancer. I understood the logic of this theory, but I still thought my idea was more reasonable.

I never mentioned it again, however, I did now start giving serious consideration to medicine as a career. I had thought about this before. Once in high school when my friend Karen and I had visited a nursing school, and again in my senior year of college when I realized that my Natural Science degree could qualify me for medical school. At Tulane I became friends with some of the medical students, interns, and residents and I enjoyed listening to their stories about their patients. A favorite story involved an elderly black man, in his 80s, who was told he would need to have his penis removed due to some serious disease. He did not want this surgery, and when the doctor tried to tell him it would be okay, and that at his age living without it would not be so bad, the old man replied, "That's true, but Doc, it sure does dress a man up fine."

Dr. Roy suggested I spend some weekend time in the emergency room, saying: "It's a good way to know if you really want to go into medicine." The following Friday night I went to the emergency room. There was a nurse and some interns at the reception area, and a place in the back where residents could go to try to get some sleep between incoming emergencies. The job of the nurse (and now I was asked to participate) was to decide if an incoming patient's situation was serious enough to wake up a resident or if it was something the nurse or an intern could handle. It was quiet for a short while and then the police arrived with a young man, brought in by ambulance on a gurney, whom they said had been stabbed. He was screaming, and there was a lot of blood. It was a frightening scene and without hesitating I went to wake up the resident on call. As it turned out the stab wounds were superficial and required some stitches that the nurse or intern could easily have done. The resident asked if I had even looked at the wounds and, of course, I had not. I knew in that moment that I definitely did not want to be a doctor. The thought of people's lives depending on me, and on moments of quick decision making, was impossible for me. I knew that

I would never have that level of confidence, nor the ego-size necessary to go along with it.

I loved living in New Orleans and spent my time, evenings and weekends, becoming familiar with the city. I walked everywhere. I loved the walk along St. Charles Avenue, from Canal Street to Tulane University, where I would spend hours enjoying the unfamiliar plant life in the Botanical Gardens. I got to know every alley and most of the establishments in the French Quarter. There was one coffee shop I especially liked to frequent and one day I met two high school boys there and we became friends. One, Eduardo, was an exchange student from Ecuador. He said he was the son of the President of Ecuador. I believed him. The other, Tim, was a native of New Orleans, and he taught me a lot about the city including one amazing revelation — homosexuality.

I had never heard of it before and did not know that different sexual orientations existed. Tim's sister was a lesbian and had a life partner. They lived in an apartment in the French Quarter and, I would occasionally have dinner at their house or join them for a drink or a cup of coffee. Once I went with them to a gay and lesbian bar off Bourbon St. I watched the clientele and came to better understand their life. I tried not to act shocked at the sight of women kissing women, men affectionately dancing together, and the continuous entourage of cross-dressers. Once I had a flashback of a guy in Madison whom I had frequently seen riding his bike across campus. There had been something 'unusual' about him that, at the time, I hadn't understood. Sitting in the bar I realized that there would be nothing at all unusual about him here, off Bourbon Street.

One Saturday I decided to go to a motorcycle dealership to see if there was any way I could afford to buy one. While there I met a guy named "Skip." He had a BSA 441 motorcycle that I really liked, but of course could not afford. We started dating and at first it was a lot of fun. We would sometimes spend whole days together walking along the Mississippi River, having dinner, and listening to late night street musicians on Jackson Square. Mostly we went on long motorcycle rides to the nearby little bayou towns or out along Highway 10 to the Gulf of Mexico. He told me that he had been married and had an infant son, but that his wife had left him and how angry it had made him.

During Spring break that year my former college roommate, Herbie, my brother Gary, and Gary's roommate, Jim, drove down to visit me for a few days. Together with Skip we all went to Biloxi, Mississippi, and camped out on the beautiful white sand beaches. We built a big bonfire and boiled a huge pot of crayfish ('crawdads', as they are referred to locally) suffused with wonderful Cajun spices. Eating crawdads and drinking beer on a hot night by the sea is a true southern pleasure. You can eat all night and not get full since shucking these small arthropods takes time and results in little real 'meat'. A few days later when Gary and the others started their drive back to Madison I felt somewhat 'down'. Homesick, I guess. I realized how much I missed Gary and the rest of my family.

The following weekend when Skip came by to see me, he got angry about something, I don't even remember what it was. In any event, his temper flared and he picked up a pan from the hot plate and threw it at me! I was completely shocked. He apologized profusely but from that moment on I was frightened of him. I realized he could be violent, and wondered if that was why his wife had left him. I decided I did not want to see him again and told him so. This also made him angry, but he left and said he'd be back in a few days. I started spending the evenings in my neighbors' apartment, after explaining to them why I did not want to be alone in my own apartment. A few times over the following week I heard Skip come by and knock on my door. Sometimes he would yell loudly and kick at the door saying he knew I was in there. Now I was really frightened and wondered if I would ever feel safe in my apartment again.

My ex-boyfriend, Woody, got in touch with me and told me he was currently stationed in Norfolk, Virginia, and asked if I could come and visit. Memorial Day Weekend was coming up so I bought an airplane ticket and flew to Washington D.C. where Woody met me. This was a weekend that only two completely naive 'country bumpkins' could have experienced! I arrived with what I thought was enough cash for the weekend, Woody did the same. However, not watching what we spent, we were nearly out of money by Saturday afternoon. My flight was leaving from Norfolk on Monday night so we decided to hitchhike and got to Richmond by Saturday night. We spent the night in a dorm room on the University campus, staying with some of Woody's old friends. The next day we hitchhiked to Virginia Beach where, having spent the last of our cash on food, we looked for an inexpensive room by the ocean, and hoped to pay by check. We asked the young people at the beach about an inexpensive place to stay. They directed us to a boarding house run by an old woman who said she had a room that we could stay in. Reminiscent of a scene from a prior century, she started walking us down a hall, a lit candle in hand, wearing a long night gown. She knocked on the first door and people in there yelled out at her. She then went to the next door and the same thing happened. After trying four or five rooms she finally found one with no response, so she opened the door with her key and said we could stay there. But when we entered we noticed that there were already other belongings in the room, so once again we were walking down the hall with her, knocking on doors. Finally she found what appeared to be an empty room, and then demanded cash in advance. We told her we had no cash, but would write her a check. Angrily, she said she did not accept checks and threw us out! We walked down to the ocean and crawled under a pier to try to get some sleep as a light rain had begun to fall. Within moments we heard all these rustling noises, lighting a match we discovered that we were not alone under the pier. There were literally hundreds of crabs scurrying about! We hurriedly left and walked over to the main street. Much to our delight we found an all-night coffee house and so, with just small change left in our pockets, we bought bottomless cups of coffee and spent the night there.

The next morning we hitchhiked to Norfolk in time to see the Memorial Day Parade, which was big. Norfolk is home to large military bases so the whole town came out for the parade.

Woody and I were starving since all we had eaten in the past 24 hours was some penny bubble gum we had bought. As we walked along the parade route we came to a park and saw a big wishing well with lots of quarters and dimes in it. While everyone was busy watching the parade we sat on the edge of the well, reached our hands down into the water behind us and scooped up handfuls of the coins. When we had retrieved enough to buy a hamburger we left and had lunch. With a full stomach, Woody hitchhiked with me to the airport and I got on my flight back to New Orleans, worrying the entire time how I was going to get to my apartment with no money for a taxi. Upon arrival I just got in a cab and gave him my address, thinking I would simply pay by check. When we got to my apartment and I handed him the check he got very angry and said he didn't accept checks! I told him I had no cash, and assured him the check was good and he should cash it. I left him an extra-large tip and said good-bye. He never cashed the check.

In early June a most wonderful event happened. Dr. Mo hired another lab assistant, Barbara. She had just graduated with a degree in biology from Southeastern Louisiana State. She was tall and thin and blonde with a great smile and a fabulous New Orleans accent. She came from a well-known local family who were conservative Catholics. Her father was an elected judge. Barbara was the oldest of nine children and had moved back home following her graduation. We became great friends almost immediately and within a few weeks got an apartment together in a different section of the Garden District. She wanted to get away from home and I wanted to get away from the apartment in which I no longer felt safe.

Barbara and I had wonderful times together. I liked everything about her, especially her flexible mind. She was willing to try anything and she loved music! We got in the habit of coming home from work, going to bed and sleeping until about 11 p.m., then going uptown to the French Quarter. We would frequent our favorite bars to listen to music and dance. One bar, "The Seven Seas," was in a rather seedy area near the Mississippi River. It had a beautiful big juke box, so huge that one could dance on top of it; and this we did, nearly every night.

We met an old black man named Babe Stovall who played a twelve string steel guitar. He would go from bar to bar in and around Bourbon St., playing for tips and drinks. We loved his music and would sometimes follow after him just to hear him play and sing. We used to beg him to record his music so we could buy an album. Some of the songs he played regularly were: "Ain't Gonna Study the War No More" and "Let That Circle Be Unbroken." I don't know whatever happened to him or if he ever recorded any of his music. I do know that the night we left New Orleans we went to say good bye to him, and, midst lots of hugs and tears, he played those two songs for us.

Very early one hot and humid Sunday morning when we were sitting on Bourbon Street watching the hookers go home and the Gospel singers arrive, we met David. We were soon a 'threesome'. Like Barbara, David was a native of New Orleans, but they did not know each other. He was from the "other side of the tracks"; his family was uneducated, Catholic, Cajun, and poor. He was very out-going with a 'wheeler-dealer' kind of personality. I don't remember what he did for a living but he always seemed to have some money, and, best of all, he had a nice big motorcycle! I never dated David; I wasn't attracted to him in that way, but he wanted me to be his girlfriend. We agreed to just be friends. I loved spending time with David, he made me laugh a lot and I learned a great deal from him. He was the first truly 'free spirit' that I met. Later in the 1960s there would be many free spirits among my friends, but at this time David was a novelty. He loved Mexico and made a number of trips there on his motorcycle. He had a big straw hat which he gave to me when I left New Orleans. I still have it. He liked to play games of all sorts. He taught me how to play chess until I learned the game well enough to almost beat him, at which point it was no longer fun for me. I didn't like to be competitive, it made me nervous. We played running around outdoors kind of games — like hide and seek in the famous cemeteries with large, above ground tombs. And he also liked to play 'mind games' that were meant to shock people. For example, he would stare at water fountains which were still labeled "colored only" and "white only" and then draw attention to himself by loudly slurping from the "colored only" fountain. Or, when we went to a movie, he would make a point of sitting up in the balcony where the "colored only" were to sit. During the Veterans Day Parade, he held up anti Vietnam War signs, and this was in 1966, before the nationwide demonstrations had begun.

David was a great dancer so he and Barbara and I were familiar faces in all the places with good music. We got to know a lot of the "street people" since we all hung out in the same places each night. These were young people, from various parts of the country, traveling on their own. We spent a lot of time with them but didn't really get to know much about them, not even their names. We just knew them as "Coon" from Missouri, "Stinky" from Pennsylvania, "Cougar" from Texas, and so on. Coon had a guitar and sometimes we would all sit down by the river and he would play and sing for us. He was really good looking and I was attracted to him, but he definitely had a wild side and I knew enough to keep my distance. Before the year was out Coon disappeared and we heard he was in jail. Our friend, TS, had a sports car and one weekend he and Barb and I all rode in that small car to Galveston, Texas and back!

Me with the straw hat David gave me

David and Barbara and I liked to visit the stripper bars but the waiters came around often to make sure you weren't sitting there with an empty glass. We learned to sip our drinks slowly since they were expensive and we were only there to see the show. Sometimes the bouncers would come and tell us we had to order another drink or leave; we

Me in the sports car we took to Galveston

left. New Orleans food was another one of our pleasures. We had favorite restaurants where the prices were cheap and the food was fantastic. David liked jambalaya, the hotter the better, and he loved oysters on the half shell. They were a big deal in New Orleans. Everyone talked about eating oysters on the half shell so I thought there must be something really special about them. I tried eating them many different ways: with lemon, with lots of lemon, with hot sauce, with lots of hot sauce, and followed with a shot of tequila, but I did not like them. To me they looked and tasted like one could imagine a glob of sandy fish oil! I did, however, enjoy fried oyster po'boys. And I loved cajun spices, anything "blackened," and vegetables like okra and fried tomatoes that were foreign to this northerner. Shrimp boils were my favorite; washed down with a cold beer they were perfect. Beer was my drink of choice back then. I had not developed a taste for wine and I was afraid of "hard liquor." I thought people who regularly drank liquor were alcoholics or would soon turn into one. Other than an occasional Pat O'Brien's "Hurricane Drink" and an even rarer shot of tequila, I didn't drink any liquor. And so the hot and humid summer in

New Orleans passed. I liked my work in the chromosome lab and tolerated the work for Dr. Mo. Nightlife with Barbara and David was always entertaining.

In late July my sister Jane, who was seventeen years old at the time, came to visit. I was certainly not the best 'chaperone' for a minor. She met a boy and I let her stay out with him until all hours of the morning. I had a wonderful time showing her all my favorite things about New Orleans. We walked all over the French Quarter, visited the large Farmer's Market and of course we had the city's famous chicory coffee and beignets.

When Jane left I again had a feeling of homesickness. It had been nearly six months since I left Wisconsin and I missed my family again, and my friends in Madison. So, I began planning a trip home. I asked Barbara, the head lab technician, to request Dr. Mo to approve some vacation days in the first week in October and I booked a flight.

As summer ended and a new group of students came to Tulane Medical School, I found myself longing to be back in college. The world of work was not nearly as much fun as life on a university campus and I missed the life style of my student days. I started looking into graduate schools and was soon busily studying catalogs and considering where I might like to live next. One of my favorite classes at UW Madison had been Plant Pathology and I began to think this would be the perfect field of study for me. Why not be a plant doctor? It would be interesting and research based. If a plant died on my watch, who would care? Most important to me though, was not the field of study nor the particular university, but where I was going to live. I quickly narrowed the possible locations to warm climates, and decided to apply for graduate school in plant pathology at the University of Florida, Florida State University, and the University of Hawaii.

My October trip to Madison began with a flight to Baton Rouge in a light rain on a Friday afternoon. From Baton Rouge I took another small plane to Memphis, but by now, we were flying through a severe thunder and lightning storm. A short while into the flight the pilot made this announcement in a long, slow southern drawl: "Folks, Ah'm a fair weatha' pilot, and I gotta find us a place to set this here plane down as soon as I kin."

An eerie, white-knuckled half hour later we landed on a wet airstrip in Natchez, Mississippi, and promptly slid off the runway into a field of mud; the plane tipped sideways and came to a stop with one wing stuck in the mud. The pilot had called ahead to prepare for an emergency landing so fire trucks were on the ground, waiting and ready for us. Unfortunately, when they came to help us deplane, their ladders were not tall enough to reach the door that was pointing straight up in the air. The doors on the other side of the plane were buried in mud. There were only twelve passengers on the plane and we were all hanging by our seat belts, otherwise unharmed. Eventually extendable ladders were brought and, in the pouring rain with lightning all around, we were helped off the plane. The airline put all of us up in a hotel for the night and allowed us to make one long distance call. I called my parents and told them that I would be arriving the next day due to bad weather. I did not tell them that the plane I had been on was now nearly upside down in a muddy field.

The next morning was sunny and beautiful and I woke up feeling absolutely wonderful; completely rested, having had the best night's sleep I had had in months. It was as if angels had plucked me out of that plane and put me to sleep in that dry, comfortable hotel bed. Nothing was going to diminish my sense of joy on this day. The weather was perfect and I was alive and headed home.

Tom met me at the airport in Madison and we picked up our relationship where we had left off. I always enjoyed his company and there was something comfortable about having a 'boyfriend' tucked away back home. This situation would continue for the next twelve years. I did imagine that one day I might marry Tom, although I had no idea what he was thinking about our relationship. We never really talked about a future, and we never lived in the same city after I graduated from UW Madison. I certainly never considered giving up my life preferences to move to the cities he later lived in, like Chicago and Peoria.

I had not told my brother Gary that I was coming home for a visit since I wanted to surprise him. Gary was by far the most important person in my life at that time. I absolutely adored him (still do) and I was incredibly pleased that he was now studying at the University of Wisconsin and was so happy there. He was studying agriculture, dairy science in particular. He said he didn't really want to be a dairy farmer, but still wanted to be involved in the research and science of agriculture. It was October, 1966, and Gary and I were like-minded with regard to politics, religion, a desire to travel and a need to be independent. We could talk openly about any subject and we always seemed to be on the same wavelength. I was very excited to see him again and immediately went to the house he was sharing with five other guys on campus. They let me in; I walked softly up the stairs to his room, entered and threw my arms around him. He backed away with a frightened look on his face. It took him a few seconds to realize that he was not seeing a ghost! I realized what a shock it was to him and regretted my decision to surprise him.

My week back in Wisconsin was pure pleasure. Autumn has always been my favorite season and being back with my family and friends at this time of year was wonderful. I stayed in Madison for the first few days, spending as much time as I could with Gary, Tom, and old friends who were still in school. I walked from one end of campus to the other and realized again how much I missed university life. The weather was perfect, sunny yet cool, and the scenic walk along Lake Mendota, through Bascom Woods, with all the leaves in full color, brought me to one of those profound moments in my life. I found a quiet spot on some large rocks along the lake and talked to myself, out loud. (I have continued this practice whenever I come to crossroads in my life; it helps me to focus, prioritize, and put things in perspective.) I vowed that not only would I apply for graduate school, but I would apply for second semester admission, which meant that I had less than a month to complete the paperwork. As I thought about my options, I realized that Hawaii was definitely my first choice, so I would concentrate first and foremost on that application. And I vowed that no matter what the cost, or how much I had to do, I would be in Hawaii by February.

I spent the second half of the week at my parents' house catching up on all the family news, seeing how much my niece Tammy and nephew Kurt had grown, and sharing the stories of my life in New Orleans. My mother was particularly interested to hear the details and she had lots of comments and questions. We also talked a lot about my future plans and I shared with her my thoughts of going to graduate school. I told her that I was going to apply to the University of Hawaii because it would be so "exotic." I could tell that she was thrilled about the prospect, happy to see me back in school, and she was also probably happy to see me leaving New Orleans since she never thought of it as very safe. I think my descriptions of staying out all night would have put fear in any mother's heart. Dad didn't ask much about my life in New Orleans, he just seemed glad to have me home and wanted to make sure that all my needs were taken care of: was there something special I would like Mom to cook, did I want to ride a horse, borrow the car, did I need any extra cash? And he once again called me by the pet name he had given me as a child: Ruby Ann. As a child I had a special bond with my father and that special name was part of it.

When I returned to New Orleans I felt absolutely weightless, as high as if I had been on drugs. I immediately talked to Barbara about my plans, as I knew that she too very much wanted to travel, and I asked her if she wanted to come to Hawaii with me. She said "yes" without hesitation and the two of us set about planning our departure. We saved as much money as we could. I applied to the Graduate School of the University of Hawaii, Department of Plant Pathology, and I took the Graduate Records Exam (GRE) which was required for acceptance. I really knew very little about the University of Hawaii before I applied and was thrilled to discover that they did not charge out of state tuition so the cost was very reasonable. Within a month I received my acceptance and was to begin my studies at the start of the second semester, beginning at the end of January.

The next few weeks were filled with departure plans and farewells to our friends and Barb's family. The Greyhound Bus Company was advertising a special fare: $99 for ninety-nine days around America. This was perfect for us since I had friends and family around the country with whom we could stay, making this an inexpensive yet adventurous way to get to the west coast; from there we could catch a flight to Hawaii.

We left New Orleans right after Christmas to the first of our many Greyhound bus destinations. We had about six weeks to travel around America before classes started. One of our first stops was Greenville, North Carolina, a town I will always be grateful to even though I was only there for one hour. We stopped there for lunch and a change of bus drivers on our way to Washington, D.C. I carelessly left my purse behind when we left on the next bus; it contained my identification and $500 in cash which was all the money I had in the world. We were about a half hour up the road when I realized I had left my purse. I immediately told the bus driver who said that he could not turn around but that he would stop at the first gas station and call back to Greenville to see if it had been found. I was extremely anxious, realizing that without money, my plan to get to Hawaii and go to graduate school would be over. Fortunately, after the driver made the phone call, I was immensely relieved to hear that my purse would be put on the next bus, and that I could pick it up at the next bus station. Within an hour I had my purse back and all the cash was still in it!

My former roommate Char was living in Washington D.C. at this time, working for the federal government in some nondescript office job. We had reconnected via letters and so our first visit was with her. She lived in a nice apartment on Wisconsin Avenue just north of the National Cathedral. We had a wonderful time together, with lots of laughs and little visible strain apparent in our relationship. She shared with us that she was not very happy with her life; she found her job unchallenging and she had not yet made many new friends. Barbara and I visited the famous monuments and museums by day while Char went off to her job. By the second day there, we realized that Char's life was more complicated than she had admitted. We noticed many half empty whiskey bottles badly hidden around the apartment, in the bathroom among the towels, in the hall closet under an umbrella, and in the pantry behind the cereal. When we left Washington a day later I was feeling sorry for Char and worried about the direction her life was taking.

From D.C. we took a bus to New York City to visit Dee who had graduated from UW, Madison and returned to New York. She was working as an artist/illustrator for Columbia University, and was living in a most unusual apartment in Spanish Harlem. The apartment was long and narrow like a bowling alley. Dee said they had converted a hallway to make this apartment. I loved being back in New York, and Dee was the perfect host. We spent time in underground coffee houses in Greenwich Village, saw "Hello Dolly" on Broadway, ate fabulous ethnic foods, and talked long into the nights trying to catch up on each other's lives.

Wisconsin was the next Greyhound adventure stop. We arrived in Madison on one of those freezing cold days when a strong wind coming over the lake makes the cold even more miserable. We went first to visit Gary and were shocked to find our friend David from New Orleans there with him. He had driven his motorcycle all the way up from New Orleans to see me! I was definitely touched by the gesture and wished that I could feel for him what he obviously felt for me. I felt guilty when I went out that night with Tom.

Barbara and I spent a week in Wisconsin, a few days in Madison and the remainder of the time with my family. I loved being with Mom, Dad and my siblings, and especially June's children, Tammy and Kurt. They would squeal with delight whenever they saw me!

We left Wisconsin in a snow storm, taking a bus south to Oklahoma where Josie was now living. In Norman, Oklahoma we visited a fantastic coffee house, the likes of which I had never seen. Along with the usual folk singers for entertainment it featured coffees from all over the world. Josie was engaged to 'her Tom' and he was stationed there with the army. He had enlisted as an officer rather than wait to be drafted. In this way he felt he would have a better chance of choosing where he would serve and could avoid Vietnam. Josie was planning to get married in the summer and I could see that our lives were going to take very different paths.

From Oklahoma we went to Lincoln, Nebraska where M.L. another ex-roommate of mine was living and attending graduate school. She was working on her Ph.D. in plant physiology and still in love with Alan, a British student she had met at UW-Madison. He was working on his Ph.D. in astronomy. The University of Nebraska's campus was definitely unique. It had a well-established agricultural school that included pastures and barns along with greenhouses and laboratories. Most amazing to me were the students from nearby who rode their horses to campus, keeping them in university pastures while they attended class. We spent a few enjoyable days with M.L. and then headed west to Denver. Neither of us knew anyone in Denver but we were interested in seeing the city so we thought we would find a room in a YWCA and stay a few days. Denver was cold, the YWCA was expensive by our standards ($8 per person per night), and so we only spent one night and one day. I do not remember much about the city, perhaps because of the harrowing ride that followed. We left Denver on a bus crossing the Rockies on a sunny late afternoon. As we reached the highest section of the route over the mountains we ran into a blizzard. The only passengers on the bus were Barbara, myself, and five young men in the back who were obviously drinking. As we moved along the winding, slippery mountain roads Barb and I got quieter and more alarmed by the situation while the young men got louder and seemed completely oblivious to the danger. Suddenly, in the dark and with heavy snow falling, the bus slid off the road. Fortunately it was in an area with no steep drop off and so we simply got stuck in a wide, treeless ditch filled with snow. The next vehicle to come by stopped and the driver told us he would call for help as soon as he reached a phone. A few hours later another Greyhound bus came to rescue us. Other than being cold and rather uncomfortable with our fellow now quite-drunk passengers, we were soon once again on our way, no harm done.

We arrived in Los Angeles the next evening and I called Terry, an old friend from UW-Madison who had moved out to California in order to work in the film industry as a cameraman; he was studying filmmaking at USC. Terry picked us up at the bus station and we stayed with him in his campus apartment that he shared with three roommates. The most memorable thing about this visit was my first experience with getting 'high'. All four of these guys smoked marijuana and once I realized what marijuana was all about, I couldn't help but smile at the memory of that childhood film on the evils of using "dope."

I didn't really care much for Los Angeles. The weather was sunny and beautiful but the city was sprawling and seemingly without a heart — no core area that could really "wow" me — and anyway we were now in a hurry to get to Seattle where we planned to catch a flight to Honolulu.

Our next stop was in San Francisco where we were hosted by a former friend and physician from Tulane who was now living in the city with his wife and new baby. They were wonderful about showing us around San Francisco, taking us to all of the famous tourist sites and treating us to its fabulous seafood. We stayed two days and it rained nearly the entire time, but I thought the city was beautiful and I wished we had more time to spend here.

The final leg of our long bus tour took us up the coast of Oregon on high winding roads with scenic views of the ocean where hundreds of seals sunned themselves on the rocks below. We drove through Portland with snow-covered Mt. Hood in the background, and crossed the Columbia River where it emptied its powerful waters into the Pacific Ocean.

This last day on the Greyhound Bus was enjoyable, and though we were both more than ready to be done with bus rides for a while, this final trip sealed my desire to come back one day and revisit these places. I knew I would love to have more time to spend to really see America, and maybe next time I would have my own car and could travel on my own schedule.

Seattle felt more like spring time than late January. The city was green, flowers were actually in bloom, and trees had leaves.

We were met at the bus station by Chuck and Kathy whom I had become friends with through Woody. Chuck had been Woody's best friend from high school and we had double dated a number of times. They had recently married and moved to Seattle where Chuck got a job as an engineer with the Boeing Company. We stayed three days; the first two were cloudy and overcast, but on the third day we woke up to sunshine, and Mt. Rainier was in clear view. I had no idea that Seattle was so beautifully situated, nor that the climate was so mild in the winter. I realized that this too might someday be a place where I could live.

Catching a flight to Honolulu was relatively easy. In the 1960s anyone under the age of twenty-one could fly stand-by for half fare. Barb and I were over twenty-one but we both had sisters who were only seventeen years old at the time. We had duplicated their driver's licenses, put their names on our luggage I.D. tags and then passed ourselves off as our younger sisters. I became "Jane" and she became "Annette." We got seats on an afternoon flight for $65 each and were as excited and giggly as teenagers to be on our way to Hawaii. Obviously it was not hard for us to pass as our sisters!

HAWAII

We landed in Honolulu late in the evening and left the plane via stairs to the runway, outside, on a beautiful warm and humid night. We were completely in awe of our surroundings since the airport was like a jungle with banana trees and flowering plants we had never seen before. The entire area surrounding the terminal was beautifully landscaped, including even Japanese style goldfish ponds. Barbara and I were so excited to see it all that we forgot about our luggage and spent more than an hour walking through the fantastic gardens. When we finally did think about the terminal and our suitcases the baggage area was already shut down for the night. We had to beg an official to open it up for us, which he did because I think he felt sorry for us, believing that we were just seventeen years old. With luggage in hand we took a taxi into town and got a room at the YWCA.

Our first few days in Hawaii were busy and very productive. We found a furnished apartment near campus and moved in. I then contacted a doctor who had previously worked at Tulane and relocated to Hawaii as head of the Children's Hospital. He put me in contact with Dr. Uemura, the chief pathologist there, who offered me a job to set up a laboratory to do chromosome studies. At that time there was no one in the newly formed state of Hawaii who could do chromosome studies so it was an exciting opportunity for me, especially since once again I was low on money and knew I would have to pay tuition and other graduate school expenses. Next I went to the University of Hawaii's Department of Plant Pathology and met the key people in the department, including Dr. Buddenhagen, the Chair. I was surprised to be given an oral "entrance exam" by a committee of three professors. Dr. Buddenhagen then told me they were prepared to offer me a graduate assistantship and that I had a number of research projects to choose from. I was thrilled with this turn of events, realizing that the graduate assistantship covered my tuition expenses and gave me an adequate monthly salary to live on.

The University of Hawaii's campus was small in comparison to UW Madison and did not have old historic buildings nor a famous Ratskeller, but it was beautiful nonetheless. The grounds were covered with tropical flowering trees and bushes. The newly built East West Center was open and airy and backed up to a very large Japanese Garden inclusive of small ponds with lily pads and colorful fish, beautifully shaped bonsai trees alongside large rocks to sit on, and small paths and bridges to walk on. The East-West Center and this Japanese Garden became a favorite spot of mine throughout my two years on campus. The Plant Pathology Department was located nearby, in a row of old Quonset huts. Professors and graduate students were crowded into offices, classrooms, and labs that resulted in some bickering and discontent. Even Dr. Buddenhagen was reduced to cleaning off his desk top, sterilizing the surface, and using the space to try to isolate pathogens from infected papayas. I liked him from the beginning. He was young (thirty-seven years old) and quite handsome. He was the divorced father of six children and was dating a lab technician in the department. He had recently received an NIH grant to study the airborne spores of plant pathogens and I chose this project to work on for my graduate assistantship / Master's Thesis.

Taking classes and doing research in the Plant Pathology Department was enjoyable both academically and socially. Members of the department, professors and students, were an interesting and diverse group. Besides me, there were students from England, Hawaii, the Philippines, Iran, Sri Lanka, Brunei, Canada, Nepal, California, and the Sudan. The professors were from Japan, North Dakota, England, Panama, and Hungary. This little international community gave me an education in and out of the classroom. We worked and studied together during the day and socialized in the evenings. I learned to love hot and spicy foods, to eat and cook with chopsticks, enjoy musical instruments like concertinas and wooden flutes, to say hello/goodbye in different languages, and to appreciate the stories and circumstances of their lives. More than ever I wanted to travel, to see the places they came from and talked about so passionately.

Early on while having breakfast at the East-West Center I met Roger. He was a graduate student, working on his Ph.D. in Marine Biology. He was movie star handsome and very outgoing. Within minutes he had asked me out! We dated for about five months and I very much enjoyed his company. We mostly joined his friends Mic and Lilian. Mic was a stock broker and Lilian was a high school English teacher. They lived in a small house in Waikiki and were avid surfers. So was Roger. The three of them would be out in the ocean most mornings before dawn, waiting for daylight when they would catch their first wave. I tried to learn to surf but was too afraid of deep water at that time in my life.

Every Wednesday night the four of us would go to T Pier in the Honolulu Harbor for "gin and tonic" on one of the sloops owned by Roger's other friends. These were people who lived on their boats and the sea was their life. One was owned by Mathieu, a French professor, and his Japanese wife. Their sloop was about twenty-eight feet long and they had sailed it together across oceans until settling in Hawaii. When I met them his wife was pregnant. When her delivery time came, Mathieu described how he helped her into their skiff and rowed her across the harbor to the mainland and a beachfront hospital. Another friend, Jim, owned a twenty-five foot sloop which he had sailed solo around the world and was therefore a member of an elite club of fewer than one hundred who had done so. Usually we just sat on board, drank our gin and tonic, grilled fish and talked. The conversation was always stimulating and carried on late into the night on topics from local politics to world travel. Sometimes we would take one of the boats out to sea for a few hours where Roger and Mic would don scuba gear and get lobster for us to feast on.

Barb and I got to know a number of the other residents in our apartment building, mostly university students. One day a friend from across the hall stopped me and said, "You know that guy, Roger, you are dating? Well I think it's only fair that I tell you he is married!" Needless to say I was in shock and disbelieving. I immediately called Lilian and asked her about it and she confirmed this news. She told me that she wanted to tell me and had recently told Roger that if he didn't tell me, she would. It turned out that Roger had a wife and two children. His wife was the daughter of the sheriff, and she and Roger had been married for ten years, with a nine year old daughter and a new baby girl. Roger came over later that night to talk to me about it. I told him what a jerk I thought he was, especially to his wife, and I never saw him again. About a week after this last encounter a baby girl was admitted to Children's Hospital where I worked. She died a few days later from heart failure related to Down's Syndrome. The baby was Roger's daughter. I stayed in touch with Lilian and Mic and learned that a few months later Roger and his family moved to California. He had finished his doctorate and took a job at a

California university. I continued my friendship with Lilian and Mic and attended the Wednesday "gin and tonic" nights on T Pier.

I've always been an early riser, and for me it was off to the East-West Center where I could enjoy the beautiful views of the mountains, read the paper, have a cup of coffee and a cigarette, and meet up with some of my international friends. Mostly I sat with a group of about twenty Iranian students at what I fondly called "the Persian Table." I was taking a meteorology course where I met and became close friends with Kamran. He was an Iranian who was intelligent, well-travelled, dark, and handsome. Everything about him was "exotic" to me and I loved spending time with him and his friends. I called him "Kami" and he became an important part of my life.

I also met Alan, a Jewish graduate student from New Jersey who was in the Department of Asian Studies. He was bright and very opinionated. He did not like "small talk," thought it was a waste of time, and would let people know if he thought the conversation was drifting in that direction. We started dating. At first it was almost accidental. We would run into each other at the East-West Center and grab a cup of coffee or go for a walk in the gardens. Soon we were going to parties together, a movie now and then, and often shared study nights in the library. He was more serious than my other friends, and was the only one I knew who was not in Hawaii to enjoy the beautiful beaches, ocean sports, or tropical climate. He was at the university solely because of its well-known Asian Studies department.

Setting up the chromosome lab at Children's Hospital was a rewarding endeavor. Dr. Uemura was a wonderful man to work for, always interested and appreciative of my progress. I ordered the necessary equipment: a good binocular microscope with an attached camera, an incubator, and a scale to measure micro amounts of materials. I also ordered the necessary supplies: specific chemicals, petri dishes, microscope slides, and micropipettes. Within a few weeks I was ready to do my first chromosome study. It was right around this time that Dr. Uemura told me that his assistant pathologist had resigned and he would need someone to assist him at autopsies. He asked me if I was interested. I immediately said "yes!." I knew where the autopsies were conducted and had seen Dr. Uemura walk through those thick doors at the end of the corridor a number of times. My curiosity was always aroused and I had thought about asking Dr. Uemura if I could observe an autopsy some time. I never did because I was worried he would think I was a bit crazed, after all it did seem somewhat morbid to want to watch an autopsy.

The first autopsy I assisted with was on a five-year-old boy who had died of cancer. I was very nervous and definitely "freaked out" by the experience. My brain kept telling me over and over again, "this is a human being," "this is a little boy." I did my best to watch as Dr. Uemura went to work, to assist with tweezers and scalpel when asked, and to keep my emotions in check. Dr. Uemura carefully moved organs aside and pointed out numerous tumors along the backbone. In this case the parents had signed permission for an autopsy of the body only, not to include the head, which was fortunate for me since I had seen enough for one day. We did this autopsy on a Saturday morning and later that afternoon I went to the large Ala Moana shopping mall in downtown Honolulu. I intended to buy a new dress for an upcoming party but the mall was full of children and my mind kept picturing them as they would look if they were dead. I had to leave.

Over the course of the next two years I assisted with numerous autopsies and slowly it became just a routine lab procedure. I no longer saw those bodies as human beings, but rather as cadavers. Eventually I did the initial cutting that opened the body cavity, to have it ready and waiting when Dr. Uemura entered the room. We had a small radio and would sometimes listen to music. When an autopsy involved the head, Dr. Uemura would do the work since it involved skill in using an electric saw. There were a number of cases that were difficult to forget; like the brother and sister who burned to death in an automobile accident, a young boy who died of malnutrition from neglect, and a two-year-old who died of hepatitis. In this case I accidentally nicked myself during the autopsy and had to have a series of gamma globulin shots as a precaution.

Children's Hospital was located in a rather rough neighborhood about a twenty minute bus ride from the University. During daytime hours going there was not a problem, however, often I would work late at night doing chromosome studies in my lab. The closest bus stop was two blocks from the hospital on a rather dark residential street. I was never comfortable waiting there late at night so I always had my little tear gas gun with me. I had purchased it while living in New Orleans. It looked like a little pistol but just had one tear gas "bullet" in it. One night after work I was waiting at the bus stop about 2 a.m. when an old clunky car full of young men drove by and started whistling and making crude remarks. It was obvious to me that they could mean trouble and I figured they would be back so I got the little pistol out of my purse to be ready. My heart was pounding and I was silently "willing" the bus to arrive. But as I feared, the next vehicle to arrive was the return of the old car with the threatening men. They stopped the car where I stood. The guy on the passenger side in the front seat got out, opened the door, and demanded that I "get in." As he took a step closer to me, I raised the gun, pointed at him, cocked the hammer and said loudly, "Get out of here or I will kill you dead!" My heart was still pounding, adrenalin was rushing through my body, but a wonderful calmness had taken over my brain as I spoke those words. The guy stared at the gun with obvious fear in his eyes and jumped back in the car as they quickly drove away. A few minutes later the bus arrived and I was safely on my way home. As I relived this event in my mind over the next few days I tried to put myself in the one guy's shoes, the guy who I pointed my tear gas gun at, and I realized that of course he thought the gun was real and for all he knew I was some crazed murderess waiting on a dark street corner for the opportunity to kill someone!

The smart thing to do was to get my own transportation so I didn't have to rely on buses in the middle of the night. I bought a motorcycle, a Yamaha 100 Twin, and I loved it. It was just my size and easy to get around on, except when it rained. Somehow it reminded me of my childhood and riding horses which I had always loved. I know in my mind I romanticized these two means of transportation, because I think they made me feel free and strong. About a month after I bought the motorcycle I had an accident. I was making a right hand turn onto a major road near campus from the right hand lane while a car in the left land also made a right turn and ran into me. It was a big shock, especially when the driver apologized profusely and said he did not see me! I kept thinking, *How could you not see me!* Anyway, I had a small fracture in my left foot and a few scrapes and bruises on my hands and arms. About two weeks later, with a small foot cast, I was riding my motorcycle home from the University and a campus maintenance pick-up truck pulled out in front of me. I hit him broadside, flew off the bike, and landed in a grassy ditch. Luckily other than a few more scrapes and bruises and a broken cast I was fine. Imagine my shock when the driver apologized profusely and said he didn't see me! I got the message: people simply do not "see" motorcycles.

My 1961 Rambler

I sold the motorcycle and bought a used car. It was a two-toned, light green and white, 1961 AMC Rambler that I purchased from Dr. Meredith, one of my professors. He liked to find old cars and fix them up. Apparently this one had been used to haul pineapples and was pretty muddy when he found it. He sold it to me for $200 and it was perfect. Over the next two years it was a big part of my life. I drove around the island numerous times and often on roads labeled impassable, hauled camping gear, partied from it, slept in it, shared it with friends, visited orchards of passion fruit and papaya as part of my university research, parked it on the beaches of the North Shore for weekend getaways, and appreciated its comfort during the rainy seasons. I had never owned a car before and knew nothing of upkeep. When things went wrong I relied on my friends to help. I remember my friend Kami changing the tire for me once in the pouring rain. I learned from my friend Hassan to park it on a hill when the starter went out so I could let it roll down the hill to get it going. I was stopped by a policeman once and cited for having a tail light that was out. I don't remember ever getting anything fixed on the car, I just continued to drive it with all its faults. When I left Hawaii two years later I traded the car to my brother for his 35mm camera.

Sometime within the first few months we were in Hawaii, Barb met Ken. Ken was stationed in Honolulu with the Navy. He was a very interesting guy, fitting none of the stereotypes one would think of for a military "career" man in the 1960's from Tennessee with a southern accent. First of all, he was really a "hippy" in uniform with short hair. He was an avid reader and a member of the genius Menses group. Ken was very kind and personable, and I liked him from the beginning. He and Barb became an item early on, so much so that I can barely remember a time in Hawaii without Ken. He lived on the navy base by Pearl Harbor so on weekends we would sometimes net lobsters there for dinner, and of course on a few occasions Ken gave us a personal tour of the USS Arizona Memorial.

In August of 1967, six months after our arrival, Barb and I decided to move into an apartment closer to campus with two girlfriends, Chris and Phyllis, who were looking for roommates. The apartment was small, and with four of us, it was quite crowded. However, it was right across the street from campus which was very convenient, and with four of us sharing the rent it was really inexpensive. Chris was quiet and studious, with short, dark hair and pale skin. She spent more time in the library than at the beach. Phyllis was blonde, athletic, and always tanned. She loved the ocean and did a lot of snorkeling and surfing. She had a big aquarium full of little critters that she collected while snorkeling. Some of these critters were nocturnal and would wake us up at night with their underwater fights. It was mostly the hermit crabs, knocking on each other's shells, always competing for a better "home." Phyllis was dating Kimo, a handsome guy whom she later married.

One weekend in early October, Alan and I, and Barb and Ken, took an Aloha Airlines flight to the Island of Kauai. We had no specific plans other than to explore as much as we could in two days. The plane was small and we arrived on a runway with a little bench at one end and a rough wood roof overhead. It looked somewhat like a bus stop and this was the terminal! We packed light, each of us with just a small shoulder pack, and we took off walking down the highway. We walked past numerous waterfalls, rocky cliffs leading down to the sea, and thick, lush forests going to the top of the mountains. We had arrived around 4 p.m. and walked about an hour before we saw our first car. We weren't hitch-hiking but the car with a few local people stopped anyway and asked us if we wanted a ride. We explained that we were just planning on hiking so they wished for us a wonderful visit and drove off. This experience was repeated about a half a dozen times over the next few hours until we finally gave in and accepted a ride in the back of a jeep with a father and his young soldier son coming home for R&R from Vietnam. When the jeep entered the long driveway of the soldier's family it looked like the whole island was there to greet him. It was a very emotional scene and I was amazed that at such an important homecoming which meant so much to all these people, that they would stop to offer four strangers a ride and then invite us to be part of their celebration. We stayed for a while, thanked them over and over, and set off walking the remaining short distance to Hanalei Beach where we camped for the night.

To say we "camped" is an overstatement. We actually just stretched out some towels on the sand, laid down, and fell asleep only to be shockingly awoken in the early morning when the tide came in and soaked us and our belongings! Fortunately it was a beautiful weekend and as soon as the sun came up we dried out and continued our hike. Hanalei Beach was famous for having been the site of some of the filming of the movie "South Pacific." It was a very beautiful place but other than four or five thatched roof houses, some local fishermen, and a few little fruit stands there was no development in the area. (NOTE: Hanalei is now a well-known tourist destination with numerous resorts and restaurants)

We decided to hike inland to a State Park well known for its waterfalls and rainbows. We started off on the highway and after coffee and pastries at a small roadside outdoor stand we found a trail leading into the park. There was no office building or park ranger in sight so we just walked in and began the long, slow climb up the mountain. We spent the day enjoying the most beautiful scenery from thick flowering bushes to expansive vistas. When we had climbed high enough we were actually '"on top" of multiple rainbows, looking down at a valley of sunshine filled with that famous Hawaiian mist. We had a few snacks with us and ate fruit along the way, mainly guavas and "mountain apples," a very delicious fruit, and one I have never seen outside of Hawaii. We drank freely from the clear, fast moving streams that were everywhere. Throughout the day we had come upon small huts owned and run by the park service. With darkness approaching we found one of these huts and decided to spend the night there. It was locked so we pried a window open and crawled in. We found a lantern to light and then built a fire in the fireplace and enjoyed our warm cozy shelter as the expected rains came. During the night there were many jungle type noises, most notably wild boars rooting around outside of our hut. In the morning we hiked up to the road at the very top of the mountain and hitch hiked back to the airplane runway near Lihue where we caught our return flight to Honolulu. It was an absolutely incredible weekend and the joy and exhilaration of the experience stayed with me. I loved the land and the people and that's how Kauai became my favorite of the outer Hawaiian Islands.

I continued to date Alan through the fall semester, but as each week went by I found myself wondering if our relationship was worth working on. He became too possessive, always wanting to know where I was and who I was with. And he demanded too much of my time, so much so that I felt I was losing track of my other friends. The final straw came when his parents came to visit from New Jersey and he introduced me as his "fiancé!" I was very shocked by this, but in front of his family I was too embarrassed to speak out and dispute this fact. It was early December and they were in Hawaii for one week, a very uncomfortable week for me. His mother bought me expensive gifts and I felt so guilty about receiving them. His parents argued all the time and Alan argued along with them. From my Midwestern prospective they were disrespectful of each other by being critical and using hurtful terms, always in a loud yelling voice. I began to realize that given time, Alan would probably be as verbally abusive to me as his father was to his mother, and I decided to end the relationship. He had applied for a transfer to McGill University in Montreal and had been accepted into their Ph.D. program. He was planning on leaving Hawaii at the end of the fall semester and moving to Montreal, so I took the coward's way out of the relationship. We said good bye at the airport when I flew home for Christmas and he left for Canada. He told me he wanted me to join him in Montreal as soon as I could. I knew I never would!

I was so excited to be home for the holidays, that for once, the cold weather was just a minor inconvenience. Our family was changing and I felt a real need to be able to stay connected, to be a part of all their lives. June and Gene had built a new house and their children, Tammy and Kurt, were already both in school. Audrey was pregnant with her first child, Jane was engaged, and Gary was in love. Dad's trucking business was doing very well and everyone seemed to be happy. It was a great trip.

When I returned to Hawaii my good friend, Richard, picked me up at the airport. We drove to his parents' house where they were having a holiday party. Richard was Japanese American and his family was the complete opposite of Alan's family. They were soft spoken, always polite, and very gracious hosts. They made me feel not just comfortable, but important. It was the perfect welcome back experience because I knew that in my life I wanted to be around people like Richard, not Alan.

At the end of that semester my roommates and I decided to give up our crowded little apartment. They each moved in with their boyfriends and I rented a little place of my own in the mountain foothills behind the campus. I left no forwarding address so Alan could not find me and that was the end of that. I never saw or heard from him again. The apartment I rented was actually the basement of the home of a Belgian family who had fled the "Belgian Congo" when that country gained its independence in a bloody uprising. This was a white, multigenerational family in which the grandparents only spoke French, even though they had been in Hawaii for nearly nine years. My apartment was dark and a bit damp but it was mine alone. And anyway, I didn't spend much time there. I had no TV and no radio, and I didn't cook very often since good, cheap, local food was always available on or near campus. The apartment had a big bathroom, a living room, small kitchenette, and a bedroom. The shower in my bathroom always had lizards on the ceiling. I grew used to them and appreciated the fact that they were good at hunting insects. However, having to go to the bathroom in the middle of the night was not a pleasant experience since occasionally I would step on one with my bare feet! This apartment was near the old Chinese cemetery and I liked to walk around in there. The tombs were above the ground and relatives would come and leave "treats" for the deceased on top the tombs. The sight of little plates of fruit and flowers placed atop the stones struck me as a very moving and quiet act of love.

I felt so free and independent without Alan. It was his absence that made me finally realize how controlling he had been and how wonderful it was to have my friends back again and be in charge of my own life. I scolded myself repeatedly for my behavior over the past few months. "Annabelle, how stupid of you! How could you let someone do those things, say those things, and passively accept it? Remember this lesson and never, ever let anyone control your life again!" (When talking to myself I often called myself Annabelle whenever the situation I had gotten myself into was stupid or silly and I felt a scolding was in order).

It was now January, 1968, and a beautiful time in my life. I loved the music and the changing pace of American culture. For the first time I became actively involved in politics. The Vietnam War continued to escalate and the sad evidence of this result could be seen in the Punchbowl National Cemetery on Oahu. Student demonstrations were becoming commonplace on campus, right alongside of pot smoking and psychedelic light shows, LSD and outdoor concerts, beer and campfires on the beach, amphetamine and all night parties. My circle of friends grew large and there really was a feeling of "love" or at least a deep caring for each other. And my friends were a very diverse group: black, white, Asian, Hawaiian, Middle Eastern, African, European, straight, gay, male, and female, and all young. My friends were in different groups, and for the most part these groups didn't really know each other. With each group I had a different kind of friendship and was involved in different activities. When with my Persian friends we often spent an evening on the Waimanalo Beach around a big bonfire with someone playing the concertina. These wonderful gatherings never involved drugs, just beer and food. The conversations were interesting and accompanied with much laughter. Among those in regular attendance was Hassan, who was always entertaining. He reminded me of the character, Zorba the Greek. He was less inhibited than the others, liked to sing and dance, and had the most fantastic smile and beautiful eyes. Kamrouz was in love with Judy, and vice versa. She was the fun loving, very blonde American from Minnesota who I later traveled to Syria with. He was more serious, a graduate student of economics. Bijan seemed more French than Persian, and was very trendy and fashionable. He always had a gorgeous girlfriend. Abdullah dated Mary Jane, a Canadian. They seemed a bit older and more reserved than the rest of us. Ali was tall and handsome and had recently acquired a bride, Parveh, through an arranged marriage in Iran. She was young, beautiful and shy. They seemed to be very much in love and were inseparable.

As for me, I spent most of my time with Kami. He seemingly had nothing; a few T-shirts, some jeans, and an old bicycle, but he was so much more worldly than I. We would lay on our backs in the sea oats by the beach, listen to the ocean, and gaze up at a billion stars while discussing existentialism. Kami talked to me about Kierkegaard, Nietzsche, Camus, Sartre, and Kafka—philosophers I had not even heard of before then. Other times he spoke of the beauty and wonder of nature, at a time when I had mostly taken it for granted. Kami brought me a new view of sunsets, the feel of a breeze, rainbows, wild orchids, and lush green covered mountain tops that I had previously just simply acknowledged. Sometimes we compared our childhoods and marveled at how different they had been: me on a small farm in rural America, he in the midst of a revolution in Iran when the American government helped to overthrow their elected leader, Mosaddegh, and put the Shah back on the thrown. Kami had a pilot's license, newly acquired, and sometimes he would take me flying in a small two-seater he could rent at the airport. Once we flew to the island of Maui which was a real adventure since we weren't exactly sure how to get there. We had no radar and it was far enough away from Oahu to lose sight of land altogether. Kami was probably more nervous about our situation than I was since I knew nothing about planes, and sometimes ignorance is bliss.

With Barb and Ken and their friends George, Pan, Robbie and many others, we lived a "hippy" life. We, men and women, wore our hair long, dressed in flowery clothes, drove to the top of the mountain overlooking Honolulu, smoked pot, and marveled at the beautiful city lights below us. The best experience up there was during the Chinese New Year when most of the residents set off fireworks. From our safe perch above the city, stoned on marijuana, we lay down in the tall grass and enjoyed this fantastic light show. Periodically we would attend concerts by famous musicians such as Ray Charles and Glenn Yarbrough. Often we just walked the beaches of Waikiki and listened to Hawaiian music. Once we even attended a show by the famous Hawaiian entertainer, Don Ho. Mostly we went to each other's apartments and listened to music by Dylan, the Jefferson Airplane, Steppenwolf, and Donovan to name a few. And we talked politics.

This was a presidential election year and we were very much opposed to Lyndon Johnson by this time. We did not understand why the U.S. government kept sending more and more young soldiers to Vietnam. The reasons given seemed completely irrational. The "domino theory?" How could a small nation like Vietnam turn the world into communism? As I watched our leaders of the day, like Johnson, McNamara, Westmorland, and Rusk, I became so angry. I saw them as old white men, and knew it was their decision to keep sending more young men to die in this useless cause. President Johnson came to Honolulu and was scheduled to give a speech on campus. Many of my friends and I went. I really wanted to hear what he had to say, but unfortunately the demonstrators had become so angry and loud by this stage of the war that Johnson was shouted down, and he left in frustration. The main slogan chanted by the protestors was "Hey, hey, LBJ, how many kids did you kill today?" In March of 1968 Bobby Kennedy announced he would run for the Presidency. I began to campaign for him almost immediately and felt excited and thrilled at the prospect of having a president who was against this war, and was "young."

Throughout my two years in Hawaii the war in Vietnam escalated, U.S. troop numbers increased along with the anti-war protesters. I became involved with a student group on campus that was engaged in helping fellow students go AWOL when the Hawaiian National Guard, 29th Infantry Brigade, was called into active duty in May of 1968. One of those impacted by this call up was my friend Richard. Our campus group helped him hide out and then go to Canada and finally Sweden where he was given asylum. He still lives there today. A few weeks after Richard left, Bobby Kennedy was assassinated in California. For me this was devastating. Protesting, campaigning, fund raising, and helping soldiers go AWOL was hard work, but it was energizing. With the death of Bobby Kennedy I felt completely deflated. I no longer wanted to even think about the upcoming presidential election.

During this tumultuous political period, Barb and Ken decided to get married. It was a small, beautiful wedding in May of 1968.

Barb and Ken's wedding

I was Barb's Maid of Honor and Robbie was Ken's Best Man. We wore Hawaiian leis and the celebration after the ceremony was held outdoors.

My sister Jane was getting married in early September and I was also her Maid of Honor. I flew into Chicago in late August to spend a few days with Tom. The Democratic National Convention was just getting started. There was a lot of hype in Hawaii around the convention, especially since our senator, Daniel Inouye, was the keynote speaker. Tom was in Medical School and was busy during the day, so I went downtown with two young ladies I had met on the plane to join the protesters. I was shocked by the size of the crowds on the street, even more so because it seemed like there were more police and other men in uniform than there were demonstrators. I spent the better part of two days on the streets of Chicago before and during the first day of the convention. There was a lot of name calling on both sides, but it was clear that the power was on the side of the police. The smell of tear gas was ever present, along with the burning sensation in my eyes.

I felt a sense of camaraderie with the young people in the streets, but my heart was just not in it. I no longer had a candidate that I could wholeheartedly support. I did not believe that Eugene McCarthy or George McGovern was electable, too lackluster, and I viewed Vice President Humphrey as part of the establishment and a supporter of the war. I took the Greyhound bus home and watched the remainder of the convention on television with my mom. What was going on inside the convention was even more upsetting than what was going on in the streets. The nomination of Humphrey frustrated and angered me more than it saddened me. The highlight of the convention for me was when someone offered to place Julian Bond in nomination. He had to gracefully turn it down since he was not yet old enough to serve as president.

Jane's wedding was a huge event and a great reunion of family and friends. Jane married Dick, the "boy next door" so to speak.

Dad, Mom, Me, Jane, June, Audrey and Gary, September 1968

They had dated since she was fourteen-years-old and now, at the age of nineteen, she was marrying him. I had tried to talk her out of it, asking her to come to Hawaii and stay with me for a while. Though Dick seemed like a nice guy, I thought she was too young to marry. (The marriage lasted seven years).

My brother, Gary, married Rosie over the summer in a small ceremony in Madison. I was unable to make it to the wedding, but we had a celebration of sorts for them a few days before Jane's wedding. The neighbors surprisingly planned a "shivaree." They came unannounced banging on pots and pans and demanding food and drink! This was all in good fun and done whenever someone married and didn't have a big wedding where everyone was invited.

My two weeks in Wisconsin were a joy. I loved spending time with the family and catching up on everyone's changing lives. Audrey had a baby that spring so little Mikey was added to our growing clan. Tammy and Kurt still squealed with delight when they saw me. Mom and Dad seemed happy with their new lifestyle. Their trucking business was growing and they had a few animals in the barn to tend to, though no cows to milk. I've always been close to Gary and we talked for hours about our future plans and similar political views. At that time we were both considered "hippies" and out of the mainstream with regard to the rest of the family. Gary had managed to fail his physical for the draft by registering high blood pressure. I worried about this but thought it was safer than going to Vietnam. Dad had high blood pressure most of his life so it seemed logical that Gary may have inherited it.

Back in Hawaii, I was beginning my final semester of coursework for my Master's degree. I had collected data on airborne plant pathogens by placing sticky microscope slides on the wings of small inter-island planes. This had been done over the course of a year and provided me with very interesting information. I could count and identify various fungal spores on the slides, and since I also had detailed weather data for the year I could determine which conditions were optimal for the spread of disease-causing pathogens. I was simultaneously taking a full load of graduate credits and working about twenty hours a week in the chromosome lab at Children's Hospital. Somewhere in the middle of my stay in Hawaii I was introduced to amphetamines, and I used them when I had no time for sleep or when deep concentration was needed. I found that with amphetamines, I could hone in on a problem and utilize my entire, uninterrupted brain power to find solutions. Using amphetamines I figured out how to use micro amounts of blood cells for chromosome studies, rather than needing a vial of blood. I memorized the Latin names of phyla and species of numerous plants for my final exam in Plant Taxonomy. What would have been a boring task, was interesting and actually pleasurable on amphetamines. And most important of all, I analyzed pages of data from over three hundred slides of numerous microorganisms and correlated the results with weather patterns over three hundred and sixty-five days. I was amazed at how clearly I could "see" overall relationships and then draw significant conclusions. Bob Dylan had a song out at the time called "Amphetamine Annie" and I knew without careful planning that could become me. I decided that when I left Hawaii I would leave amphetamines behind, forever. And I did.

My personal life, outside of school and work, was filled with new experiences. I loved the food which was a combination of island cooking and Asian cuisine. Saimin was a particular favorite since it was tasty and cheap, and sold at numerous outdoor stands. It was a kind of noodle soup with Japanese, Chinese and Filippino influence but unique to Hawaii. Pupus were another local favorite. All the bars offered these numerous plates of small samples of seafood and other delicacies for free with drinks. As students with little money, we learned to visit bars (especially those in the large hotels along Waikiki Beach), buy one drink and then eat delicious pupus until we were stuffed. Nearly every weekend there was a Hawaiian show along the beach to entertain the tourists. The shows were outdoors and free and I loved them because the dancers were really amazing. They did hula dances which were stories in motion, and Tahitian dances that were very fast moving and rhythmic. After admiring these dancers for a number of weekends, Barb and I decided to take Tahitian dance lessons. These were group lessons and we each wore a bikini with a matching wrap around short cloth skirt. I wanted to be able to move my hips as fast as they did so one day I could really shake a grass skirt, but it was a lot harder than it looked. Oddly, the action was mostly in the knees and feet, not the hips.

I lived in Honolulu, on the island of Oahu, in the Manoa Valley, where the University of Hawaii is located. In the 1960s there were only about one hundred thousand people living in Honolulu and the whole island had a very rural feeling. There were only a few tall buildings and they were hotels on the beach in Waikiki. The island was small so I became very familiar with its towns and fishing villages, mountains and rain forests, pineapple fields and deserted beaches, Pali Lookout, Diamond Head, and the popular surfing spots of the North Shore. I took my car on just about every road on the island and sometimes on dirt paths that were clearly not meant for cars. With my friends we would drive through pineapple fields, sometimes picking a few for a later picnic, or across small river beds to remote beaches where we would snorkel in the sea and then camp for the night. We returned often to our most favorite places, like Hanauma Bay where we could snorkel in calm waters, or the waterfalls near Waimea. The waterfalls were accessible via a hiking trail about a mile long through lush jungle along a river. Once at the waterfalls we could swim in a deep clear pool with the water crashing down nearby.

I loved to just take day trips and drive along Kamehameha Highway with friends, stopping now and then in villages like Liae where there was a Polynesian Culture Center and a Wayside State Point where one could swim out to small odd shaped island-like rocks where big fish frequented. I also visited each of the outer islands over the course of my two years. Kauai was my favorite because I thought it was the most unspoiled, lush and tropical with vast expanses of empty beaches. Maui has a large inactive volcano, and hiking on the crater is like an imagined walk on the moon. The Big Island, Hawaii, had an active volcano while I was there and once I flew over it in a helicopter with one of the professors in our department. Other than Oahu, I spent more time on "The Big Island" than all the others because the University was doing research on large papaya and passion fruit farms here and I came often to help collect data. Once I came with a fellow graduate student who was from this island. He took me to see the town where he was born. It had been completely buried in lava in 1950 and only the top of a church steeple and a few telephone poles were still visible.

Hawaii truly was a scenic paradise, but as a young woman in my twenties it was not big enough to satisfy my adventurous spirit. I grew impatient with the smallness of the islands, always driving around in "circles." I began to long for wide open spaces and highways that actually took you further and further from your starting point. After two years I realized that I had what the islanders affectionately called "rock fever." One night Dr. Buddenhagen took me out to dinner in Waikiki and we sat near a window overlooking the main "drag" filled with tourists and soldiers and young people from all over. He said he found it sad to see these young people, always "looking" for something and never satisfied with what they had or where they were. He told me he thought Hawaii in particular attracted these young people, these "hippies," and he wondered if their generation (my generation!) would ever find happiness or would their restlessness, their constant questioning of the older generation, eventually settle into a pessimistic, doom and gloom kind of future. He was only about fifteen years older than me but what a difference that time span meant. From my age and my view of the world at that time I saw hope and excitement and the possibility of a real change in how people viewed each other. I believed in "flower power," the power of love, and saw all these young people, these "hippies," as the caring and optimistic leaders of the future. My generation was going to see the world, unite the world, and put an end to war!

On another day toward the end of my stay in Hawaii I experienced an event which would impact my decision-making for the rest of my life. I was in Waikiki with friends, enjoying a beautiful afternoon at the beach, when a bus load of tourists arrived. This was a tour of senior citizens, all very excited to be in Hawaii and to see the ocean. They walked along the beach in street clothes, some using canes, and one old man was in a wheel chair. He looked at me and said, "This is a dream come true, all my life I wanted to come to Hawaii, to experience this beautiful island, and now I'm here!" I smiled at him and congratulated him for getting here, but my unspoken, shocked reaction was, "You waited too long!." This was my instantaneous realization: our life spans aren't long enough, nor our bodies healthy enough, to put dreams off. Do it all while you can!

Gary and Rosie moved to Hawaii around Christmas of 1968. He had been in graduate school in Oklahoma but the Agricultural College there did not appreciate a Dairy Science student from Madison, Wisconsin who looked more like a "hippy" than a farmer. He transferred to the University of Hawaii with my help, convincing him that no one at this university would be wearing a suit, nor expect students to wear one. Shorts and colorful Hawaiian shirts were the dress code of the day. They arrived a few weeks before I completed my degree and quickly moved into some of the life I was leaving behind. They met my friends, got my car, and enrolled in classes at the University. I taught Gary how to do chromosome studies and he then took over my job at Children's Hospital and worked for Dr. Uemura.

As I was nearing the end of my graduate degree I was very busy analyzing data, summarizing the results in graphs and charts, and writing my thesis. This was all done by hand. With pen and ink I created the graphs and charts, and after the text was written I took it to a professional typist and for $25 she typed the forty some pages of manuscript into the format required by the university. I was proud of the research I had done and received many compliments on my work during the oral defense of my thesis. Two of my professors suggested that I stay on and continue this research, turning it into a Ph.D. dissertation. I certainly had enough data now, and knowledge of airborne plant pathogens to continue this study. However, everyone in the department knew that I had saved some money and planned to travel and "see the world." I told them I would think about it, and perhaps be back in the fall to start my doctorate. I had been planning for weeks, months even, to fly to Luxemburg and begin a new adventure by backpacking around Europe. I had been in these discussions with my friend Judy from Hawaii and Herbie and Char, my ex-college roommates from Madison. All of us had wanted to do this for a number of years and talked about doing it together. However, when the perfect time came for me to leave, January of 1969, none of them were free to go. Judy wanted to stay in school and not take the semester off, Herbie had moved to Boston and just started a new job, and Char had met someone and was planning on getting married. Much to my parents' horror, I decided to go alone.

The night before I left Hawaii I went with my friends, Barb and Ken, to the Punchbowl National Cemetery and was shocked to see that it was now nearly full. Hundreds and hundreds of gravestones had been added, all from soldiers killed in Vietnam. Richard Nixon had been elected President and was about to be inaugurated. I was completely disgusted with the politics of the United States at that time and did not want to be there with "warmongers" in office. I did not believe that Nixon had any "secret" plan to get us out of Vietnam, and was happy that I would be leaving.

My exit from Hawaii was sad and exciting at the same time. About twenty of my friends (mostly Persians) came to the airport to see me off. They brought me leis, and I had so many of them around my neck that I could barely see out of my eyes! We spent quite a while in the airport since I was flying standby (half fare for those under the age of twenty-five) and soldiers on R&R from Vietnam were also there flying standby. Rightfully so, the soldiers were given priority, so I had to wait a number of hours before I finally got a flight to the mainland. The day I left Hawaii my long straight brown hair reached my waist, my skin was brown from two years in Hawaii, my clothes were light weight and summer-like, and of course there were all the leis I had on. Arriving in Wisconsin in the coldest month of winter I felt so exotic, and judging by all the stares I got, the Wisconsinites felt the same.

CHAPTER 5

RULE # 5: Enjoy and Support the ARTS

Music, poetry, art, and literature are what make us human. Enjoy the fabulous talent of our many ancestors and creative contemporaries. Seek out your own talent by trying your hand at artistic endeavors such as dancing, writing, painting, singing, or perhaps playing an instrument.

BACKPACKING THROUGH EUROPE TO THE MIDDLE EAST

I spent a week at home in Wisconsin, enjoying every minute with my family. I packed and repacked my suitcase. It was winter so I needed some warm clothes for northern Europe, but I wanted to spend more time in the warmer climates of the Mediterranean countries so I needed summer clothes too. And I didn't know how long I would be gone since I really had no plan at all, other than to go to Europe. The hardest thing to leave behind was my guitar, but I had a full sized suitcase and knew that was enough to have to be responsible for.

Mom and Dad tried to talk me out of going on this trip. Dad asked what I would do for money and I explained that I had saved about $2500 by working in the chromosome lab and doing autopsies. He was shocked! He thought about it for a while and then said, "Well Ruthann, you could buy yourself a brand new Mustang with that much money!"

I smiled, patted him on the shoulder, and said, "But Dad, I don't want a Mustang or any other car. I want to travel." (Years later I teased him about this by saying, "Dad, remember that Mustang you wanted me to buy? Well by now I'm sure it's a pile of rust in some landfill, but what I bought with the money are memories I will have all my life.")

Mom was glad I wanted to travel and thought it would be great to go to Europe, BUT she said, "Why would you want to go by yourself? Why not wait until summer when some of your friends might be free to go with you?" Though she never actually said it, I knew she was afraid for my safety. I assured her that I did want to go by myself rather than wait to see who might be available in the summer. I was twenty-five years old and had been dreaming of this kind of adventure for a long time. I had planned a trip like this before, with Josie, then with Char, and with Barb, and finally with Judy, over the course of six years, but events in our lives led us in different directions. I knew this might always be the case and since this was MY big dream, I alone needed to make it happen.

I flew stand-by to New York City for about $25, and called one of my friend's family when I got there. This friend, Susan, was someone I met at the University of Hawaii and she insisted I should stay at her house in New York even though at the time she was doing a study abroad in El Salvador. Her family were wonderful to me, they met me at the bus station at the end of the George Washington Bridge and drove me to their house. Her mom fixed New England clam chowder for me which I had never heard of and I loved it. They drove me into the city the next day so I could go to an international travel agency and get a Eurail Pass and an International Student ID. I knew from friends who had backpacked around Europe before that these two items were essential. I also went to the office of Icelandair and bought a one way ticket to Luxemburg. This airline was well known among my peers for having the cheapest tickets to Europe.

I spent a few nights with this very hospitable family and then called my friend Mic from Honolulu who was in town for the week visiting his dad out on Rockaway Beach. I soon learned this was a very Irish area of New York City. Most of Mic's friends and neighbors were firemen or policemen. His Dad was a retired fireman. I spent a couple nights in Rockaway enjoying the Irish pubs, music and food with Mic. It was winter and cold so I was wearing my dark brown suede jacket, the only winter coat I had. When we came home from an evening of pub hopping I realized that the pockets on my jacket had been neatly cut, probably with a razor blade, and my gloves were missing. I supposed it was a thief, looking for a wallet or cash. I loved that jacket and was really unhappy about my torn pockets. I bought a little travel sewing kit and fixed it the best I could.

The next evening Mic drove me to the airport. As I sat in the airport waiting for my flight, I thought about Mic and his Dad, and Susan's family, and how kind and generous they were to me. Over the course of my travels I met many more people like this and had no way to really thank them enough for all they did for me. As I aged and acquired some assets I have tried to return the favor by being generous and kind to other people, a sort of "passing it on" endeavor.

The flight to Iceland took about six hours and it seemed that all of us were smoking on the plane. By the time we arrived the air inside the plane was blue in color and my eyes burned. There was a six hour time change between New York and Iceland so it was early morning when we arrived. We had a long layover here and the airline offered a bus tour of Reykjavik which I was happy to take. The city was smaller than I imagined and much more colorful. The buildings had roofs of blue and red and green. There were no skyscrapers, in fact most buildings were only a few stories high. We stopped at the famous old Hotel Borg in the city center for coffee and pastries, and when we left there about 11 a.m. the sun was finally beginning to rise. Back at the airport I visited a store filled with beautiful Icelandic sweaters. They were relatively inexpensive and I really wanted one, but I stuck with my plan: no souvenirs. I wanted to travel as long as I could and see as much of the world as possible on the money I had. I knew

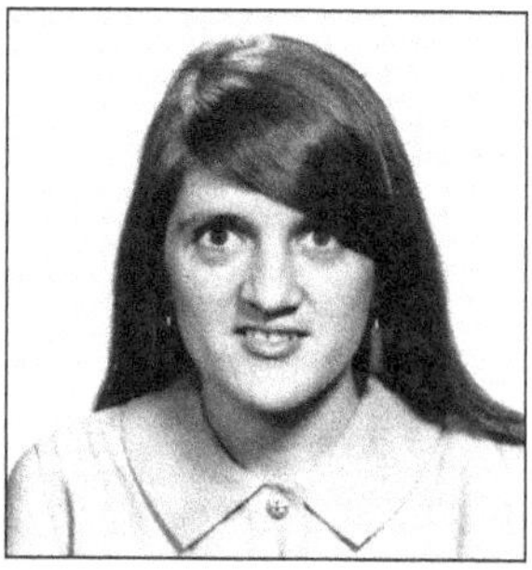

First passport photo

this meant being frugal, and besides I had one suitcase and it was already full of the things I thought I needed.

EUROPE

Luxembourg City was dark when I arrived and I had no plans, no idea of what I would do or even where I would spend the night. I followed the other passengers, took a shuttle bus into the city center, and got off at the train station. There was a young German man on the shuttle who seemed overly attentive and presumptuous about a "friendship" he was trying to establish with me. He said he knew the city and would help me find a hotel room. He explained that I needed some local currency, and since I only had dollars and American Express travelers' checks, it would be better to go with him. There was a little 'pensione' hotel near the station, so we walked over there. He did all the talking, in German, and paid the woman at the desk some money. With a big smile on her face she handed him a key. When he started walking up the stairs, I asked him where my key was. He said, "Oh, we'll be sharing a room. It's safer and cheaper this way." I immediately realized how stupid it was of me not to trust my gut feeling regarding this guy. "Absolutely not!" I responded. He then sheepishly apologized, asked the woman for another room for which she gladly accepted my cash of $4 U.S.! The room was tiny, but the bed was fantastic. It had an eiderdown quilt with a duvet cover instead of a double sheet and blanket like in the States. I loved it and adapted this style of bedding when I later returned to America.

That night as I lay there jet-lagged and trying to fall asleep I had a serious conversation, out loud, with myself that went something like this: "Annabelle, don't be so gullible! How could it not have been obvious to you that this guy was simply after your bod? Now use this situation as a needed learning experience. You need to find a tourist office or a book store and get some accurate information on each place you visit. Try to figure out for yourself where you might spend the night and things you want to see and do. And most important of all...follow your intuition! When you get a 'gut feeling' about someone or something, pay attention! That little 'inner voice' is always right." (NOTE: I don't know when this habit started, but from a young age I, Ruthann, would talk to my "other" self, Annabelle, whenever I was upset about something I had done; or when I needed courage and encouragement; or when I just wanted to get an important idea or concept in my head. These "conversations" are always out-loud, and when I am by myself.)

I awoke early the next morning with a renewed sense of determination and self-confidence. I walked over to the train station and picked up brochures and maps and then spent a few hours drinking coffee and pouring over this literature. It seems strange to me now, that I arrived in Europe with no specific plans. I had put a lot of thought into getting there, but none into "what then." Feeling very much "the stranger in a strange land" I decided that I would start my adventure in England. I reasoned that the culture would be different, but the people would speak English, so that would be one less barrier to deal with. Also, two of my former college roommates (M.L. and Molly) lived in England now so the thought of staying with old friends while I familiarized myself with this new lifestyle was very appealing. I took the afternoon train to northern France, and then a ferry across the English Channel. After arriving in England, everyone on the ferry was ushered into a large warehouse-like building. A misty, chemical smelling spray was then released from the ceiling and descended on us like a slow moving cloud. I think it was some kind of disinfectant but the sight of it reminded me of the gassing of Jews during the war. My fellow passengers were obviously used to this since no one seemed to think this was unusual except me.

Calling my friend M.L. in Brighton, England was another strange experience. First I had to exchange some dollars for British pounds including the necessary coins to make a phone call. When I called the operator to get the telephone number I could not understand what she was telling me. She was speaking English but was talking fast and had an accent very unfamiliar to my ears. Finally I turned to a Pakistani man behind me in line at the phone booth and asked him for help. He listened to the operator for me and then in an English accent I could understand he explained what she said. I needed him to translate her English into my English! Soon I was talking to M.L. and with her directions in hand I boarded a train to Brighton where she met me at the station. My time with M.L. and her husband, Alan, was relaxing and enjoyable. They were both working at the local university and M.L. was also pursuing her Ph.D. while there. They seemed very happy with their decision to move to England. It was winter and I was cold all the time. Their house had no central heat and one had to insert coins to get hot water for a bath. At night we slept under piles of blankets.

We walked in the afternoons to the cliffs by the sea and spent our evenings in the local pub where we could sit by a roaring fire in the old stone fireplace. We talked over a glass of ale and cheap pub food and enjoyed the short-lived warmth. I was disappointed to find out that the pubs closed at 10 p.m.! I thought back to my British professor at the University of Hawaii, how he criticized American bars and told me how wonderful the British pubs were. I therefore thought that they would be wild and crazy and open all night. I didn't realize he meant they would be more like a comfortable living room where everyone went home to bed at ten. Another disappointing thing about England was that places of business were not dependable. They might post their hours as 9 a.m. to 5 p.m. but in reality they might not be open until 11 a.m. or noon, depending when the owner/worker arrived. This was even true of the post office and the ticket windows at the train station. Not that it mattered so much since the trains rarely ran on time.

My next visit was with Molly, her husband, and young son, Travis, in London. They lived in an apartment, again no central heat. Molly was a stay-at-home-mom so we had lots of time to see London together with the baby in his stroller. We visited old churches, flea markets, and parks, ate lunch in cafes with cold sandwiches and no option for black coffee other than "Nescafe" which was an instant coffee bag served next to a cup of hot water. I loathed it, but even worse would have been coffee with hot milk already added.

On my own, I visited many of the famous tourist spots like Big Ben, the Tower of London, and Westminster Abbey. One afternoon while lost in a back passage of the abbey, I sat on an old stone bench to rest and glanced down to see a burial site underneath! It was a rustic stone carving of a man in a robe lying face up with his arms crossed and an inscription stating that this was the burial site of an 11th Century Benedictine monk. I wondered when the last time someone noticed him there, tucked away under that bench. And was it an honor for him to be buried here (after all it was the Westminster Abbey) or was it meant as some kind of punishment since he was hidden away in the back of the building. But most of all it reminded me of how long we will each be dead, and how short our lives actually are. I secured the memory of this monk in my brain and linked it with my determination to live my life to the fullest. In whatever time I had, I would carry out my dreams and see the world.

Before leaving London I took one last metro ride to the American Embassy. Throughout the world this is where most young traveling Americans received their mail. Mine was addressed simply: Ruthann Zimmer, c/o The American Embassy, City Name, Country Name. Getting letters from family and friends made the trip to an American Embassy worth it, but in England this trip also brought warmth. The building had central heat! I went there often during my month long stay in England because it was the only place where I felt completely warm. Having lived in Hawaii for two years where temperatures were always around 80F, adjusting to a cold damp winter climate was difficult and negatively influenced my feelings toward England for many years.

I left England the same way I arrived, train to ferry, ferry to France, only this time the sea was very rough. Sitting in warmth in a lower lounge area I was feeling quite nauseous. The French at that time smoked these little cigar-like cigarettes, and even though I was a smoker myself, the combination of that warm air and smoke filled room was unbearable so I went up and stood on the top deck by myself. It was really windy and cold but that fresh air was rejuvenating, and soon I was singing to myself and feeling so excited for whatever my next adventure would bring.

My destination was Germany since my other college roommate, Josie, was living there with her husband, Tom, and their baby son, Heinrich. Tom was in the U.S. Army, stationed near Bamburg. Germany had a big impact on me for a number of reasons. First, most of my ancestors came from here so I was very interested in the country and the culture. Second, this was where the war began and signs of it still existed in bombed out buildings and military cemeteries. I found myself staring, almost rudely, at older Germans who had to have been involved in some way in the war effort. I wondered what they were doing back then, were they soldiers, were they anti-Semitic, and did they feel guilt for what Germany did? Looking at the faces of those around the age of my parents sometimes made me angry. I knew they were about my age during the war and I wanted to ask them what they were thinking back then. How could they have supported someone as hateful as Hitler? How could they not have known about the murder of so many Jews?

Josie gave me two books, both of which I carried with me throughout my travels in Europe. One was *Europe on $5 a Day* which became my sole tour guide. The second was *The Rise and Fall of the Third Reich* which I read from cover to cover as I traveled from country to country.

While Tom was busy with his military duties, Josie and I took Heinrich with us and we did various side trips. We visited nearby towns with old cathedrals, Nuremberg where the war criminal trials were held, and Heidelberg with its charming old university. Once we did a boat ride on a stretch of the Rhine River with beautiful views of old castles built on top of cliffs. I had to admit that the countryside of Germany was in some ways much like Wisconsin, especially the farmland with the Holstein cows in the pastures. I could see why my ancestors ended up in Wisconsin.

I wanted to see Berlin but going through East Germany to get there was off limits for Tom and Josie, as a U.S. military family, so it was a side trip I made on my own. At the train station in Bamberg I bought what I thought was a round trip ticket to Berlin. Since no one there spoke English this whole transaction was made using hand signs. The train ride through East Germany took many hours since the train stopped often and various guards got on and checked passports each time. West Berlin was a marvel of modern buildings, crowded sidewalks, busy traffic, numerous restaurants and cafes, fashionable shops, and a very colorful night life. I stayed at my first Youth Hostel there and went out to some of the night clubs with my fellow "roommates." The following day I toured East Berlin. There was very little traffic and buildings were still bombed out with no repair work done. Even the large museum in the center of the city did not have complete walls or roof. Inside were many stone carvings from Egypt, too large for anyone to steal, not bothered much by the rain and wind, and miraculously not harmed during the war. The biggest attraction in the city was a cemetery where Russian soldiers were buried. They boasted of the fact that all the soil and plant life there were brought from Russia. Finding something to eat was difficult since there were no openly visible restaurants. For me being in East Berlin was like stepping back in time about twenty years and being in West Berlin was like stepping ahead in time about twenty years! The contrast between these two cities was truly shocking.

I left West Berlin on the same train I had arrived on and headed back to Bamburg where Josie was scheduled to pick me up. A few hours later the train stopped in East Germany and I was asked for my ticket and passport. Lots of conversation ensued and I was informed that my ticket was "no good." I was removed from the train to a small station where about six or seven guards / railway employees worked. The train left and I was the only one in the station with these men. A slow fear began to creep into my body. They were in uniform and speaking loudly in German, obviously about me! I imagined that they were lying, that there was nothing wrong with my ticket, but that these men were dangerous and that I was now in serious trouble. Finally they explained to me in minimal English that my ticket was only one way. "Ticket Bamburg — Berlin, ya; ticket Berlin — Bamburg, nein!" They wanted an additional amount equal to about $12 in German marks. I only had U.S. dollars and travelers checks which they would not accept. My fear dissipated when they realized I was worried and upset and began speaking softer, trying to communicate with me in some English. They served me coffee and sweet rolls, and after a few hours the next train came. These men then took up a collection among themselves and gave me a handful of German marks for the ticket to Bamburg. They shook my hand "gute-bye" and helped me on the train. I have never forgotten their kindness. I learned a wonderful lesson on understanding cultural differences and situations before passing judgement of any kind.

After another week of Tom and Josie's warm friendship, I left Germany on my own and set off to see as much of Europe as I could. The 1960s were a time in which many young people were out exploring the world as cheaply as possible. I started out alone but met many fellow travelers along the way – some were going my way, but often I would change course and go their way. After months of traveling I looked back and realized that I had only been on my own for a total of four days. This was the glory of the 60s, it really was a time of "smile on your brother, everybody get together...." The conversations would go something like this: "Hi, where you headed?"

"Barcelona."

"Ah, nice place. I was there about a month ago for the Grand Prix. Be sure to stay in one of the 'pensiones' off the Ramblas. They are quite nice and yet inexpensive."

Other times it was, "Hi, where you headed?"

"Vienna."

"Hmmm, I haven't been there. What takes you there?"

"We met a Swedish couple a few weeks ago and that was their favorite city in Europe so we decided we have to see it. There are four of us going there, taking the overnight train. Want to join us?"

Travel tips would be shared along with biographical information such as name, where from, and college alma mater, etc. Then as casually as the conversations began, they would end with new traveling companions or a "good luck" and "see you around." A Eurail Pass and no commitment to time or direction made it all possible.

One of my traveling companions was an Irish-American girl named Kathy. We spent a few months together mostly in Spain, Portugal, and France. She was my age but was already widowed. Her husband had committed suicide after years of depression and she had left to try to "find herself." She was quiet but smiled a lot and very much enjoyed the people and places we visited. She was pretty with brown hair and brown eyes and that beautiful smile of hers made it easy for us to meet new friends. We met an Israeli couple on the train from Barcelona to Madrid and the four of us toured Spain together. While in Madrid with the help of the Israelis, Kathy and I went to a flea market where we sold our suitcases and some of our clothes. Our American Levi jeans were the hottest items. We each had two pair so we each sold one pair. Getting rid of the suitcases was the beginning of a new travel experience. I felt so free not having to haul that heavy thing around. I bought a small leather shoulder pack, just big enough to fit the few items of clothing I had saved. My entire wardrobe now consisted of a small plain black dress, pair of black sandals, one pair of levis, one pair of loose fitting travel pants, a couple T-shirts, a couple blouses, a sweater, a silk head scarf I had purchased in Holland, a bikini, a sun dress, a few under garments, a pair of loafers, and my brown suede jacket with the sewed up pockets. I took the money from the sale of my "stuff" and had a guitar made to fit my size and playing style. It was gorgeous and I loved it! I felt so free, being able to easily travel from place to place with my leather pack (I named it Ramblas after the main street in Barcelona) slung over my shoulder and my guitar in hand. We visited the rich beach towns on the Costa del Sol and the historical Moorish towns of Granada and Toledo. On Sundays I would wear my black dress and head scarf and we would visit a cathedral, church, synagogue, or any other place of worship just to take in the awe of these foreign rituals. I carried this habit with me throughout my years of travel, continuing my interest in world religions.

We met three young Canadian guys one day near Gibraltar and they were planning to go to Morocco on the ferry boat from Spain to Tangier. We thought this sounded like a great adventure. The Israeli couple did not want to go so we said good-bye to them and left on the ferry with the Canadians. We bought the cheapest tickets which gave us nothing but a deck chair on the top of the ferry. Part of the top floor was made of glass and we could see the wealthier travelers below enjoying a fancy dinner at tables with table clothes. They were drinking wine and having a great time. Still, I was enjoying my stick of French bread and a bottle of coke since from on top we had such beautiful views. The ride was only about three to four hours, but about half way across the seas got rather rough and soon the ferry was rocking wildly. We saw diners below with plates on their laps, bottles tipped over, and people falling down. Our chairs were fastened tight to the deck so we just hung on and enjoyed the ride!

Morocco was a world away from Europe. We only spent three days there and our entire visit was in Tangier. The Canadians left for Fez and places beyond, but because Morocco was not part of our Eurail Pass Kathy and I decided to head back to Spain where we could ride the trains for "free." Still, the three days in Morocco were interesting on one hand, and unpleasant on the other hand. The moment we disembarked from the ferry boat we were accosted by small boys, around eight to twelve–years-old. They worked in groups and followed us everywhere, always asking for money. The Canadians, one in particular, was very friendly with the boys, which the boys loved. They would laugh and giggle and try to stay close to him. When we ate in restaurants the boys would come in and sit at a nearby table and order a meal. When finished their bill would be added to our bill! The Canadians never seemed to mind and always paid their tab. Walking through the bazaar was like stepping back in time. There were hundreds of small stalls with merchants selling everything from buttons to baklava, chickens to chess sets, and lemons to leather. The bazaar was like a giant maze and around every corner were more merchants and street performers. We saw snake charmers, fortune tellers, magicians, dancers, and local musicians. After three days I was exhausted, physically and mentally, and glad to get back to Spain!

Kathy and I visited Portugal, much of Spain, and then Paris together before she flew to America where she intended to go to school. She was kind enough to take my guitar with her and put it on a Greyhound bus to Appleton, Wisconsin for me. She sent it in care of my sister, June, who was living there at the time along with a letter from me asking June to keep it for me. (Unfortunately, June's young children and dog managed to destroy the guitar before I returned to America so I never got to play it again). Traveling without the guitar though was much easier. Now I just had Ramblas, my small leather shoulder pack.

Europe as a whole was a great "education" for me. I enjoyed the people, the historical buildings, scenic views, the food and wine, the ease of travel with an American passport and the strength of the U.S. dollar at that time. I could live on close to $5 /day not counting the Eurail Pass. Food and lodging was inexpensive. I usually stayed in youth hostels or small pensiones for less than a dollar a night. I rarely ate in restaurants except for small cafes. I learned to eat in outdoor markets or from small kiosks. Breakfast was always some strong black coffee and a pastry of some sort. Lunch was a deli item like a piece of pizza, small sandwich, bowl of soup, or whatever was on special for the day. Dinner was usually bread and cheese and fruit and wine, often as a picnic in a park or while riding the train to a new spot. Sometimes I would use the train as my hotel room. The Eurail Pass back then was a First Class ticket. I could get on any long distance train around 9 or 10 p.m. and sleep in my compartment until around 3 or 4 a.m. and then I would get off and take the next train back to where I was the day before. This was especially useful in countries like Switzerland where even the youth hostels were "expensive" by my standards, and it was easy to ride trains in and out of the country and get my sleep coming and going.

I was in Zurich for May Day and witnessed the celebratory

big parades mostly honoring union workers. The hostel was booked full so I rode the trains at night. I loved the mountainous countryside of Switzerland and Austria. I traveled to Innsbruck with a Canadian girl I met in a youth hostel and her Norwegian boyfriend. They were both skiers and since Innsbruck had hosted the Winter Olympics it was high on their list of places to go. We joined some other Americans and headed to Vienna, a city that really fascinated me. I loved our visit to the grounds of the former Hapsburg dynasty. I thought of it as truly a land of "old King Cole and his merry old souls"" There was a beautiful opera house in Vienna and with our International Student IDs we could get tickets for the upper balcony for a few Austrian schillings, about ten cents. If there were no seats available they would let us sit in the aisles. I loved it. It was all in Italian so I couldn't understand what they were saying but the music was wonderful and the opera house was one of the most beautiful, ornate buildings I had ever seen. Most of the Austrians on the streets were very well dressed; men in suits and overcoats, women in dresses and heels. They were not very friendly and looked at us with disapproving eyes. At one point as we were walking under a small bridge the Austrians overhead started shouting anti-American slogans and something about Americans in Vietnam and then one of the women actually spit at us. It was my only personal encounter with anti-Americanism on my entire European trip.

I zig-zagged the continent, and visited all thirteen of the countries covered by my Eurail Pass, plus Great Britain and that short sojourn into Morocco. I liked Spain most of all, because it was warm and I could use some of the Spanish I learned in college to get around. Barcelona was my favorite city. It had a great night life and was colorful and exciting even in the day time. On one trip to Barcelona I met a French freelance writer/photographer who lived there and he spent time showing me around. We went to a bull fight together and also to the Grand Prix which was in town. The famous Scottish driver, Jackie Stewart, was in that race. We had tickets to the inside of the track which was a very exciting place to be. I tried to photograph these futuristic looking race cars as they zoomed around the track but when I developed the film later it was obvious that mostly what I photographed was the empty track after the car had already gone by!

In Belgium I met an Australian on the train. I was impressed to learn that it was common for Australians to take time off, up to two years, between college and the world of work to go off and see the world. We were sharing a compartment with a Belgian lady who spoke fluent English. She told us she learned English solely by watching British TV programs. I was amazed, and thought it was too bad we didn't have Spanish TV or French TV in America! I traveled through Belgium, Luxembourg and France with the Australian boy and then he went on to Spain and I went to Scandinavia. He was kind and cute and I missed him when he left. I took the train to Hamburg, then a ferry to Denmark. I met some Danish college students on the ferry and they showed me around Copenhagen, including a very entertaining trip to Tivoli. I could have spent more time there since I really enjoyed their company and Copenhagen, but I was anxious to get to Sweden to look up my friend Richard who was then attending the University in Lund after receiving political asylum there. Nearly a year had passed since I helped him go AWOL from the U.S. Army in Hawaii.

Richard was sharing an apartment with fellow engineering students and seemed well adjusted to his new life in Sweden. He had learned the language and was receiving help from the Swedish government to continue his studies. I was very happy to see him and to know that he was succeeding with his plans to finish his engineering degree and eventually become a Swedish citizen. I spent about a week with him and had a wonderful time reminiscing about life in Hawaii and our mutual friends back there. I also spent time with him and his roommates discussing life in Lund and the adjustments he had to make. For one thing, credits from the University of Hawaii did not transfer so he had to start his entire degree program over again. Saying good bye to Richard was hard. I felt a longing for the life we had both left behind in Hawaii, and sad to realize that he might never be allowed to return. (NOTE: Since I traveled a great deal in the following years I lost track of him. Forty years after this visit Richard and I got back in contact via Facebook. He received amnesty under the Carter Administration but still lives in Sweden where he became a citizen, married, had two children, and works as an engineer. He has since traveled to America, including visits to Hawaii.)

From Sweden I traveled to Amsterdam to meet my friend Judy from Hawaii. I got to Amsterdam about ten days before Judy's arrival. I checked into a third floor tiny room at the top of a small steep, staircase typical in Holland in the old buildings along the canals. Across the hall from me was an American soldier, Steve, waiting for his orders to return to the States. I spent some time traveling around the city with him. Unlike the

From top: Me, Judy, and friend on gondola in Venice. Molly at flea market in London. Josie with her son, Heinrich, in Bamberg. World War II cemetery in Germany.

other vagabond backpackers in Europe this guy had a job and money and a timeline to his travels. We ate in real restaurants and for the first time I had Indonesian food, which I loved. We visited the home of Anne Frank and the Rembrandt Museum and the Heineken Brewery among other tourist attractions. Most of all I loved the coffee houses in Amsterdam. After Steve left for the States I went to the coffee houses every night. They had big booths or tables and one just joined any group of young people that you wanted to. I would listen for a group speaking English (always many) and then choose one with a topic of interest to me. Sometimes it was political like the war in Vietnam. Sometimes it was travel talk. Sometimes heated arguments on things like existentialism.

Judy arrived with her usual high level of energy. No jet lag visible with that girl! She was always wonderfully optimistic and traveled with a beautiful, never ending smile on her face. We spent the summer together and once again I was zigzagging around Europe, this time focusing on countries she was most interested in seeing. We first went to Germany and in a Youth Hostel in Frankfurt met a young German woman whom we traveled with for a while. The three of us went to Norway together and hitchhiked from Oslo in the south to Hammerfest above the Arctic Circle. We stayed in Narvik for a few days, hiking the fjords and falling in love with the most beautiful scenery I had ever encountered. I was absolutely mesmerized by the steep snow covered fjords, harbors filled with ships, beautiful blue skies, and the amazing midnight sun. Baked, boiled, or fried shrimp were sold in paper bags like popcorn and we ate plenty of it. The people were very friendly so getting a ride by hitchhiking was no problem.

Judy and I traveled well together. In general, we both enjoyed adventures of any kind. We both loved to dance and so we sought out night spots with live music and dance floors. With Judy's blonde hair, big blue eyes, and general attractiveness meeting dance partners was not a problem. It didn't matter that often our dance partners could not speak English, it was the music and each other's company that mattered. We danced our way through

Germany, France, Spain, and Italy and enjoyed many laughs along the way. Once in Italy, while staying in a room in a high rise "otel" in the center of Rome a note tied to a string came floating to our window. We opened the window and retrieved the note. It said simply, "I love you!." We looked up and saw this cute young man looking out the window in the room above us. We became "friends" with him and his buddy and they showed us around Rome. They were Italians and only spoke about ten words of English, but they were good dancers and knew the best clubs to visit at night. Judy and I loved to dance. I thought of myself as a good dancer, but Judy was by far the best. One evening after hours of dancing and a few drinks we were sitting in the courtyard outside our "otel" just laughing and trying to communicate with our Italian friends when an old woman yelled at us from an open window above and then threw a bucket of water at us!

In Rome we visited many of the classical tourist spots, and for the first time on my European travels, I paid for tours. It was Judy's idea. She wanted a guided tour so we could hear details of these places in English, and it was indeed a good idea since there was so much to see in Rome. We went to the catacombs, the Coliseum, and the Vatican as well as many museums, art galleries, and cathedrals. We took a hydrofoil to the Isle of Capri where we watched the wealthy parade around in their designer sunglasses and beautiful suntanned bodies. One night with our new found Italian friends we took a picnic box of wine and cheese and built a fire on a beach not far from Rome by the Tyrrhenian Sea. As I sat near that fire I thought of all the beaches I had sat on watching a bonfire, eating, drinking, and just being in love with the sound of the sea and my good fortune to be there enjoying the company of the people I was with at the time. And I thought of those beautiful beaches of Hawaii so far away and it made me a bit homesick.

For Judy and me there were a few times when one big difference in our lifestyles got in the way. I wore my hair long and straight and I rarely used makeup. I could wake up early, shower, get dressed, and let my hair dry in the sun. Twenty or thirty minutes were the most time I needed. Judy on the other hand moved slower in the morning, and needed a couple of hours to get ready. She had shoulder length hair which she curled and fussed over. And she wore makeup every day. Usually it didn't matter. Wherever we were I could get ready and go for a walk in the morning, get coffee and breakfast and come back to our room a few hours later to meet up with her when she was ready. However, there were a few times when this trait of hers was definitely frustrating. For example, we missed a morning train out of Madrid, the only nonstop train to Paris, and had to wait until the following day. We missed the free early morning student tour of the Louvre. And our late starts meant that we sometimes waited in long lines for entrance into tourist attractions. Still, I very much enjoyed my time with Judy as a traveling companion. She was adventurous, interested in all there was to see and do, and maintained an upbeat, positive attitude through it all.

In mid-summer we left the ease and comfort of our Eurail Passes and boarded a freighter sailing from Brindisi, Italy to Patra, Greece. Brindisi was a sailors' town and I felt almost physically molested by all the men ogling us and making noises and seemingly lewd hand gestures and comments. For once I was glad I didn't understand the language.

The freighter was large and the passengers on board were all relegated to the top deck with little or no comfort, but the inexpensive tickets and the short passage time made it worthwhile. Most significant for Judy and me was our meeting and subsequent close friendship with Paul, the French Canadian, who would accompany us all the way to the Iranian border. Paul was a great compliment to our little traveling group, making it a perfect threesome. He was like a brother to us and we both felt safer in his presence. We were heading to the Middle East and we knew that as two women traveling alone we would feel as vulnerable as we did in the Italian sailing town of Brindisi. Traveling with Paul changed all that. He was big and bearded, but his relaxed and smiling demeanor was disarming. He was very personable and made friends easily, so we were always in conversations with local people in local establishments even when we didn't speak the same language and had to rely on hand motions. Judy and I were definitely heading to Iran and Paul wanted to go to Iraq. Other than that we had no specific plans. We poured over maps and a few old tour books, and asked a lot of questions of fellow travelers. We listened to each other's ideas on where to go next, what to eat, and what to do, and then decisions were carefully made and equally balanced.

Our first night in Greece was magical. We arrived close to dusk and stayed in a little inn by the sea. The nearby restaurant served dinner outdoors on tables by the sea. As the sun went down numerous local people began arriving for drinks and laughter and music provided by two men playing concertinas. I felt ecstatic! Much like the night we spent around a bonfire along the Tyrrhenian Sea outside of Rome. But this time it was the Ionean Sea with smiling, welcoming Greeks, yet under the same stars and with that same sense of camaraderie that so often overwhelmed me amongst complete strangers in my travels around the world. I felt so privileged just to be there to share in that experience.

Athens was not what I expected. It was a large sprawling city, but not tall with skyscrapers. The people were friendly and polite, but it seemed like such a male dominated society. The coffee houses were filled with men. At an afternoon matinee Judy and I were the only women in the theater. Most of the women that we did see in the streets wore black dresses and scarves, nothing like the modern women of Rome. The ancient ruins of the Acropolis did their magic on my mind, and made me promise to read and learn more about the history of the people who built this so long ago.

It was July, 1969, and we were staying in a large, rather modern hotel in the center of Athens. Judy and I in one room, and Paul in another. We almost never stayed in hotels but the dollar was strong and everything in Greece was therefore reasonably inexpensive. And besides, it was very hot and this hotel had air conditioning, so we splurged. One night as we walked outside into the streets we noticed people were gathered around store windows watching televisions inside. We got close to one group and asked them what was happening, why was everyone trying to watch these televisions. From our looks and our English language they recognized us as Americans and started applauding us and offering to buy us drinks. They explained that they were watching the televisions to see Americans land on the moon! Crowds gathered and they all wanted to touch us and congratulate us. We were treated as heroes just for being Americans, and we stood there in awe surrounded by all these excited Greeks and watched Neil Armstrong walk on the moon.

On our last night in this comfortable hotel a strange event happened. In the middle of the night someone knocked on our door loud enough to wake both Judy and me up. Then we heard someone speak in a spooky, heavily accented voice saying, "I'm going to keeeelll you." We assumed it was a prank, but still listening to someone threatening to kill us made going back to sleep difficult. We decided to pile furniture in front of the door so no one could get in, even with a key. Satisfied that we were secure, we happily went back to sleep, and never did find out who it was that made the threat.

Paul and Judy and I left Greece on a freighter bound for Istanbul. We were all very excited to be leaving the western, Christian world which we were so familiar with for the unfamiliar exotic, Muslim world. At this point I had been on the road for six months and felt comfortable and competent as a seasoned world traveler. I was definitely ready for the next adventure: the Middle East.

CHAPTER 6

RULE # 6: Learn the art of "Letting Go"

Know when a situation is beyond your control and simply allow yourself the pleasure of relaxing and as John Lennon would say, "let it be."

IRAN

Istanbul was the perfect introduction into the contradictory culture of the Middle East. On the northwest side of the Bosphorus tributary separating the Black Sea and the Sea of Marmara was the European-like part of the city, while on the east side lay the true Oriente of famed historic accounts. The eastern part of Istanbul was an astounding site with its many mosques and minarets as well as the scattered existence of old Christian churches, some turned into museums or even mosques. And at the center was the Grand Bazaar, a huge labyrinth of narrow covered streets and thousands of little shops. We stayed in a small "otel" near the Grand Bazaar and tried to soak in as much of this overpowering exotic culture as we could. The owners of our hotel were very friendly and each night one of them would go out on the town with us. This was a wonderful experience because it allowed us to participate in many local traditions that we would never have known about. For example, there were small squares in the city where each evening puppet shows were put on. These were well attended and quite elaborate, involving huge puppets with amazing costumes and interesting sets. Kids were always seated on the ground up front. There was much laughter and hand clapping from the audience, children and adults alike. Another interesting event was the late night "soup kitchens." After an evening of dancing, closing time at the clubs, or late night shows the people of Istanbul loved to stop for bowls of soup featured in many of the restaurants and street cafes. The soup was a broth with little round dumpling-like things floating in it. We of course had to try it, not knowing what it was. I didn't care for the taste and later found out it was made from sheep brains!

I loved the Grand Bazaar and spent hours weaving my way through all the narrow covered streets with the merchants hawking their wares in a variety of languages. They would look me over and then after deciding where I came from they would beckon to me in that language. Usually they started speaking to me in German and when I didn't respond they would switch to English. Each shop was small, maybe a hundred square feet at most, and specializing in one type of item. Shops with similar items were all located in the same general area such that there was within the Grand Bazaar a "gold bazaar," a "shoe bazaar," a "carpet bazaar," even a "button bazaar!" Really, anything you could possibly think of could be found somewhere in the Grand Bazaar. I loved Istanbul and its people, and have returned a number of times in my life. It is still my favorite city in the world.

We traveled from village to village on small Turkish buses called "dormes." They were not air-conditioned, always crowded, noisy, and late, but they were cheap and easy to find. We preferred these to the larger long distance buses that smelled like diesel because the engine was located behind the driver's seat inside the bus. It was July, and it was very hot. Even though temperatures neared 100F, Judy and I wore our mini-dresses as "tunics" over our blue jeans. This, along with penny loafers and a silk headscarf, made up our conservative wardrobe necessary for travel in the Muslim villages in the central and eastern part of the country. We rode one of the large buses from Ankara to Marvan, over the mountains on an all-night trip.

It was following this bus ride, with its important lesson, that we boarded that fateful train for Bagdad and ended up having the harrowing experience in Syria that I have described in the opening chapter of this book. After escaping from Syria we decided that the easiest route for us would be to skip Iraq altogether and go northeast to Iran. We found a bus going to Van which was up near the Iranian border and began a long, uncomfortable, and as it turned out, embarrassing ride. During our "captivity" in Syria we had survived on adrenalin, but once safely back in Turkey, our bodies gave in to the amoebic dysentery we had contracted through the contaminated water we had drunk. We sat in the front of the bus and the driver obligingly stopped each time we tapped him on the shoulder. We would then get off the bus and deal with our diarrhea. Fortunately, we were driving through mostly unpopulated desert and mountainous regions. We arrived in Van and stayed in a hotel for a few days, too sick to go anywhere or do anything.

It was now the beginning of August, and Paul needed to start his long trek back to Canada. He accompanied us to the Iranian border and we said our sad good-byes. The three of us had been through a lot together and I knew I would miss him since by now he felt like a "big brother." We vowed to stay in touch and we did for a while, but I never saw him again.

The border consisted of two large shed-like buildings, one on the Turkish side with Turkish border guards and one on the Iranian side with Iranian border guards. Passing through neither side was easy since we were perceived as American hippies, probably carrying drugs, and were females traveling alone. The Turkish border guards immediately started rummaging through Ramblas, my Spanish-made leather shoulder bag. Having removed everything and finding no drugs they began cutting open the lining and the pockets. When they were finally finished the bag was in shreds and they handed me my small pile of personal belongings in a brown paper grocery bag and this is how I entered the country of Iran.

The Iranian border guards were no more friendly than the Turks were. They looked at us and our belongings with a hint of disgust on their faces. We asked about a bus to Tehran and they said all the buses were full and we would have to wait there until tomorrow. There was paperwork to be filled out and one of the questions asked, "Will you be visiting anyone in Iran? If so, please give a name and address." I knew my friend Kamran was still in

Hawaii, but his brother, Kambiz, was in Tehran so I answered the form saying I would visit Kambiz in Tehran and handed the paperwork back to the guards. Within moments our entire situation changed. The room was abuzz with loud conversations in Farsi and we were hurriedly ushered into a nice room with comfortable chairs, served tea and cookies, and assured that we could take the first bus to Tehran. A half hour later we were given the front seats on a big air conditioned nonstop bus to Tehran! It was then that I realized that Kamran's family were probably not farmers as he had told me.

Kami on his horse

Our bus ride took all night and we arrived in Tehran in early morning. We took a room at the Roosevelt Hotel and I called the number Kami

Kami and me at Farahabad

had given me for Kambiz. Amazingly Kami answered! He told me he had unexpectedly returned to Tehran and would come and pick us up at the hotel. He arrived an hour later wearing dress pants, dress shirt, and leather gloves with a car and a chauffeur! I had never seen him in anything but jeans and an old T-shirt. We drove through the crowded streets of Tehran and out into the desert until we came to a huge archway with guards at the entrance. When they saw the car and Kami they saluted and waved us through. We had entered Farahabad, the estate that Kami and his family lived on and the home of the Royal Stables and Hunting Lodge. It was absolutely beautiful with tree lined roads, pomegranate orchards, and three large palaces. One was where Kambiz and his family lived, the other two were for Kami's parents: one for his father and one for his mother. The palaces were surrounded by huge, tall trees and green lawns.

I never visited either of his parent's palaces but spent quite a lot of time in Kambiz's home since that is where Kami was staying. Upon entering it, the first thing one saw was a beautiful, large music box. It was very ornate and with many moving parts. It looked like something one would find in a museum, possibly built in the 17th or 18th Century. This wonderful piece of art was the only object in the large entrance and the doors on either side led into a large living room. The ceilings were high, the furniture ornate and in the French style of Louis XIV. A large formal dining room was off to one side with a table that could seat about twenty people. The whole place reminded me of Versailles!

After a night in the Roosevelt Hotel, Judy and I went to stay in her boyfriend, Kamrouz's, parents' house. They were a nice family and certainly happy to meet and get to know Judy. We slept on small beds on the second floor of the non-air conditioned home and I remember enjoying the siestas in the heat of the August afternoons. On about the third day, Judy informed me that the family wanted to spend time with her alone, and that they felt Kami should find me a place to stay since he was my friend. I have to admit, I was very naïve and completely oblivious to the fact that I might be an imposition!

Kami picked me up the next day and I moved to the Hotel Elizabeth, which was managed by his Aunt Fifi. It was a very nice hotel in a wonderful location and only cost me $3 per night, which was at a very good discount, but still it was high for me since I had less than $100 left to live on!

I continued to spend a lot of time with Kami. We went horseback riding out at Farahabad, visited his Aunt Fifi and family up at the Caspian Sea, and took long drives out in the country. We went to a big outdoor birthday party at Farahabad for Kambiz. I really liked Kambiz from the moment I met him. He was very charming and handsome, and with a wonderful openness in his personality that allowed me to let my guard down. He never seemed judgmental to me, unlike so many of his countrymen. Late in the evening after hours of wonderful food and conversation we continued the party inside with music and dancing. It was then that Kambiz asked me to dance and told me of the death by suicide of his and Kami's younger brother, Kamrouz. I was stunned. Kami had not mentioned it to me at all, but it was now clear to me why he had unexpectedly returned to Tehran for the summer. I felt a terrible sadness for them all, but especially Kami. I remembered the night we drove his brother Kamrouz to the airport in Honolulu for a flight back to Tehran. Kamrouz was just seventeen years old and had been going to a boarding school in Hawaii while Kami was attending the university. Kamrouz was in danger of being deported since he had gotten into some trouble at school. He was very westernized, and definitely did not want to return to Tehran at that time. The departure scene at the airport was sad and unpleasant, and I now realized that was the last time Kami saw his brother alive.

It was getting late in August now, and Judy left to return to Hawaii. Kami planned to leave at the end of the month. I was not ready to return to the States. I always knew I could call my parents for money to get back home. They were my "security blanket," but I wanted to make it on my own. I knew I had enough money to take the train to India where I might find a job since the official language spoken is English, but I really did not want to leave Iran. The next day I went to the American Embassy and asked about getting a job in Tehran. The embassy was not far from the hotel and was a beautiful big building with a nice courtyard. In my travels I had become very familiar with American Embassies and I loved going to them. Everything in them from the smiling fellow Americans to the soft toilet paper in the bathrooms reminded me of home. Of course the mailroom was my favorite since letters from family and friends awaited me there. The young American employee I spoke to about getting a job was helpful. He didn't seem at all surprised by my request. Guess I wasn't the first American citizen running out of money in Iran! With his suggestion I went to visit an officer in the Iranian Air Force to apply for a job teaching English to young recruits who would be sent to Texas for flight school. There were a few other Americans waiting to be interviewed and one was a young lady from California named Ginger. We both had long brown hair, hippy style, and immediately knew we had a lot in common. We exchanged brief stories of what brought us to Tehran and I invited her to visit me at the Hotel Elizabeth. The interview went well; the officer only had one question on "American English." I was asked to use the word "hit" in as many sentences as I could with different meanings. So I said,

*Hit the road Jack!
*Give me a hit off that cigarette, please.
*My favorite hit tune is one sung by Bob Dylan.
*In the bottom of the ninth he got his first big hit.
*I'm tired so I think I'll hit the sack.
*You should never hit anyone no matter how angry you get!

I passed the quiz and was offered the job, but first he asked if I were sure I wanted to work with the Air Force since I had a college degree and could make more money working at one of the international schools. He gave me the names and addresses and I went immediately to apply for a job at Iranzamin International School. I was offered a position teaching chemistry and physical science. Classes had started the day before but the British teacher they hired had not shown up. I accepted the job and agreed to begin work the following day.

I returned to my hotel room with a copy of the chemistry student textbook, lab book, the teacher's manual, and a grade book. I was relieved to know that I would be earning a paycheck and would not have to rely on my parents to get back to the States. Still, I was very nervous about the idea of teaching teenagers! I had no idea how I would be able to relate to them. I had no idea how I would maintain discipline. And I really had no idea how to teach. My two university degrees in science provided me with a broad chemistry background, but knowing something and teaching it are two completely different skills. I read the first chapter in the book and took a few notes, but it just made me more anxious. I reread my contract, computed my take home pay and cost of living and decided that if I could just make it through November I would have enough money to buy a plane ticket home. Surely I could at least last that long!

As it turned out, from my first day in the classroom I was hooked on teaching. The teens were not scary at all! They were in fact fun loving, funny, challenging, interesting, and inquisitive. Discipline was never an issue. I genuinely liked them and they liked me in return. This is not to say they didn't do crazy things at times. One morning I walked into class to find Kriton, a Greek student having a great time standing on top of my desk! He smiled and pretended to do a "Zorba the Greek-like" dance. The rest of the students were staring at me, wondering what my reaction would be. All I could do was laugh and start clapping at his antics. Immediately the whole class was laughing and smiling. Kriton got off the desk top and class began as usual.

The class sizes were small, from one student in an advanced chemistry to fourteen or fifteen in my other classes. Most of the students were trilingual, speaking French, English, and Farsi or whatever their native language was. They came from highly educated families. Their parents were government ministers, ambassadors from other countries, members of the Royal Court, heads of corporations, doctors, and professors. I admired my students more than they could possibly have understood, and I did my very best to teach them as much science as I knew how. I spent hours every evening and on weekends trying to organize the material and find as many ways as possible to explain the concepts. This was an International Baccalaureate (IB) school with a very specific curriculum. The students were tested at the end of the year on tests sent from the IB headquarters in Geneva, Switzerland. I felt a great deal of pressure to make sure all of the required concepts were covered and that the kids understood it enough to pass.

In early September I left the Hotel Elizabeth and moved in with Kami's other aunt, Shishi. She had a two-bedroom apartment not far from the old Roosevelt Hotel and she was very welcoming. She spoke no English and so began her continuous smiling attempts to teach me Farsi. She would point to all the objects in her house and then name them in Farsi. And in general, she just talked and talked when I got home from work at night. She was a widow and lonely so I'm sure she would have enjoyed a real conversation. Sometimes I would go to bed exhausted and dream in Farsi. When I awoke I would jot down, phonetically, what I remembered of the "conversation" and later asked Kami if it was really Farsi or just gibberish. Amazingly, the phrases I repeated really were Farsi and he could tell me what they meant! It was as if my brain knew some Farsi, but "I" did not.

Meanwhile Ginger and I had become good friends. She was living in Tehran with her brother and sister-in-law and their children. Her brother was an engineer and had been living in Iran for some time. He came over to work and to be a "missionary" of sorts. He and his wife were devout Christians of the evangelical, Pentecostal kind. He bought a restaurant that he managed in an area of Tehran near the American Embassy. Ginger and I went there often for meals and just to sit on the beautiful rooftop with a view of the Alborz Mountains north of the city. And we both spent wonderful times out at Farahabad with Kami. Ginger was certainly one of the most colorful friends I've ever had. She had a great sense of humor and had fewer inhibitions than most young people I knew.

Me and Ginger in Tehran

She loved dogs and did a very good job of impersonating them. She would bark and growl and sniff at things, grab a handful of her long hair and perk it up resembling a dog's ear, and slide her head next to one's arm waiting to be petted! The servants at Kami's house were always entertained by her fun-loving antics.

That September Kami was in a bad accident with his jeep and ended up in a hospital in Tehran. He had suffered a badly broken leg and was in the hospital for a long time, a month maybe. The severity of the injury forced him to change his plans to return to Hawaii that fall. I stopped every night after work to see him. Sometimes while I was there his father would stop by for a short visit. He was a classic gentleman from a seemingly bygone era. He was always impeccably dressed and always followed accepted protocol of his highly ranked status as a close family friend of the Shah. He was about seventy years old at the time, with silver hair, a beautiful smile and a caring, soft spoken voice. I liked and admired him, though he spoke no English and I spoke no Farsi, I felt comfortable in his presence. His attention to me, and his kind manners made me feel welcome. The same was not true for Kami's mother. I didn't see her often either, but when I did she was kind in her greeting but lacked sincerity in her smile. I think at the time she thought of me as a threat since she was busy trying to interest Kami in prospective brides from the wealthy echelons of Persian society.

Ginger and I decided to rent an apartment together. Her brother had found one not far from where he lived, and in October we moved into this rather new building. It was a two bedroom, two bathroom (if you counted the Eastern style toilet room. This was the size of a closet and contained one "hole in the floor toilet" with porcelain footprints to squat on and a water tank overhead for flushing capabilities). There was also a small kitchen and rather large living room/dining room combination. Out back was a small walled-in yard and an open dirt floor cellar. Kambiz loaned us some furniture that consisted of a nice large Persian carpet, wood dining room set and an office desk. Ginger and I each bought a cot-like bed with a straw mattress, some cushions for the living room floor, and finally most important of all, a stereo! It was the 60s after all, and we both loved the music! There were western bookstores and music stores in Tehran so all the latest hits were available. We bought albums by the Rolling Stones, Bob Dylan, and Crosby, Stills, Nash and Young among others. Somewhere we found this large, smooth river rock that we used as a candleholder in the middle of the floor. And life was good! We frequented a newly opened pizza place (the only one in Iran) owned by an Iranian who had returned from years of living in Los Angeles, as well as the Iran American Society that was close to our apartment. We met many interesting young people that fall and winter, smoked hashish on more than a few occasions, and took a couple trips on LSD. It was all part of an exploratory time in my life. I was genuinely interested in how it felt and what it meant to "trip." But I also had a healthy dose of precaution and knew I would not get hung up in any drug world.

Once we were given some psilocybin (psychedelic mushrooms) and we took it before going to the hospital to visit Kami. Of all the drugs I have ever tried this one had the most enjoyable mind altering effect. It made everything seem beautiful and funny and possible. It was a full moon that night and so we decided that it would be really great if Kami could get outside to see it. There was an elevator at the end of the hall that was large enough to accommodate a hospital bed so we pushed him in his bed out to the elevator with the intent to ride him up to the roof for a view. We managed to get the bed out of the room and half way down the hall before alarms went off and people came running. We were all laughing so much we had tears in our eyes. Unfortunately, the staff did not find our attempt humorous and thought at first that Kami was crying and not laughing. Maybe they also thought we were trying to kidnap him.

By December Kami was well mended and getting ready to return to the States. Before he left, he managed to deliver a large live Christmas tree to our apartment. We decorated it the best we could and loved every minute of having that cheerful reminder of America over the holiday season. In January I met a young American military man stationed in Iran and dated him

Ginger and me in Shemiran, North Tehran

for a short while. Through him I learned of an entire world of Americans living in Tehran in an excluded compound. I went with him to parties where all the food and drink were from America. Their houses were also built and furnished American style. They were mostly military families or employees of Bell Helicopter and were very much pro the war in Vietnam. I really had less in common with them than the Persians who lived on my street, but still I enjoyed some of their conveniences of "home." My last date with this American guy was on Ginger's twenty-fourth birthday. She was at home that night, sick with chicken pox, and I felt guilty later about going to this American party without her. Fortunately I had chicken pox when I was very young so did not have to deal with that. And by this time my dysentery had finally subsided after multiple series of antibiotics. Through it all I had lost a lot of weight and was thinner than I had ever been in my adult life. I only weighed around a hundred pounds but felt good for the first time in months.

The school year was going well but when the principal asked me if I intended to stay for the following year I said "no." It was late January and I had always intended to stay until I had enough money to get a plane ticket back and then return to Hawaii to work on my Ph.D. in botany. I had by now saved enough to get the ticket back but wanted to finish out the school year since I was enjoying the work and life in Iran very much. Also, I was beginning to learn a bit of the language and wanted to see more of the countryside before I left. Second semester went fast. Kami had returned to America, this time to Colorado. He was studying agriculture and in particular sugar beets. We stayed in touch through letter writing. Iranzamin was busy getting ready to put on a play. The art teacher, Douglas, was the director and the play chosen was Shakespeare's "A Midsummer Night's Dream." I agreed to help with the play and became the stage manager. This was no ordinary production. The costumes, stage set, and cast were absolutely amazing! The main characters were played by students from various parts of the world: Iranians, Americans, British, Egyptians, Canadians and others.

It was at this time that I met Juni, a wonderful young woman with a sense of self and social justice not common in most high school students. And I became friends with Susan Moss, a fellow teacher at Iranzamin. Susan taught English and history and was also helping out with the production of the play. She was a former Peace Corps volunteer who had served three years in Uganda before moving to Iran. She had a Persian boyfriend while in Uganda and had followed him to Iran. That relationship hadn't lasted and she was then dating Dion, the Director of the Iran American Society. Susan was attractive and intelligent. She also had a wonderful liberal education, was well versed on many topics, and deeply interested in the history, art, and culture of Iran.

For spring break that year she borrowed Dion's VW Beetle car and she, Ginger, and I took a trip through the heart of Iran visiting holy cities, a zinc mine, and ancient ruins. We drove to Isfahan with its beautiful turquoise mosaic mosques, and then on to Qom, a conservative holy Shiite city. We arrived just in time for the occasion where Shia men march and beat themselves with chains and whips or even stab themselves with knives to show grief for the Imam Hussein who was murdered in the year 680. We got out of the car to watch the procession but as the men reached a state of frenzy and were heading our way we wisely got back in the car and left Qom.

I don't remember how we ended up at the zinc mine but after a tour by the manager and an invitation to spend the night in their guesthouse and join them for a great dinner, a party was declared in our honor with music and drinks. There were probably a hundred or more male mine workers there and we three women! Susan soon declared she had a "terrible headache" and needed to retire for the night. Shortly after Ginger became "ill" and also had to retire to our sleeping quarters. That left me, and I was too Midwestern nice to leave the "party" so I spent the next three to four hours dancing with just about every guy there and thanking them for a wonderful evening!

The next day we drove to Yazd, a desert town in Southern Iran with an ancient Zoroastrian burial site. We hiked to the top of the site which was a circular twenty-foot tall walled in roofless tomb built on a small mountain. Upon death, the Zoroastrians place the body in this tomb and wait for the birds to come and "peck the flesh off the bones." This was an important ritual in Zoroastrian beliefs.

On our return drive to Tehran, while Ginger was at the wheel, somehow she missed a turn and we ended up driving off road in the sandy desert! No harm done, we simply backed the car up and got back onto the road. However, from that point on Susan took over the wheel. Sometime later we had engine trouble and managed to coast into a nearby auto repair shop, probably the only one within two hundred miles! The repair was minor, and after a short time drinking tea in the shade, the car was ready for our return trip home.

As the school year was coming to an end I began to realize that I really did not want to leave Iran or the teaching profession. I spoke with the principal who informed me that he had already hired a replacement for my position. The father of one of my students was the Iranian Minister of Higher Education who knew something of my background and asked if I'd be interested in teaching in a University and setting up a Chromosome Clinic since there were none in Iran at the time. I was flown to Abadan on the Persian Gulf and I met with University officials there. I didn't care much for the men I met there and the position sounded totally lab orientated with little or no teaching. While there they took me to dinner and a bar in a big western style hotel. I met a number of British men working for the oil company headquarters. I remember these Brits and their Iranian counterparts had nothing but crass things to say about the Arabs who lived on the other side of the Gulf, in Saudi Arabia. They called them "ragheads" and said they were uneducated Bedouins with no history and no culture who just happened to be sitting on a lot of oil.

My next interview was at the University of Tabriz in northwestern Iran, up near the Turkish and Soviet Union borders. Tabriz was an ancient city, with a half a million people, a grand bazaar, and a large university. It was located on the old silk route and had been a trading center for centuries. I liked the doctors I met and could see that they were very interested in doing chromosome studies and having me teach a medical genetics course. Along with this job offer that paid me more than double what I made at Iranzamin, I received a budget to build a "state of the art" chromosome clinic. I happily accepted the position that was to begin with the new school year in the fall.

My final weeks at Iranzamin were very enjoyable. The play had been a huge success, thanks mainly to the genius of Douglas, the director. I helped chaperone the prom and the after party at Juni's house where I got thrown into the pool by some of the kids. The IB exams went well and all my students who took the exam passed. When summer came one of my students, Abdullah, asked if I wanted to make a visit to a village near the Caspian Sea where his family owned some land. There were six of us who went, three Persian boys, Farhad, Cameron, and Abdullah, an American-born but Egyptian raised brother and sister, Danny and Joelle, and me. We took a bus as far as the road went and then hiked for about forty-five minutes crossing on two swinging rope bridges over a slow moving river to reach the village. Houses in the village had thatched roofs and were mounted on high stilts near water flooded rice paddies. One house was left empty for Abdullah's family to visit and we all stayed there. It was just one large room with bedding on the floor. The villagers brought us tea and meals. We stayed there about a week, enough to get a feel for living in a remote village with no electricity or plumbing or shops or stores of any kind. The river ran by the village and this is where we did our bathing. Women were allocated a section of the river around a bend and out of site of the village. I went there every day and enjoyed a cool bath, swimming with fish and an occasional long black snake. Once while there we heard this giggling coming from the shore and saw little boys peeking their heads up from behind some rocks to look and laugh at naked women! Late one evening some women brought a sick baby girl to our house. The baby looked really dehydrated so we stayed up all night feeding it tiny teaspoons of sugar water that she hardly had the strength to swallow. By morning, after hours of slowly sipping this sugar water, the baby seemed much better.

There were lots of nocturnal wild boars in the area and they would come out at night to feast in the rice paddies. The men in the village owned one gun, an old muzzleloader and they would periodically go on wild boar hunts. The six of us decided to join the hunting party much to the amusement of the villagers. I was given the honor of firing the first shot. I couldn't see the wild boars, but I could hear them. The men kept yelling, "Shoot, shoot!" I wanted to follow the hunting rule established by my father, which was to never shoot at anything until you were absolutely sure you could see and identify it. Still, they kept yelling for me to shoot, so I aimed the muzzleloader in the direction of the noise and pulled the trigger. A ball of fire shot out of the top of the rifle and singed the hair off my right eyebrow and the kickback from the gun was so powerful that it knocked me down while the end of the barrel jerked up toward the sky. After that I went along on the hunts just to help find the wild boars, and determined to never shoot another gun!

The villagers picked wild mushrooms from nearby forests and cooked them up for us. They were absolutely delicious and we decided it would be a smart thing to bring some back to Tehran. The villagers gathered up a huge basket of the mushrooms for us and we carried them back across the rope bridges to the highway and from there we hitchhiked back to Tehran. Getting rides was always easy in Iran since it would have been considered rude to drive past someone in need of a ride. The mushroom idea turned out to be a disaster since we obviously had no idea how to cook them and they tasted awful. I think they probably needed to be soaked in salt water or something for a while to get rid of the bitter taste. Anyway, after all our work of getting them to Tehran we ended up throwing them away.

Kami returned to Tehran for the summer and it was wonderful to see him again and spend time at Farahabad. He had received a pair of gold cuff links with the Royal Crest on them from the

Shah, and was upset because somehow he had lost one of them. We searched places he had been in the house, on the grounds, in the old hunting lodge, horse stables, etc. but could not find it. A few days later while riding horses accompanied by his favorite dog, we stopped in the desert for the dog to do its "business" and noticed something shiny in the pile of excrement. Sure enough, it was the gold cuff link!

I loved the horseback riding, and the mountains and desert areas to ride in were spectacular. My favorite horse was an Arab mare named Gina. I grew confident in her sure-footedness so riding in the mountains on narrow trails with high scary drop-offs didn't bother me much. I'm afraid of heights so sometimes when the drop-offs were especially steep I would simply close my eyes and let Gina do her thing. (The art of letting go!)

Judy and her fiancé, Kamrouz, returned that summer and got married in a typical Iranian wedding that Kami and I and Ginger attended. It was a very formal event and the reception was around a large candle lit swimming pool. True to Iranian style, Judy wore so much make-up I hardly recognized her! She usually wore little make-up, so the change was astounding. Following the wedding they returned to Hawaii to complete their graduate work.

Sharon, an American friend of Ginger's brother and family, came to live with us that summer. She had been married to an Iranian and had lived in Iran for a number of years, but was seeking a divorce. She had two young sons and wanted very much to stay with them, but could no longer tolerate the abuses of her husband. Sharon was a very religious person, a conservative Pentecostal Christian like Ginger and her family. She had worked as a reporter for the Kayhan, a local English newspaper and she wanted to do a story on Meshad, one of the holiest cities in Iran. I agreed to go with her and so we took a bus together across the great salt flats of eastern Iran, more than five hundred miles from Tehran.

Around dusk the bus stopped in what seemed like the middle of nowhere with nothing but a few rundown buildings, a bench that we sat on, and desert. Soon an old man walked up and started

Judy's wedding

quizzing us. Sharon was fluent in Farsi so she could answer for us. He first asked what we were doing in Iran. She explained that we worked, her for the newspaper and me for the university. Next he asked how much money we made. She told him and he seemed very impressed. Then he asked if we were married. She said that she was, but I wasn't. He looked at me for a while and asked how old I was. "Man binti-haft" (I'm twenty-seven), I said. He paused for a moment and then reluctantly said, "I'll marry you." I politely thanked him for the proposal but declined the offer. He nodded his head and walked away. I realized that he felt sorry for me being so "old" and still not married! And though he certainly did not want a foreign wife, he obviously wanted my salary. A few moments later he returned, pulling his teenage son behind him and declared with a big smile on his face, "My son will marry you!" The kid looked terrified and I had to work hard to keep from laughing. I assumed that he must have believed that I turned his proposal down because I thought he was too old so he went and brought me his son! Luckily the bus blew its horn, signally departure time so we quickly boarded. As soon as the bus left, Sharon and I both burst out laughing at this ridiculous encounter.

Meshad is an old Iranian town that is most noted for the large Mosque and adjoining domed burial site, the Shrine of Imam Reza who was killed there in the 9th Century. Shiite Muslims routinely make pilgrimages to visit the Shrine. We stayed with an Iranian family, friends of Sharon's, and borrowed chadors from the women. The Iranian chador is a head to floor veil that all women wear while visiting the Shrine. With a chador covering all our features we felt safe visiting the Shrine, even though we were not Muslims. As I remember, it was a large tomb like structure that people walked around, rubbed their hands on it, and some kissed it. I didn't get that close. The entire visit lasted only a few minutes.

Me wearing a chador

A day later and we were back on a bus to Tehran. This time around midnight, much to our surprise, the bus stopped along the road for the night. The passengers all got off and began to set up make shift campsites. They obviously knew this routine ahead of time since they had brought blankets and other supplies with them. We looked around and could see the lights of a small town not far away so we decided to walk there and look for a hotel room. We were tired and hungry and thirsty and covered in dust since there was no air conditioning on the bus and windows were open all afternoon as we drove through the sandy desert. In the town a policeman drove up and asked us what we were doing there. We explained about the bus but he didn't seem to believe us. He told us to get into the back of the car and he drove us to the police station. We asked about a hotel but after talking it over with his fellow policemen he said we would have to spend the night there in the jailhouse! They believed we were "foreign whores" in town to do business! We slept on the floor in a bare room and the next morning early they brought us tea and bread and they drove us to a local hammam (bath house) where we could have a shower and then they drove us to the bus. Obviously at some point they must have driven out there and realized we had told them the truth.

In August before my move to Tabriz, Ginger and Sharon and I went to Shiraz for the Shiraz Arts Festival. This was an annual musical event sponsored by Queen Farah Pahlavi and it attracted a number of international celebrities. It was held among the beautiful ruins of Persepolis and this particular year the main attraction was the famous sitar player from India, Ravi Shankar.

Me standing in front of the ancient ruins of Persepolis with guards who were enjoying the event

It was one of those magical evenings in my life, sitting out in that ancient place with a desert background and a billion stars overhead listening to this most strange and beautifully compelling music. I wanted that night to never end.

One other memorable musical event was the coming of the movie, "Woodstock," to Tehran. I was very excited to see it, having heard so much about it from friends back in the States. A whole group of us went to the opening night in Tehran and were shocked to realize that the entire movie had been dubbed into Farsi, including most of the music. We could do nothing but laugh when we saw Joe Cocker's voice dubbed by an Iranian singing "Little Help from My Friends" in Farsi!

Ginger's brother, Bob, his wife Joan, and Sharon were outspoken evangelical Christians and wanted Ginger and me to partake in one of their weekly prayer groups and so out of courtesy I reluctantly consented. This meeting was held in our apartment. A small group of these Christians came over, they said a number of prayers while having us all hold hands in a circle. One prayer was to "give Ruthann a sign" so she might believe. All in all it was an uncomfortable event and I was glad when it was over. After everyone left Ginger and I grabbed a cab, as we did on many evenings, and went out to join friends for some food, drink, and good conversation. In the cab I asked Ginger what perfume she was wearing since it smelled so strong. She insisted she wasn't wearing perfume. I smelled my own hands and realized the "perfume" was on me! I thought it must have come from holding hands in the prayer circle. Later that night I took a shower and tried to wash off this perfume but the odor was still there. In fact, that odor lasted for a few days, no matter how hard I tried to wash it off. The prayer group members took it as the "sign" their God gave to make me a believer. I have to admit the prolonged odor was beginning to creep me out, but it did not make me a believer. A week later I left for Tabriz and a whole new adventure.

Tabriz was a rather unremarkable big Iranian city. There were no beautiful mosaics, few carefully planned gardens of pomegranate trees or flowering bushes, but the bazaar was big and of historical significance as an important trading center for millennia. This was my favorite part of the whole city and I planned my daily walk to work on a route that took me through various parts of this remarkable ancient covered labyrinth. Some of the shops were more modern, selling things like dishware and watches, but I chose the older shops selling items like ornate hookahs and inlaid backgammon sets, handmade jewelry, carpets and samovars. One shop sold beautiful Pustin Afghan sheepskin coats. They were popular in the 60s among my hippy generation and I really wanted one. I would periodically stop and ask the price. Sixty dollars the shopkeeper would say and the bargaining would begin. It took more than a month but eventually I bought a coat for thirty dollars. It was three quarters length, with beautiful embroidery, and lined with sheep's wool. Best of all it had a hood, the only hooded Afghan coat I had ever seen and the reason I really wanted it. This coat was very warm and I was so grateful to have it when the harsh winter arrived.

The main street of Tabriz was really a wide avenue with shops on both sides including a rather western style hotel and restaurant and an ice cream parlor. Most disappointing of all for me was the realization that people here didn't speak Farsi. Just when I was beginning to be able to speak Farsi in sentences and to understand a lot of what was said, I found myself surrounded by a new language, Turkish.

I was housed in a women's dorm for nursing students when I first arrived. It was a rather modern building and I had a nice private room with my own bath. Meals were provided in the cafeteria there and I got to know some of the young nurses. They were all rather interested in me as this young American woman living amongst them. They would join me at meals and enjoy practicing their English. They would also invite me out with them on weekends. Weekend nights (Wednesday and Thursday nights in the Middle East) were huge social events. The main avenue was packed with young people sort of promenading up and down this street in same sex groups eyeing the other groups of the opposite sex. The groups would mingle a bit in the ice cream parlor but mostly just flirt from a distance.

On my first weekend in town the young professor, Dr. K, who was to be my supervisor and the benefactor of the chromosome lab, took me out to dinner in the modern hotel on the main avenue. We had steak and a glass of wine and about half way through the meal I fainted. I was only out a few seconds but it obviously really shook my dinner host. I thought back to the night in Hawaii when I fainted during a meal and realized it came about in the same way, somehow from a mistake in swallowing. I told myself it was the steak and I didn't really like steak that much anyway so I quit eating it for years! I tried to reassure Dr. K that I was just fine but I think it was weeks before he believed that I really was in good health.

There was no embassy in Tabriz but there was an American Consulate and I quickly became acquainted with it. I picked up my mail here on a regular basis and the Vice Counselor, Cliff, and his wife became my friends. I soon met everyone in the "foreign community" of Tabriz through regular parties held at the Consulate. There were American Peace Corps volunteers, British

Wearing my new "Pustin" (Afgan coat) in Tabriz

teachers at the University of Tabriz, and French doctors at the Medical School. The head of the Medical School was an Iranian, married to a French woman, and they had two daughters around my age. The oldest was married to a French photographer and the youngest was married to an American Peace Corps volunteer. All of them lived together in a big beautiful old home in Tabriz. The home had many rooms in separate quarters as well as an inside courtyard so it easily accommodated this large multigenerational family and their servants.

The daughters introduced me to the music of Leonard Cohen and the use of headsets, which made the music even better. We sometimes smoked a little hashish and then lay back on big soft, multi-colored Turkish cushions on the expensive carpets that covered the floor and listened to a variety of music or simply talked and laughed. Culturally they were more French than Iranian and had spent much of their lives going back and forth between Iran and France.

In many of our conversations they told me that they would rather settle in France but that their parents were now in their seventies and needed them there with them. Both parents were addicted to opium, a drug commonly used by the older generation of Tabriz as a way to deal with aches and pains and to sleep well at night. In their home they had a small "opium den" in the attic and each night they would gather there with their elder friends and smoke government issued opium.

On one occasion the daughters and I were invited to join them to experience what it was like. The room was small, covered in Persian carpets, with a low table in the center that nearly filled the room. Large cushions propped up against the walls circled the entire room such that there was just enough space for one to sit on the carpet with legs tucked warmly under the table and then lean back against a cushion by the wall. Very cozy. The doctor prepared the pipe and explained the process. When he lit the opium you should take three or four deep inhales and then pass the pipe to the next person. Immediately drink the small liqueur glass of sugar water that was offered, so that you would not possibly faint. The experience was a most memorable one because having done it I understood what Persian friends of mine had said about opium. They said it is an "old people's drug" and should never be used unless you were old or infirm. Young people high on opium were said to have blissfully sat back and watched their own child drown without getting up to help. The feeling I got from opium was just that. I don't think I could have moved if I wanted to, but anyway I didn't want to. I laid back on that cushion and very much enjoyed the next few hours of my life in that peaceful, blissful state. There were no visions, no dreams, no thoughts really, just pure contentment and then it was over. I never used opium again and never wanted to. As a friend once said about drugs, "they are like a phone, when you get the message hang up!" I got the message: when I'm old and if in pain this would be a wonderful medication.

Living in the nursing school dorm was free (including meals) and convenient, but I decided I really wanted more privacy and a place of my own. I wanted to have visitors, friends from Tehran who could come and stay with me sometimes, so I put the word out among the foreign community and through someone who knew someone, I found a nice two-bedroom apartment in an old home with a large courtyard. An elderly woman owned the house and she lived alone downstairs. She rented out the second floor as an apartment. It had no private entrance. I just walked in the front door of her house and took the stairs to the second floor. My apartment was minimal in amenities but I liked it. There was no kitchen, just a hotplate. A teapot sat on top of the kerosene stove that heated the place in the winter. It was furnished in the basics: beds, dressers, small table with two chairs, carpeted living room with comfortable cushions to sit on, and a very rustic bathroom with the Middle Eastern style toilet (porcelain footprints and hole to squat over) and a cement shower room. The old woman spoke no English or Farsi so we could not communicate. She had a nice smile and often came out to greet me when I entered the house.

One weekend I returned earlier than she expected and I found her in my apartment with some of her old women friends. They had gone through my dresser drawers and were holding up a pair of my bikini underwear. She was very embarrassed when she saw me, and they all quickly left my apartment. I knew she must have been very curious about this single American woman living in her house, but no more curious than I was to know her life story.

My job was going very well. My title was Cytogeneticist in the School of Medicine and my office/lab was in the University Hospital. I taught a basic class in Human Genetics to third year medical students through an interpreter. Teaching under these circumstances (lecture only) was not nearly as enjoyable as teaching at Iranzamin, but setting up the chromosome clinic was very rewarding. I was not given a budget, but simply told to order what I needed. It took about six weeks for the equipment and chemicals to arrive: a high powered microscope with an attached camera, an incubator, and an autoclave were the main pieces of equipment.

To test out the equipment I did the first chromosome study on my own blood sample. Everything went well until I took the film into the university photo shop for development. I needed them to crop and enlarge the photos of the ruptured cell nuclei so I could clearly see each individual chromosome and arrange them in an identifiable karyotype. After numerous unsuccessful attempts I went to Dr. K. We decided to put in a dark room next to my lab so I could develop my own film. Having my own darkroom worked perfectly since I learned to vary the process such that identifying individual chromosomes from the photos became much easier than ever before. I began seeing patients on a regular basis. Most cases were suspected genetical defects in newborn babies, but there were other quite unusual referrals.

There were four cases in particular that shocked me. These were not situations I would ever have encountered in the States. The first one was a young woman who was referred to the clinic because she was unable to get pregnant. When I first met her she was fully veiled in the Iranian "chador" and with her husband who looked to be only about sixteen or seventeen years old. My first thought was that she probably wasn't even post puberty yet. I took a blood sample and then Dr. K called her into his office for a physical exam. Shortly after he asked me to come into the examination room and when I entered I saw what appeared to be a perfectly normal looking naked young man! I could tell that Dr. K was as shocked as I was. The young bride was male, not female, and these two young people didn't know the difference! They came from a remote village, in a conservative culture where private parts were not seen nor talked about. What followed were weeks of providing information and counseling to the young couple. He loved his wife and wanted to stay married and have children. "She" was horrified at the idea of becoming a "boy" and losing her husband. She wanted us to "fix her" so she could have babies. Telling her she had no ovaries was not helpful because she had no idea what ovaries were. "Her" chromosome karyotype came out normal, forty-six, XY, male. In the end the doctors in the hospital decided to do a sex change operation on her to help her live the life she wanted to as much as possible. Her male sex organs were removed and she was given female hormones. Surgery was also performed to create a vagina. They were proud of the outcome and published the results in a French medical journal. I never did understand the need for this last surgery since the young couple was having a sexual relationship without it and with no other female organs it would never become the birth canal she wanted.

The second case involved a young man who was brought to the clinic by his father. The father then matter of factly told Dr. K and me to "fix him." He had found a wife for his son and wanted to make sure his son would be able to produce offspring. The young man was obviously cognitively disabled and stunted in growth and development. I was amazed to think that he was expected to marry and have children. Upon a physical examination we saw that his sex organs were deformed and not symmetrically located. The chromosome karyotype came out normal as expected. I felt sorry for them since I knew he could not be "fixed," and most of all I felt sorry for the new wife to be.

The third case involved an entire village. It began with a baby born at the hospital with Down's Syndrome. The chromosome karyotype revealed that the baby didn't just have the twenty-one trisomy expected, but a translocation twenty-one trisomy. In these cases the extra chromosome is passed on to the child from a parent who has the translocation chromosome, making the parent a carrier. I then did a karyotype of the mother and found that she was the carrier. It's not a common genetic diagnosis and I had never seen it before. Dr. K was curious about it and wondered how many others in her family might have it. We decided to investigate and a few weeks later we took a trip out to her remote village. We found what appeared to be a high number of people with Down's Syndrome. Dr. K tried to convince them to let us take some blood samples from a number of the villagers but they were fearful and skeptical. We managed to get a few samples from some agreeable adults and a child with the characteristics of Down's Syndrome. Back at the lab I found the translocation chromosome in two out of the four samples we took. Over the next five to six months that I was in Tabriz, Dr. K went back to the village a number of times trying to collect more and more samples with some success. The chromosome karyotypes I did resulted in more and more discoveries of the translocation trisomy twenty-one chromosome. His goal was to do a genealogical study of the entire village, tracing this translocation chromosome back as far as he could. It became an ongoing interesting project, but I left before it was completed and always wondered what the final study would look like.

The fourth case speaks to the culture of the country at that time. A man came to the clinic, bringing his seventh wife. He asked that we find out what's wrong with her since she was unable to bear children. Dr. K's examination found nothing wrong and the chromosome study I did was also normal. I asked Dr. K if he was going to examine the man and he said with a sarcastic smile, "Oh no. Didn't you know? Allah did not create men with reproductive issues, only women!" When the man heard the results of the tests he said, "Allah has made life very difficult for me. He has given me seven wives and they are all barren."

About every third weekend I would buy a bus ticket to Tehran to see old friends. I stayed with Ginger who was still working for IBM and had rented a wonderful small rooftop apartment near our old neighborhood. On one such visit I heard that a former Iranzamin student, Radka, was attending the University of Tabriz, living in a dorm, but had been ill and was unhappy there. I let it be known that I had a two-bedroom apartment and she would be welcome to stay with me if she wanted to. In early December, Radka moved in with me. She was Bulgarian and her father was working on a project for the Iranian government so her family was living in a village not far from Tabriz.

Winter came with a vengeance that year. A blizzard blew in from the north and lasted for days. Tabriz came to a standstill as the snow piled up and plows were not available to clear the streets. The University was closed as were most businesses in town. On about the seventh day we could hear wolves howling and the gendarmerie was called in to keep them from entering the city. I felt like I was on the movie set of "Dr. Zhivago!" The pipes froze in the apartment so we had no running water. Radka and I collected clean snow to melt in our teapot to make tea. We walked the two blocks to the public hammam to take a long hot shower. There were women in this establishment who would scrub your body with a pumice stone. We decided that two trips a week were enough! The bakeries with their hot ovens built under the streets managed to stay open so we lived on fresh bread and tea until at last the storm ended and slowly the streets were cleared. The university reopened so Radka was back in school and I went back to work.

Within days the American Consulate informed us that there was a smallpox outbreak in Tabriz and it was being hushed up. Iran had been declared free of smallpox for nearly nine years by the World Health Organization, and the government did not want to lose that rating. We were told to come to the Consulate to get a smallpox vaccination as soon as possible and so we did. We were also asked not to tell anyone that we had received the vaccine since they did not want to cause an embarrassment with the Iranian government. The following day I was called into the director's office at the hospital and was quietly told that everyone who worked there was going to be vaccinated against smallpox that day. I couldn't tell them that I already got the vaccine so I had a second shot. One week later while I was home in the apartment armed soldiers came to the door with medical assistants who were ordered to vaccinate everyone, and so I received a third smallpox shot!

The outbreak was short lived but sad and frightening. On a few occasions I saw wailing mothers bring their dead pox covered babies into the hospital and leave them there. One morning I arrived at the hospital to see a hysterical woman with a very bloody face and missing teeth. A doctor nearby explained that she had smashed her face into a rock as a way of mourning the death of her child. The entire city of Tabriz was under quarantine for about three weeks. The army set up checkpoints at all the roads and no one was allowed to leave or enter without government approval. Once again the university closed.

It was sometime during this period when I found out that Radka had been seeing my friend, Cliff, the American Vice Counselor. The situation was very awkward for me since I knew his wife and family and this secret affair was going on in my apartment. Radka was a very beautiful young woman and she had big dreams. She wanted to go to America and not return to Bulgaria where she said opportunities were extremely limited. Her family was returning to Bulgaria in the summer and they expected Radka to go with them. She had a Bulgarian passport but no permission to stay in Iran without her family. Cliff and Radka saw each other throughout that winter and into summer. He gave her a visa to the U.S. and enough money to make the trip. I helped with the plans for her "escape." She would take the bus from Tehran to Istanbul and then fly to New York with instructions to ask for asylum when she got there. I came with her to Tehran and she brought just one suitcase of clothing. She had told her parents she was going to Tehran just for the weekend to visit old friends and say good-bye. Ginger and I had a small farewell party for her and the next day she left on the bus for Istanbul. As it turned out, she met

Cal, a young American peace corps volunteer, on the bus and he traveled with her all the way to the States. A year later they were married in Pennsylvania and I attended their wedding.

My last summer in Iran, the summer of 1971, went by fast. Kami returned with his friend Vic and they moved into a new home with a beautiful pool. It was located right outside of Farahabad. His servant, Ahmad, was there to cook and clean, take care of clothes, the cars, and Kami's two dogs. Kami had come back to stay this time. He accepted a position at the Golestan Palace and prepared for a life in Iran.

I moved out of the apartment in the old lady's house and rented the basement of a home occupied by some of my foreign friends. One was an Englishman named Robin who taught English at the university. The other two were American Peace Corps volunteers, Frank and Bob. They had rented this huge old house and invited me to stay in the basement quarters that were spacious and nice. I had a living area, a bedroom, and a bathroom. They taught me how to play bridge so we could have a foursome but I didn't play enough that summer to really know the game. The weather got very hot so we, like most residents of Tabriz, moved our beds to the roof and slept outdoors under the stars. It felt fantastic to

View from the roof of our Tabriz house

sleep in fresh air and listen to music up there on that roof. I fell asleep to songs by Janis Joplin, Dylan, James Taylor, and Joan Baez among others.

One weekend the four of us decided to climb one of the peaks of the Zagros range just outside of town. It was over thirteen thousand feet high and we left early on a Friday morning. The climb started off pretty easy, more like a hike with a slight incline, but soon we were amongst huge rocks climbing hand over foot in steep terrain. After hours of this, with multiple stops for rest, I was exhausted and thought about turning back. However, my next thought was of victory, seeing myself on the top of that mountain looking across the Soviet Border! Late in the afternoon we came upon a shepherd resting in a cave like structure near the summit. He was there tending his flock of goats. I think we were as surprised to see him as he was to see us! Frank and Bob could speak some Turkish and so we sat down to rest and have a friendly conversation. He soon offered us tea and bread, a welcome nourishment since we brought nothing with us on the climb. We had assumed it would only take a few hours. The shepherd was well stocked with supplies since his goats pastured in the high altitudes most of the summer. Following this rest with food and drink, the remainder of the climb was easy and soon we were on the top. I loved the sense of accomplishment as much as I loved the spectacular view. The climb down was amazingly easy and only took us about three or four hours, even though we arrived home in the dark.

Bob had to fly back to America that summer to attend a wedding. He was the best man at the Tricia Nixon and Ed Cox wedding at the White House! Bob was not one to drop names nor boast in any way. He had roomed with Ed Cox at Princeton but had never talked about it so we were all pretty surprised when he flew off to Washington for the wedding.

Kami came up to Tabriz to visit me and we had wonderful long walks and long talks. I knew that more than anything about Iran I would miss him the most. He could make me think deeper about history and religions and cultures and he could make me laugh.

I felt completely comfortable and relaxed with him, never a need to be anyone but myself. I knew I could say whatever I wanted to, and I did. I was in love with him, as a friend. The Shah had a number of Summer Palaces around the country and Kami and I visited one on the Caspian Sea. It was in a large compound with other palace-like houses. We stayed a few nights and pretty much had the whole place to ourselves except for the servants who lived there. We ate great food, took long walks, and talked about everything under the sun. On another occasion we went to the "Pink Palace" somewhere in the countryside and Ginger and Vic came with us along with Kami's dog, a Weimaraner. Again we had the whole place to ourselves, and did a good job of entertaining the servants who had never before met a barking human like Ginger!

One week, Kami drove Vic and me in his Land Rover to an off-road village / campsite where Maryam, a fellow horse loving friend lived. She was a leader of one of the largest nomadic tribes in Iran, charming, and well educated. The four of us had a great time together, mostly riding horses from village to village in a mountainous region. The villagers were busy harvesting hay and grain for the winter, but they were very friendly and took time out to meet and greet us. At noon we enjoyed a typical Persian picnic lunch. A fire was lit and tea was brewed on a samovar. We sat on large carpets with cushions and ate fresh bread, goat's cheese, and a variety of vine-ripened fruits including grapes, melons, sweet cucumbers, and cherries. Honestly, the summer fruit in Iran is the best I have ever eaten.

Juni came to visit me in Tabriz that summer too, and later we spent some time at her little cottage on the shores of the Caspian Sea. Juni was a remarkable young lady. She had just graduated from Iranzamin and planned to attend Oxford in the fall. A beautiful, intelligent Persian princess and I adored her. Still do. She loved Iran, cared about people, and wanted to make a difference. At the same time she was playful and adventurous, with a free spirit and a sense of confidence well beyond her years. I was ten years older than her, but she felt like a peer to me.

In late August Ginger and I packed up our few belongings and shipped them to Los Angeles to her parent's address. We had been planning our trip back to the U.S. for some time. The trip would be overland through much of Asia with an expectation of arriving in America the following spring. Shortly before we left, Ginger confided in me that she was suffering from depression. That she often thought of just walking off into the desert with no intention of returning. She reasoned that it would be a nice way to die. I was totally shocked! The rose-colored glasses that I was born with could not comprehend how anyone could wish to die and leave this wonderful, fascinating experience called life. We talked long into the nights with me using every argument I could to convince her that life was so worth living. I especially played up the pleasure of the adventure we were about to embark on. I didn't realize at the time that depression is a serious illness and needs treatment. I think I eventually wore her down and she agreed to make the trip.

We each had an easy to carry canvas shoulder pack made in the bazaar along with a money belt, and that is all we took with us. I also had a pair of leather hiking boots made. I had given the shoemaker a picture from a magazine to show him what I wanted. He measured my foot and said come back in three days. When I returned to my shock he had changed the boot by adding a high heel! He explained that since I was a woman he did not think it would look good on me without a high heel. I told him that I wanted to hike up mountains in these shoes so he reluctantly undid his fancy work and made me the boot I wanted. I had about a thousand dollars in cash and traveler's checks when I left and planned to have Mom wire me more money later as I needed it. The savings I had from working in Tabriz had been deposited in an account in Mom and Dad's bank in Hortonville, WI and I had given her power of attorney over the account.

We spent our last night in Iran with Kami and Vic. We planned to leave by train and they were going to drive us to the station in the morning. I couldn't sleep at all that night, I was so excited for this trip. A new adventure into the unknown was such a thrill that the adrenalin was already rushing through my veins.

CHAPTER 7

RULE # 7: Don't Judge!

Keep an open mind and be willing to accept knowledge and truth from other people and cultures. Don't judge.

AFGHANISTAN

This was the wildest, most ancient culture I came across in all my travels. Most of the country is mountainous and the people were poor and lived in small villages. They wore home-made clothes and shoes which were reminiscent of Biblical times — loose fitting robes and pantaloons and sandals even though it was quite cold, especially in the evenings. We entered Afghanistan through the border town of Islam Gala and from there took a small, colorful bus loaded with local people headed to Herat, the closest city. Their many belongings were tied to the roof. They spoke Farsi, but with a rather strange accent, making it difficult for us to understand what they said. The bus passed through an agricultural area with pastures and orchards, people riding donkeys, and small villages with no electricity. This was one of a very few paved roads in Afghanistan and it followed a winding river valley tucked between mountains. It was the route taken by many young travelers in the late sixties and early seventies and had become known as the "hippy trail." However, on our trip to Herat, Ginger and I were the only foreigners on the bus.

Herat was a pleasant enough town, but the people expressed disapproval of the many young visiting foreigners. They would shout, use hand gestures, and sometimes call us "foreign whores" in Farsi. We stayed in a small cheap hotel already occupied by some young Swedish men. They looked like they had been on the road a long time. One was barefoot, with multiple sores on his legs, and was wearing the loose fitting pants and tunic top worn by the locals. All three had long hair, few possessions and spent time begging on the streets. I felt sorry for them but did not give them money. There were plenty of beggars in Afghanistan, needy sick children and elderly women, all of whom I felt needed my help more than these guys who had somehow made it all the way to this part of the world. Deciding which needy beggars I would contribute to became a daily unpleasant task, and one that I would grapple with over the coming months as I traveled through Asia.

We spent only a few days in Herat and decided to take a bus to Kabul, via Kandahar. We thought maybe the capital city, Kabul, would be more modern and safer for single women to travel freely in. The ride to Kandahar was very unpleasant. Again we were the only foreigners on the bus, and of course, we were two unveiled women traveling alone. Soon we could hear the men calling us "foreign whores" and speculating where we came from. They had no idea that we understood some Farsi and knew what they were saying. They chewed some kind of leaf and would spit large cuds of a reddish color on the floor. Unfortunately our backpacks were under our seats and received more than one of these spit balls! They continued to talk about us in Farsi, so finally we said to them in Farsi, "Allah hears, and you will be punished for what you are saying." That did shut them up, but it was still an uneasy ride, even after we silenced their disgusting comments.

Kandahar was far more shocking than Herat. It was a cold and dirty city. The bus station was a big parking lot full of trash, beggars, and opportunists (young men hoping to prey upon the arriving travelers). The buses parked there looked hand-made, a result of all the "jerry-rigging" and crazy paint jobs. People were scattered about in small family groups with their personal possessions tied in cloth bundles and accompanied by small animals like chickens and lambs. Ginger and I needed a bathroom so we asked a group of men squatting and talking in a circle, chewing that red leaf, where we might find a "toilette" — Farsi word for bathroom. One of the men got up and said in very limited English, "Ah you want the shit hole," and pointed us to a location behind some rusted out old remains of cars. Back there behind those frames were piles of human excretion. We had found the "toilette." We laughed at the thought of the previous hippy travelers who must have taught that man those English words for toilet, realizing that "shit hole" was the perfect description of that place!

A few hours later and we were on another bus, this time to Kabul. The bus was packed with the people we had seen in the parking lot, cloth bundles, animals and all. Alongside the many bundles, more than a few male riders were also strapped to the top of the bus! Again we were the only foreigners, and the only unveiled women on the bus. It was about a two hundred mile ride on bad roads and uncomfortable seats, with fellow passengers who looked at us like we were aliens. The men ogled, the women hissed, and the children giggled.

Kabul, the Capital city, was somewhat modern with restaurants, tea houses, and hotels and beautiful handcrafted artifacts in the main bazaar. We found an inexpensive, rather sleazy, hotel room above one of the shops in the bazaar. It was a small hotel with just five or six rooms, all occupied by young "hippy" men. We discovered that the room next to ours was occupied by a very sick young American man who had been in his room for a few days, lying on the floor in the dark without food or water. We brought him food and drink and looked after him until he was well enough to take care of himself.

I loved walking through the big bazaar and bought a few beautiful hand embroidered tunic tops for about fifty cents each. We visited the American Embassy in a lovely garden area of Kabul and collected our much appreciated mail from family and friends. There were some modern looking little cafes in this part of town and we decided it would be safe to eat a real breakfast here, scrambled eggs and toast, a rare offering on Middle Eastern menus. We were wrong. We ended up with food poisoning and were sick for 24 hours. This was the only time I got sick on our entire trip through Asia, and I did not eat eggs again until I returned to America.

Afghanistan was a country of beautiful rugged scenery and an ancient culture influenced over the centuries by the Silk Road traders who had crossed through this country, as had the Persian armies, Genghis Khan, and Alexander the Great. Most Afghan men were bearded and armed. The women wore burkas that completely covered their faces except for a small netting over their eyes to allow them to see out. Ginger and I had mixed feelings about how much of the country to explore. We discussed leaving Kabul to travel to Bamiyan, known for the tall Buddha statues carved into its cliff sides, and a popular destination. In the end we decided to head east and cross the border into Pakistan. (A decision I have since regretted since the statues were destroyed by the Taliban in 2001.) We were simply weary of being foreign women traveling in conservative Islamist places. We decided that, in fact, we had been living under Islam for over two years and longed for the freedom to be accepted as women again, unveiled and not ogled or sneered at by judgmental men.

We left Kabul on another rickety bus, headed for the Pakistani border. We planned to pass through Pakistan as quickly as possible in order to get to India, a non-Muslim country. It was a long journey, winding through mountain range after mountain range. We spent the first night in a Caravanserai, a fort-like structure where the animals, mostly camels and goats, were herded into the inside courtyard. Women were housed in a small quarter on one end of the structure and the men occupied the other three quarters of the living area. Our bus parked inside the courtyard with the animals for safety. We had noticed signs along the road as we crossed the mountains which read, in English, "Travel at your own risk, highway robbers present." I felt relatively safe inside the Caravanserai since most of the Afghan men staying there were armed and could protect themselves and their women.

Around midnight, to the surprise of everyone, a late bus arrived. The biggest surprise for us was to see an American woman get off that bus. She was from Chicago and had traveled alone through Asia and was now on her way across the Middle East. Until then we had thought that we were very brave and adventurous, but for

Our main means of travel through Afghanistan, Pakistan and India was by colorful bus and rickshaws a woman to travel alone though all those countries was a whole other step up! The next day, as we were crossing yet another mountain peak, our bus broke down. There were two other foreigners on our bus, a man (Roger) from Michigan and a woman (Jan) from New Zealand. The four of us entertained ourselves by sitting alongside the road in the grass and playing gin rummy all afternoon. It was a crazy yet very memorable experience — playing cards near a broken down old bus under signs warning us of highway robbers! (Forty years later, with no contact in between, I received a notice from Roger on Facebook, asking me if I remembered him. Of course I did!)

Early in the evening another bus arrived and took us the final distance through the Khyber Pass of the Hindu Kush and on into Pakistan. The pass was more spectacular than I imagined it would be. It was wide and expansive and I could see how easy it would have been for Alexander the Great to bring his entire army through to enter India.

After an easy border crossing and passport check we boarded a Pakistani bus to Peshawar. There were five German guys on the bus and we soon became friends. We arrived in the city of Peshawar after dark. It was crowded, poor, and noisy. Most noticeable of all was the lack of women. It appeared to be a city of all men and here, more than ever, we felt terribly out of place. As the men stared and pointed at us, fear crept into my body. We wisely stayed close to our new German friends and found our way to the train station for an overnight train ride to Lahore. We celebrated when the train left the station. Even though I was only there a few hours, to this day I remember Peshawar as one of the scariest places I've been.

Lahore was actually a beautiful city, with wide streets, flowering trees, and most important of all, there were women everywhere. And a few of them were even wearing colorful clothes and head scarves, not the still common oppressive heavy veils. We all found rooms in a small hotel and then Ginger and I took a ride around town in a one horse buggy with a kind and smiling driver. Lahore was definitely an improvement from our experience in Peshawar, but we were ready to leave the Muslim world; it was October of 1971 and Pakistan and India were about to go to war. We only spent a few days in Lahore, left our German friends there, and took a bus toward India. The border was swarming with soldiers, but they were friendly and some actually had flowers placed in the barrel of their guns! We went through passport control and walked into India.

The talk of war had been escalating for months, and a visit by Senator Ted Kennedy had clearly put the U.S. on the side of Pakistan in this conflict. The Indian soldiers were everywhere and they appeared hostile and intimidating toward us as Americans. Clearly being an American in India during this time was not going to be easy. The border post was stark, no nearby town, and no means of transportation other than a few ox carts. We piled onto one of these and rode the few miles into a nearby village. There was a bus station in the village and a little outside eating stall selling bowls of hot curry sauce and rice. I was starving by then and ate a bowl full in a matter of minutes, loving every bite of it! I had forgotten how much I loved hot spicy food. Persians have great cuisine and they use lots of spices, but not hot peppers.

As we rode through the Indian countryside on our bus to Amritsar in the Punjab State we noticed many camouflaged tanks and anti-aircraft guns. Amazingly some of these war armaments were mounted on bridges and "camouflaged" with tree branches making them very noticeable! Shortly after boarding this bus I realized that I was losing my voice. My throat had been on fire since I ate that Indian curry and now it felt like my larynx was swelling. This bout of laryngitis lasted until the next day, but even so, I was still glad I had eaten that fabulous curry.

Amritsar was a beautiful city, well lit up at night. We stayed in an inexpensive hotel room near the train station and enjoyed a great night's sleep. We were both completely exhausted and relieved to have made it into India. We spent an enjoyable day in Amritsar, with its warm weather and beautiful central lake. This area of India is home of the Sikhs and once again it felt very much like a male dominated culture. We didn't spend much time here since we thought it was too close to Pakistan and the constant talk of war. Besides, we wanted to get to New Delhi to meet up with Frank, my Peace Corps friend from Tabriz who was there on leave.

Late in the afternoon we got on the train and were on our way. The train was crowded in the second class compartment where we sat. This was an overnight ride and we got little sleep but, happily, we had window seats and the early morning views were amazing. At first sunlight people were up and about everywhere along the railroad tracks. Eventually we realized that this is where people went to pee or poop; squatting along the tracks with their back to the passing trains. Mile upon mile of this routine was shocking, to say the least, and it continued on into the outskirts of New Delhi.

We stayed at a well-known very nice Youth Hostel in the newer part of the city. It had an American style restaurant attached that we also liked. It was clean and comfortable and removed from the noise and crowds we had grown accustomed to. It cost more to stay here than our meager budget allowed, but, for a few days, it was worth the splurge. We met Frank here and the three of us toured the city together, visiting sites including the old Red Fort (an historic structure from the 17th Century which was built and occupied by the Mogul emperors), back alleys with the money changers (i.e. the "black market"), and, of course, the American Embassy to collect our mail! We learned that President Nixon was planning a trip to China and that Americans were allowed to apply for a visa and travel there if they wanted to. Ginger and I went to the Chinese Embassy to apply for a visa. We were told we had to interview for it and that very few would be accepted. The same was true at the Burmese Embassy. We applied in both places and did an interview. Neither embassy accepted our applications. In hind-sight, I'm sure they were not interested in a couple of American "hippy chicks" traveling on a very low budget.

In the shops along the Red Fort I bargained for and bought trinkets — little seeds painted red which, when you opened them, contained up to a dozen tiny, tiny elephants carved out of ivory. There were also dried tree leaves with beautifully hand painted scenes. These were mounted on cards, so I bought some and sent them out as Christmas gifts to my family. And finally, I bought myself a silk sari, hand-made and tailored to fit me. (I've never worn it!) Visiting the money changers was a rather scary experience since we knew it was illegal. However, we went because the banks would only give us seven rupees per dollar and the money changers gave us double that amount. We rationalized that the government was cheating us by over valuing their currency so we continued to use the money changers.

The late sixties/early seventies was the era in which long haired young people from all over the world were traveling to India and we often encountered psychedelic colored vans with the words "India or Bust" painted on the side. One interesting tip learned from our fellow "hippy" travelers was that there was no need to stand in long lines to buy a train ticket in India; one could simply ride in the third class cars where no conductor ever bothered to come and you could ride for free! We took their advice and as we boarded trains going in many directions, zigzagging around India, we found that riding in a third class car was indeed free; it was so overcrowded that there was no way a conductor could even get in there. The aisles were full of people, and children would sit on any available lap, including ours. Toilets were inaccessible so sometimes folks simply urinated or "did their business" on the floors.

We spent days riding these trains through cities, small villages, and ancient looking farmland. At one point we saw oxen on a yoke being made to walk around and around in a circle turning a giant wheel that removed wheat grains from the shafts. I remarked on how resourceful the people were to still use this antiquated method of harvesting grain in the absence of modern machinery. Ginger, on the other hand, was outraged by the treatment of the oxen. She felt very sorry for the animals that wore blinders and looked sickly and tired. I was surprised by her comments and a long discussion between us followed. After all the poverty we had seen on our travels, all the beggars, lepers, starving children and diseased old people, Ginger expressed sorrow for the oxen!

Clearly a love of animals was a core part of her being. (NOTE: Ginger later became a medical doctor with a passion for helping anyone in need.)

The number of beggars in pathetic circumstances was always difficult to deal with. Beggars were everywhere and we learned that it didn't work to give any one of them money because it brought more and more who would surround us, not seeming to understand that we had only a limited supply of rupees. We discovered that buying a bag of fruit and giving these out worked much better. When the bag of fruit was gone the beggars could clearly see that there was nothing left to give. Our dilemma was choosing who to give it to: young vs. old, sick vs. healthy, the most desperate vs. the least desperate. Since there was no way we could afford to help out all these people, we first focused on the oldest and sickest looking. One night we encountered a very old woman laying on a train platform. She was wrapped in a filthy blanket and was very frail, almost unable to speak. We left her some food, a couple oranges and some bread. The next morning when we came back to the station to board another train we saw that she had died during the night. The food was still there. We decided from then on we would give what we could to the healthiest looking children, where our meager assistance might actually do some good. It seemed more rational to us, and so, for the remainder of our time in India, we bypassed the oldest and sickest looking beggars and went right to the children.

I have to admit that I was also a bit afraid of contracting a disease from some of the sickest people, those with leprosy or elephantiasis or those bearing a host of unidentifiable and scary looking open wounds. We noted that the merchants in the fruit and vegetable markets would angrily chase the little begging kids away but then allow free roaming cows to keep on munching undisturbed. It was definitely difficult to accept.

India was a true feast for the eyes, the opposite of the Muslim world in so many ways. First of all, there were so many bright colors! I had become so accustomed to the black and grey and brown clothing in Iran that all the Indian women looked shockingly beautiful! And their faces were not only unveiled and visible, but often adorned with gold and paint. Secondly, there was music everywhere — in the restaurants, bazaars, and out on the streets. And thirdly, we were able to walk anywhere dressed casually in jeans or whatever, without feeling frightened or shamed. The men did not ogle and the women did not hiss. And never once did a man try to pinch my butt or grab my breast!

The Taj Mahal was truly one of the major highlights of my visit to India. We walked to the site from the train station feeling hot and sticky and a bit grubby from our third class train ride. As we neared the Taj Mahal we saw a big new air-conditioned bus pull up and disembark a load of well-dressed American tourists. They had flown here from New Delhi and were driven to the site in that bus. I couldn't help but think what a different experience they would have in India as compared to mine. Ginger and Frank and I spent the day on the grounds of the Taj Mahal admiring the workmanship, the design, and the story behind the construction of this beautiful mausoleum built nearly five hundred years ago. We walked the entire grounds and stayed to watch the sun set on the marble structure.

The busload of Americans had left hours ago and by now were most likely back on their airplane, destined for another tourist site, while Ginger, Frank, and I took another third class train ride, this time to Khajuraho, famous in India for its twenty-five temples built about a thousand years ago. The temples are famous because of their erotic carvings. The carvings were pretty shocking to my naive eyes. The outside sandstone walls of each temple are adorned with hundreds of figurines in various sexual acts including beastiality and orgies of all manner and composition. The temples are scattered around a beautiful agricultural setting amidst golden wheat fields, vegetable crops and free range chickens.

From this quiet, peaceful farmland with its strange temples, we took a train to Benares (Varanasi), among the holiest sites in India. Nothing in all my travels prepared me for the experience of Benares, where I finally understood what "culture shock" means. We got off the train to face what looked like a thousand rickshaw drivers all begging for our business. It was truly a mob scene. The rickshaws were only built to hold one person so we each quickly jumped aboard one and headed toward a hotel we

Our crowded means of transportation in India

had heard about that was located right on the banks of the River Ganges. Since we were each in different rickshaws we could only hope that we would all arrive at the same hotel. My driver took off peddling his rickety contraption through the narrow streets of this ancient city. There were people everywhere, on foot, riding camels, driving ox carts, seated in the thousands of rickshaws , all cruising in and out of side streets and even sharing the road with a few cars. I looked around and became aware that some of the passengers in the rickshaws were not among the living!

Strapped into many of the rickshaws were deceased bodies, wrapped in white cloth and (I learned later) were headed to the Ganges where they would be cremated on funeral pyres along its bank. I was told that the Hindu belief is that if a person's ashes are scattered into the holy River Ganges, it would mean that he or she was no longer destined to rebirth, but could immediately enter Nirvana. Consequently those who could afford it had their loved ones cremated here and spread their ashes in the river. So I was riding through the streets next to bouncing corpses, cows deemed holy and running loose, half naked children, beggars everywhere, and dogs so thin and hairless I could see through them — skeleton, internal organs and all. The place was teeming with life and death, so much so that I was feeling smothered. I leaned back and closed my eyes, hoping to catch my breath and calm myself. When I opened my eyes we had turned onto an even narrower street and suddenly, whizzing over my head and jumping across the street from building to building, were dozens of monkeys! There was no place in this city, not even up into the sky, where one could rest one's eyes and enjoy some personal space. I was experiencing culture shock.

The hotel was actually very nice by our now adapted-to standards. It was a very old building with thick stone walls and high ceilings and small windows. Our room was quite large and clean and it actually felt cool inside. We were so happy to be there, away from all that faced us outside. We decided to rest and spent the remainder of the day in that private, peaceful room.

The next morning we ventured out to rent a small row boat and paddled ourselves down the Ganges to view the city from the relative peacefulness of the river.

Along the banks were hundreds of people bathing in the river and scooping up cups of water to be held high in a symbolic way of giving thanks, and then to our shock, they drank it! The river water was brown and visible nearby were floating carcasses of cows and even a few human bodies wrapped in white cloth. We learned that for families who could not afford the cremation ceremony at river's edge, an alternative was to simply dump the body into the river. Cows belong to no one, and are considered "holy," so when they die their bodies too are dumped into the river. We were also told that if someone dies from snake bite or from small pox they are not allowed to be cremated so their bodies are just dumped into the river. Along with all of this there were numerous little colorful floating offerings of thanks to the Hindu gods for special occasions like marriages, births, etc. These were made of wreaths of flowers and held little food samples and burning candles. In the evening when all was dark the sight of these numerous floating candlelit offerings was quite spectacular.

I don't remember how long we stayed in Benares, in my memory it seems longer than it probably was, but we decided to leave when anti-Americanism began heating up. We had sewn Canadian flags on our backpacks and introduced ourselves as Canadians, but still it was unnerving as US flags were being burnt and there were loud demonstrations against the United States for siding with Pakistan in the escalating dispute. People were saying that a war with Pakistan was imminent so we decided to take a train north into Nepal to avoid being in a country at war, especially when our own government was supporting "the other side."

Frank headed back to Tabriz, and Ginger and I took a bus to the town of Raxaul near the Nepali border, truly one of the low points of all my travels through Asia. I rudely referred to this town as "the armpit of the world" for years thereafter. The Youth Hostel was a large tent like structure located next to a hot, mosquito ridden swamp. We arrived at sunset and there was literally a black "cloud" that arose from the swamp: billions of mosquitoes in flight! In the Hostel tent there were dozens of cots, each with its own mosquito net hanging from the overhead rafters. We each climbed on a cot with all our belongings and lowered the mosquito net over us. Then spent the next half hour killing all the mosquitoes that had managed to get inside with us. Without supper or even a drink of water, we tried to get some sleep. This proved next to impossible since the netting was old and there were holes that the mosquitoes eventually found. Throughout the night I heard the slapping of hands swatting mosquitoes and the restless tossing of my fellow travelers' hot, itchy bodies. We were all up early and ready to board the bus and leave this place. There was a trough of water for brushing teeth, washing hands, etc. outside of the tent. Some of the brave backpackers took advantage of the water, but I decided against it, thinking I would rather just stick with my own germs and not risk exposure to others.

As soon as we crossed the border into Nepal a number of passengers started smoking hashish! I had known that hashish was legal in Nepal but it was still surprising to see it used so openly. We arrived in Katmandu on a sunny but rather cold day, and I loved it from the minute we got there. It was wonderfully colorful with beautiful mountain views. The people were very friendly, greeting us with hands together in prayer fashion, saying "Nameste." The city was much more quiet and serene than the cities in India. There were no signs of anti-Americanism nor of war. In fact, the town was getting ready for a celebration of the six-month birthday of King Mehendra's son. This is the age at which Hindu children are finally allowed to eat rice and touch the ground, or so we were told. The festivities lasted a few days and culminated in a colorful parade with elephants draped in flowers and with painted heads. There were dancers, musicians, and in a richly decorated carriage rode the king, the queen, and the six-month old son.

Katmandu was a perfect place for us to be during all the talk of war. It was safe and inexpensive. Lots of young backpackers from all over the world were there, because hashish was legal. There were restaurants we would frequent that served American-like food such as pancakes and brownies, and you could order them with or without hashish baked inside. One restaurant in particular, called Aunt Jane's, was popular with the young foreign travelers. It was right next to the little pensione type hotel we stayed in, so we ate there often. Days turned into weeks and we became more and more familiar with our surroundings. We walked all the narrow streets of the bazaar area, bargaining for trinkets and souvenirs, some of which I still have, like silver rings and bracelets, silk scarves and incense burners. Once while standing outside a little shop and admiring the wares within, I was quickly yanked inside by Ginger. Shocked and wondering what happened, I heard people screaming and saw this wild elephant on the run, passing right where I had just been standing! All I could think of was how would someone tell your family that you were run over by a wild elephant?

In the center of town was a large square marked off by a stone wall about six feet tall. On the sidewalk along the outside of the wall were various venders and this is where one found the barbers. As the men sat for their haircuts, monkeys climbed and chattered on the wall above begging passersby for bits of food. It was a site I very much enjoyed and visited almost daily. One day we decided to rent bicycles and rode to a Monkey Temple outside of town. Here there were hundreds of monkeys climbing all over and around an ancient Hindu Temple. On the ride back we passed a long haired hippy dressed in a saffron colored monk's robe and he yelled out my name, "Ruthann!." It took me awhile to recognize him as a friend of mine from my graduate years in Hawaii. We spent time catching up on each other's news and then said our good byes. He said he wanted to move to Tibet and I often wonder what happened to him.

We visited the American Embassy on a regular basis to pick up our mail and to get news of the war. The border had been closed between India and Nepal as soon as the war talk heated up. Gasoline was in short supply in Nepal and, because of this, airplane flights were limited; besides, flight patterns over India and Pakistan were not safe. The embassy officials told us that they would get word to our families in America informing them that we were safe, but unable to leave. If the war lasted longer than three months they said they would bring in planes to evacuate American citizens. We took advantage of their offer, wrote a message to our parents, and the embassy officials called our homes and relayed our messages. During our stay in Katmandu, one of the letters I received at the embassy was the birth announcement of my niece, Sarah, daughter of my sister Jane. I remember the announcement was so thrilling to me that it kept me up that night, just thinking about this new baby girl halfway around the world from me.

Ginger knew a woman, a friend of her brother's, who lived and worked in Pokhara, Nepal. Her name was Kate and she was a nurse from Los Angeles working for a British Medical Clinic there. We had her address and since we had lots of time to spend in Nepal we decided to go and visit her. We flew in a small plane from Kathmandu to Pokhara. The airport was nothing but a dirt runway on the edge of a small village. Local people met the plane which carried supplies to this remote area. One amazing site was a rather small woman who actually strapped a boxed refrigerator to her head and back and carried it in to town! Ginger and I walked into town to look for the clinic. We had notified Kate that we planned to come and visit but were unable to give her an exact arrival date since the flights were not dependable. In town we saw a young woman working in a very tiny dirt floor shop selling vegetables. She had a toddler and a little baby with her. When we walked by she said, "Hello, are you Americans?" Since she seemed fluent in English we stopped to say "hello" and ask if she could give us directions to the British Clinic. To our amazement we learned that she was Nepalese but had lived in Chicago for a year. She spoke excellent English, and was now married and back home living in Nepal. She directed us to the clinic, and during our stay in Pokhara we visited her often.

The "clinic'" was actually a series of tents set up along the river at the foot of the Annapurna Mountain range. We arrived at dark and couldn't actually see the river or the mountains that night.

The tents were of varying sizes and were for varying purposes. We were given one rather nice sized tent right next to the river as our guest quarters for the duration of our stay. It had two small cots, two lanterns and a small table and two chairs. It was large enough to stand up in and was quite comfortable. I loved going to sleep there to the sound of the river water. Other tents included a large one used as the dining area, another one serving as a latrine, and then a number of smaller ones where the nurses and doctors lived, all of whom were women. And they were all British women except for Kate. The "clinic" itself was simply a few Quonset houses, sitting side by side. There were no shower facilities, we washed ourselves using small pails of cold water! There were no electrical facilities, the staff lived and worked with lanterns, and generators to provide electricity for refrigeration of medical supplies and for equipment in the clinic. The first night we were there we had dinner with Kate and her colleagues and they were telling us how beautiful the area was. We could not tell since it was dark and fogged in. We couldn't even see the river, we could only hear it. When we woke up the next morning and opened our tent flap we were both totally astonished. The river was only feet away, and the high Annapurnas not much further. We stepped out into sunshine and blue skies with those high mountain peaks towering straight up over our heads!

We visited the clinic only a few times during our stay. It was a very busy place where people came from miles around seeking medical help. I remember one case in particular where a man had brought his wife down from a high mountain village. She was carried in a large basket by himself and some of his friends. The trip had taken a few days. She was in labor, in pain, and unable to birth the baby. The British doctors were able to deliver the baby girl, but the mother died shortly after. The father was very distraught, saying they already had eight children and he was unable to care for this baby. He left her in the clinic and went back up the mountain with his friends. The nurses, in particular Kate, took care of the baby. They named her Lisa, and Kate eventually adopted her and brought her back to America.

It was now November and the nights were getting quite cold. We had brought some hashish with us from Kathmandu and on about the second or third night there we decided to crawl under our covers and smoke a little. After a few hits on our little pipe I snuggled into the blankets on my cot and dozed off. When I woke up I could see Ginger in her cot, reading by the light of her lantern. I had no idea what time it was, no idea how long I had dozed off, but I was in a state of panic. I could not move nor talk. I wanted to get Ginger's attention to tell her something was drastically wrong with me, but she was faced away from me and had no idea I was awake and seemingly in trouble. So many thoughts went through my mind. I could feel myself breathing, feel my body against the hardness of the cot, but I could not move. I knew I was "stoned" like never before. I thought of Jimi Hendrix and how he died by suffocating on his own vomit. I realized now how that could happen. I did not feel sick, but knew that if I were to get sick the same thing could happen to me. My state of panic lasted for hours, long after Ginger had turned out the light and gone to sleep. It was a very thought provoking time, mostly questioning why I ever smoked hashish, and I realized there was no good reason. The truth is I did it only because it was available and part of my 60s generation experience. I awoke the next morning, happy to be alive, happy to be able to move and talk, and happy to be in this beautiful country. Though I spent the next month in Nepal where hashish was available, legal and cheap, I never in my life smoked it again nor had any desire to do so.

We were told that there were two American Peace Corps volunteers, a young husband and wife, living in a small village a few days hike away. We decided to go and visit them so we got a guide to take us there. We walked along the river, having to cross it a few times as it twisted and ambled along the base of those towering Annapurna Mountains. The river was not deep but the water was very cold so crossing it meant drying out our wet socks and pant legs. When we arrived at their little house in this remote village they were, of course, very surprised to see us! We spent a wonderful few days with them talking about their Peace Corps experience, and sharing each other's life stories. Thanksgiving was a few weeks away and we invited them to come to Pokhara to celebrate this American holiday with us.

Winter was approaching and the local farmers near Pokhara were harvesting their crops. One day while visiting our English speaking woman in the tiny dirt floor shop, we noticed men putting what looked like pumpkins up on the roofs of houses. Our friend said that indeed they were pumpkins, stored high for food for the animals over winter. She told us that the people did not eat pumpkins. Ginger and I immediately decided to make some pumpkin pies for a Thanksgiving feast. Our Nepalese friend was very excited about this idea, saying she had not had pumpkin pie since she lived in Chicago. She said she would provide us the pumpkins if we could share some of the pie with her family. The British don't eat pumpkin either so we thought it would be nice to introduce it to them, and we knew our American Peace Corps friends would appreciate the treat.

We made the pies on Thanksgiving Day. Making these pumpkin pies was quite the endeavor, involving help from some of the British nurses and local children. Besides the pumpkins, we knew we needed a number of ingredients like milk, eggs, shortening, flour, sugar, and spices. We also needed an oven. The nurses and some of the village women built us an 'oven' using an old oil barrel. We bought rice flour, sugar, a strange "butter" and eggs in the village. Kate had received a package of pumpkin pie spices from her Mom in California as a Thanksgiving Day gift and was hoping she would find a use for it. The milk was the tricky part. There were no cows in Pokhara but they did raise water buffalo. The children were a big help because they knew how to milk the buffalo, which was a lot harder than it looked. It took the better part of the morning but the kids were able to provide us with a sufficient volume of this thick almost orangish colored "milk." We first roasted the pumpkins over a wood fire in our newly crafted "oven." This enabled us to scrape the soft pumpkin out of the shells. Next we made the crust out of rice flour and the "butter," mixed with a little water to make it dough like. We did manage to get it rolled out onto some large pans from the clinic's kitchen but I definitely can't say it looked much like pie crust is supposed to look. After mixing the remaining ingredients with the pumpkin, pouring it over the pie crust, and baking it in our wood burning oil drum "oven," the day was almost over. It had taken nearly a full day to make two trays of pumpkin pie. By this time many had gathered to taste this American concoction. Our Nepalese lady friend from Chicago and her children were the first to be served, followed by the British nurses, a number of Nepalese workers from the clinic, and our American Peace Corps friends. Everyone seemed to really enjoy the taste, though to feed everyone the pieces were cut quite small. When it came our turn to try it we were amazed at how good it was and how it really did taste like a pumpkin pie from home. We both agreed that this was a Thanksgiving Day that we would never forget.

The war between India and Pakistan was very short and ended on December 16th. The border re-opened; we said our good byes to Kate and the other friends we had met in Pokhara and flew back to Katmandu. We soon discovered that there were no buses or planes going to India. All public transport in Nepal was at a standstill. At Aunt Jane's, our old breakfast place hang-out, we met some "hippies" who were organizing a private bus to Goa, India. We decided to join them and thirty or so other young travelers from all over the world. On the bus we met two young German men, Gard and Oaf, who quickly became our friends and traveling companions. We crossed the border into India with no problems and spent our first night in a small town with just one restaurant. It was an open air restaurant with large wood tables and a tent like structure overhead held up by long wood beams. There was no electricity so we ate by lantern light. In the middle of the meal a giant rat fell from above and landed right on our table! We looked up and realized there were many other rats up there running around on those wood beams, and our dinner came to an abrupt and immediate end. We were so grossed out that we all headed for the bus. I needed to use their restroom first so I went to the back of the restaurant to find it, walking past a large pantry with bags and boxes of rice and other supplies. The room was crawling with mice! I used the bathroom, which was extremely filthy, and then got back on the bus without telling anyone about the pantry filled with mice. I figured they were all sickened enough by the rat. Some of the guys on the bus were planning an all-night "party" as we drove in the dark through Northern India so they passed around a large supply of amphetamines. When the bottle came to me I remembered how much I liked what these little pills could do for my brain. It could allow me to experience a level of pure focus that made me feel like a genius for a few hours. On the other hand, I knew the "downer" experienced when coming off that "high" would be very unpleasant. I took a small handful, maybe three or four, and put them in an outside pocket of my backpack.

After spending all night riding on this noisy, crazy bus, the Germans and Ginger and I decided to take the first available train to Madras instead of continuing on the bus to Goa. Ginger and I were both emotionally exhausted from the poverty and mass of humanity in India and were thinking that we were ready to move on to another country. We were also in need of a little comfort so we bought first class train tickets! It really was not that much more expensive and it meant getting a sleeper car and air conditioning! Our new German friends bought second class tickets but we spent time with them in the dining car and on train platforms whenever the train stopped.

The train ride was a memorable event. There were four of us in our first class compartment for the long two day ride to Madras. Besides Ginger and me, there was an elderly Indian woman dressed in a silk sari, wearing lots of gold bangles and henna in her hair which only partially covered the grey, and an Indian man about thirty-five years old in a full dress military uniform complete with medals. Both were well educated, spoke "the King's English," and were friendly, polite, and very interesting. As it turned dark outside we passed a mountainous village and could see a stream of lanterns moving down the mountainside. The old woman explained that it was most likely someone in the village using their "power" to do a kind deed. Ginger and I looked at her puzzlingly and then she went on to say, "Yes, that's right, you in the West do not understand 'powers,' and you don't even know what your own 'power' is. Every human being has a special 'power'. For example," she said, "some can read palms and tell other's future, some can predict major events, and some can cure disease or heal injuries." She went on to explain that some people have the "power" to cure snake bites. Their names are actually listed in phone directories so if you get bit by a snake you can call them and they can heal you!

Meanwhile the military man was nodding his head and agreeing with everything she said. Ginger and I were completely dumbfounded! He went on to say that his uncle could read palms and tell people's futures and that he had the same "power." So I asked if he could read my palm and he said, "Of course." I gave him my hand and he looked at it for quite a while and then started speaking in general terms about my life, of which I remember nothing. But in the end he said that I would have one daughter, late in my life. At the time I was twenty-eight years old and believed I was already older than most to be a mother, so I didn't think much of his prediction. I thought, *How hard can it be to make that prediction, since I'm already going on thirty?* Then he read Ginger's palm and we were both pretty impressed, not by his predictions, but because he described her as being the youngest of three children, and not just the youngest, but youngest by many years such that she was in a different generational culture from her brothers. In fact, her brothers, Bob and Jay, were practically out of high school and college before she was born so indeed they were of a "different generation!"

This strange encounter was followed by an even stranger event. At some point the train stopped in a small town where we all got off to stretch our legs for a short break. We could hear lots of yelling and people gathering around so we all went to see what was happening. A number of people were gathered in a large circle. In the center was a man holding a green lime. He carefully set it down and started waving some rupees at the crowd. The people began hissing and yelling at him. I asked the old woman from our compartment what was happening. What was the man doing? Why were the people angry? She said, "He is using his 'power' in an evil way. He is trying to make money from his 'power' and this is forbidden. He is saying that he will give anyone ten rupees if they can pick up the lime, but if you can't pick it up you have to give him ten rupees." Upon hearing this Gard mumbled that this was completely ridiculous as he walked into the center with a smile on his face and his ten rupee wager in his hand. The man took his ten rupees and stood back as Gard bent over to pick up the lime. Within seconds he was flying backwards and fell to the ground. It looked as if someone hit him but there was no one even close to him. He got up looking stunned with the lime still in its place on the ground. The train whistle blew to signal passengers to board so we all quietly walked back to the train, too shocked to even talk about what had just happened. That night I wrote in my journal that I would reconsider my previous beliefs that all can be scientifically explained. India had taught me that there is a lot that I have yet to learn.

The next day we arrived in Madras and the four of us went together to find an inexpensive hotel. We found a wonderful small B&B, an old British colonial house converted into a few rooms for rent at very reasonable prices. It was very clean, with big beds and big overhanging mosquito nets, and our own private shower! It came with breakfast each morning of fresh papaya and warm bread! We loved it! Ginger and I were getting weary of living amongst so much poverty and overabundance of life. We decided to just catch a flight to Bangkok where perhaps the standard of living would be higher. We wanted to walk down streets without diseased and crippled beggars, without starving half naked children, and without mangy dogs and sacred cows roaming everywhere. And besides, it had been over three years since we left America and we were definitely getting excited to get back. Gard and Oaf wanted to go to Sri Lanka so we were prepared to part ways in a few days.

Our first night in Madras we went to an open street bar/ restaurant that had a band playing a variety of music. They sang some songs in English for us and we could tell they were so proud of the Western music they knew. We were clapping loudly and complimenting them to show appreciation for their efforts even though their renditions of some familiar songs were really bad. It was nearing Christmas and they told us they would sing a religious Christian song for us, where upon they began singing "As Shepherds washed their socks by night!" We didn't mean to insult them but as soon as we looked at each other we all burst out laughing!

Madras was a colorful town with pleasant bazaars and restaurants. The seafood was especially good and of course spicy hot, the way I liked it. We visited embassies here and got visas for Thailand, a bundle of mail at the US embassy, and plane tickets at a small travel agency. We left on the same flight as Gard and Oaf. It was a flight to Bangkok, but with a short layover in Colombo, Sri Lanka. As the plane attempted to land in Colombo we could see men frantically chasing cows off the runway there as we circled and circled. Finally the runway was cleared and we landed in the most palm tree covered place I had ever seen. We decided to stay a few days and talked the airline into changing our tickets for a later departure to Thailand. Travel then was so much easier than today. For one thing, tickets never needed to be bought in advance and could easily be changed for no charge. Also, flights were never full so there was always plenty of room to stretch out and sleep.

We spent a few days in Colombo, enough to meet some fellow hippy travelers who told us we should go to Hikkaduwa where the beaches are beautiful and snorkeling is great. So the four of us were back on a train. Hikkaduwa was a small town at the end of the train line which traveled south along the coast. The houses were thatched roof wooden structures on stilts. We didn't see anything that looked like a hotel but a local man told us we could stay in one of the houses that was abandoned and that is what we did. The house was right on the beach and the views were beautiful. We enjoyed wonderful carefree days there that almost felt like Hawaii. We spent our days under palm trees, buying food from vendors walking up and down the beach. We swam and snorkeled and played in the gentle waves of the warm water of the Indian Ocean. It was like a mini vacation in the midst of our long adventurous road home.

One evening we were invited to join the villagers in a celebration carried on before the New Year to "scare away all the evil spirits." We followed them into a jungle clearing where all the kids sat around in a big circle and the adults stood behind them. Into the circle came various dancers in amazing costumes, some like scary monsters, and some like big colorful birds. Next to the gathering was a long bed of hot coals, so red hot that even standing near it was impossible for me. Yet by the end of the evening the villagers were walking and dancing on it in their bare feet! Even some of the children were able to do this! A young Peace Corps volunteer from the area had joined us there and he attempted to try it but unfortunately burned his feet badly after only two steps.

Another strange thing that happened that night involved a young Sri Lankan man from the village. He entered the circle to loud clapping and excitement. A few others joined him and they took what looked like large fish hooks and began hooking it through his skin: one on each ankle, each thigh, his abdomen, chest, and finally his cheeks. He smiled the whole while and no blood appeared where the punctures were made. Each hook had a thick string on the end and they used these strings to suspend him in air like a human hammock! He continued to smile the entire time and after they lowered him down and removed the hooks he beckoned us closer to show us that he had no sores, no visible holes in his skin, no bleeding, not even any reddening! I was totally amazed. I was standing only a few feet away and witnessed them inserting the hooks through his skin and saw the skin stretch as they raised him up and hung him by those heavy strings. Clearly science could not explain this, nor their ability to walk through those red hot coals. Again I let my mind stretch further away from the idea that Western science was the only truth.

A few days later we said good bye to Gard and Oaf and flew

to Bangkok. We both liked Bangkok and actually splurged for a nice room in a big hotel. It was a big city of modern buildings along side of old pagodas and temples and little walking bridges. It was clean in comparison to India and much less crowded. If there were beggars, I do not remember them and I didn't mention them in my journal. There were lots of fresh produce markets selling fruits and vegetables I had never seen before. Much of the produce was brought to the markets on small boats moving up and down the rivers. We could stand on the little bridges and buy food off the boats. There were also huge department stores with all the latest fashions.

We were happy to get to the embassy since once again there were lots of letters from friends and from home. I decided to call home since I was running out of money, and ask Mom to send money from my bank account to the American Express office in Singapore. We went to a big telephone exchange building to make the call. This involved paying in advance for the amount of time you thought you would talk and then waiting in line for a phone. I thought again about how long it had been since I had actually spoken to my mom (nearly three years) and the anticipation of hearing her voice made me extremely anxious. We didn't get to talk long but it was wonderful and sad at the same time. It brought on a wave of homesickness. Ginger then called her mom so in the end we both walked out of that telephone house with a lump in our throat and a desire to catch the next plane to America!

Mom said she would go to the bank the next day and wire the money to Singapore for us so I was no longer concerned about my dwindling travelers checks. The weather was beautiful, hot and humid like I prefer, and I started thinking about the surrounding areas and how nice it would be to go to Laos or Cambodia. I knew the war was going on in Vietnam but I thought Laos and Cambodia could be reasonably safe, and I really especially wanted to go to Vientiane. However, Ginger was dead set against it and thought I was crazy for even thinking about it. (In hind sight, I'm sure she was right!)

We spent a few more days in Thailand and then booked a

ride on the famous Orient Express train to Singapore. It was a wonderful train ride, past gorgeous scenery. The trip lasted two days, going through the length of Malaysia. Part of the time we rode along the River Kwai, at other times we went past miles of rubber plantations, and sometimes through thick jungles where I strained to see if I might spot an orangutan. We stopped in small towns along the way and vendors on the platform would sell us fresh fruit and tea through the windows. I thought the women looked beautiful. Malaysia is a Muslim country but the women wore colorful clothes, flowers in their hair, and always a big smile on their faces. When the train stopped in Kuala Lumpur, the only large city along the way, I was amazed at all the flowers. The train station and the platforms were full of every variety one could imagine! I nicknamed the city the "Flower Capital of the World" and kind of wished we were getting off here so I could spend more time. However, we really needed to get to Singapore to pick up the money since we were now running very low.

The border crossing into Singapore was strict and took a long time to get through. The country was obviously very conservative and did not believe in freedom of expression. There were a lot of "hippies" on the train and they looked each of us over carefully, insisting that some make changes to their clothing and telling others they could not enter unless they got a haircut! Ginger and I were wearing short sundresses and sandals and because we were women our long hair was no problem so we got through easily. We saw a number of young guys turn around and get back on the same train heading back to Thailand because they refused to get a haircut. There were other young men who agreed to get their hair cut and conveniently there were barbers right there in the train station.

Singapore was a clean, colorful, and modern city. It's right on the equator so the climate was wonderfully warm and humid. We checked into the YWCA which was a modern high rise. It was very comfortable, we had a large room and private bath, and it was quite inexpensive. On the other hand, there were signs on the doors and in the elevators notifying us that they enforced a curfew for women. We had to be back in our room by 10 p.m.! The city also had strict signs saying "No Spitting" and other demands on sanitation.

We made our first of many trips to the American Embassy to get our mail and find out about the money Mom had said she would wire to the American Express office for me. It turned out that wiring the money from Hortonville, WI to Singapore was not such an easy task and in fact it would take a minimum of a few weeks. We were very low on cash, and in those days, had no credit card, so we stayed at the 'Y' knowing we wouldn't have to pay until we checked out. We used our remaining money to buy food.

We did a lot of walking and exploring in the city. There were wonderful street food markets where we could buy really inexpensive meals. And the food was excellent. We ate very flavorful rice and noodle dishes with lots of vegetables and seafood. In a little bar by the water I tried to order a "Singapore Sling," but no one had heard of this drink. We kept returning to the American Express office to see if the money had arrived but in the end it took three weeks so we got to see a lot of Singapore. One day we walked to a park where they had all these statues depicting life in the days of the Buddha. It was quite shocking that this park was filled with large, colorful plastic figurines of frogs and birds and such for children to enjoy, and at the same time featured this huge display of ancient life including tortures and starvation and rape and murder!

When the money finally arrived we bought plane tickets to Los Angeles with stops along the way in Hong Kong and Japan and Hawaii. We went to a travel agency to get the tickets, first time I had ever done this, and was amazed to find out there was no fee for their services. I hadn't realized that they received their fees from the airlines. If I had known this earlier, it would have saved me much time and energy buying plane tickets. The other nice thing about the travel agency was the little extras we received, like a complete print out of the itinerary, a small leather case to carry all our travel documents, and a map of the Pacific area we would be flying through. Ginger was completely out of money by this time so she borrowed from me and then paid me back shortly after we returned to the States.

Flying in to Hong Kong was a rather frightening experience. The buildings were so tall and numerous and the runway so small and right over the ocean, that the view from the plane made the landing look perilous. I called Hong Kong the city of red and gold. These colors hung on buildings as banners and lanterns and in the clothes people wore. We didn't stay long but long enough to enjoy the sites, do some gift and souvenir shopping, gawk at the crowded streets and body to body street vendors, and eat lots of great food. We went to a couple interesting bars at night frequented by American and British guys who worked for Middle Eastern oil companies and were here on vacation. They seemed to have plenty of money to spend and were nice enough to buy us drinks and food. Again I tried to order a Singapore Sling but the bartenders did not know of this drink. The restaurants and food in Hong Kong were wonderful. I loved all the different Asian flavors, and began to realize that returning to America would mean a lack of all this, unless I chose a city with a large international influence. For the first time since I left Iran I began to seriously think about where I might want to live in the States. I had friends in New York, Boston, and Washington D.C., and figured I would start my search by visiting those areas.

After about a week in Hong Kong, we flew on to Tokyo. By this time we had been on the road, living out of our backpacks for about six months, and we were definitely ready to be "home." It was February and cold and snowy when we arrived in Japan. The airport was abuzz with athletes and sportscasters there to attend the Winter Olympics. It was late, the hotels were full, and we had no reservations. We met some Canadians headed to the Olympics and they offered to let us stay with them in their hotel room. We gratefully accepted and slept on the floor in their room. The next morning we took one of the "fast trains" to the outskirts of town where the embassy was and collected a bundle of mail. We spent the afternoon in that beautiful warm building reading all of our letters and deciding that a few days in Tokyo would be enough for now. We were definitely homesick and so excited to be back in the US after so much time away. We enjoyed a few wonderful days in Tokyo, sleeping in very nice accommodations, sampling food like I hadn't had since I left Hawaii, and marveling about how different it felt to be in a non-Third World country. The trains were new and spacious, the people were not loudly hawking merchandise, it was safe to drink the water, and there were no beggars! It was definitely more expensive, but at this point we didn't care since we knew we were headed to the States in a few days and would soon be employed once again.

Our flight back to the States was wonderful. We flew on Japan Airlines on an almost empty, huge 747. We each had a full five seat row to ourselves and the stewardesses brought us warm sock-like slippers, pillows, blankets, and of course great food and drink. This was an overnight flight to Honolulu where we crossed the International Date Line and were given a Certificate proving it. I still have mine.

Landing in Honolulu was memorable. I had come full circle. It had taken me a little over three years and I was back where I started, in this beautiful airport on this beautiful island. Everything was so wonderfully familiar. Everyone spoke English and I could trade in my yens and rupees and other strangely colored paper money for some easy to use dollar bills. I retrieved my backpack from baggage claim and was headed to the customs line when I suddenly remembered the amphetamines I had put in the outside pocket. I did a quick detour to the restrooms and flushed the pills down the toilet, shaking the whole while to realize that I was about to enter America with illegal drugs in my backpack!

CHAPTER 8

RULE # 8: Be a Life Long Learner

Continue to read, take a course, study, get the app for TED Lectures, etc. And always be a good LISTENER.

RETURN TO AMERICA

We spent a week in Hawaii and it was a rather frenzied visit. It was comforting to hear English spoken everywhere again. To be able to use dollar currency, and have a good old fashioned American breakfast of eggs and bacon and pancakes with real maple syrup! The island looked much the same as when I left it, sunny and beautiful, but my connection to it was completely changed. Almost all my close friends from three years earlier had now left. This was the story of Oahu at that time, young people came, stayed a short time, and left. There were now ashrams on the island and one of Ginger's close California friends (Cat) was living there. We went to visit her. The place was run as a sort of religious commune and was occupied by a number of young "hippies" along with some Indian spiritual leaders. It was a quiet, secluded place with rustic accommodations surrounded by flowering plants. We had a nice visit, met some kind people, but I knew that they too would leave in time.

I enjoyed being back, visiting my favorite places, and seeing a few old friends. However, I knew that whatever lay ahead in my future it would not involve coming back here to pursue another degree. From Honolulu we flew to Los Angeles and I stayed with Ginger and her parents for a few days. They lived in a little house in Whittier with lemon trees in the back yard and a sad looking old basset hound in the living room. We talked late into the evenings about our trip and all that we had encountered. We shared lots of stories and laughter, amid their curiosity and interest in where we had been and what we had done. Her dad was an engineer who had worked for the oil company in Aruba where they had lived for a while. They had an obvious interest in the rest of the world and of course, their oldest son, Bob, and his family were still living in Iran.

Phoenix was the next stop on my way home. Tom was doing his residency there in ophthalmology. He had definitely aged in the years since last I saw him. He had gained a little weight and no longer looked like the scrawny kid in his early twenties. His schedule was crazy busy as he was practically living at the hospital. I stayed a few days and as usual we went out to eat at some fabulous restaurants. We talked about life in general, where I wanted to live next, his imminent draft status and plans to join the army as a "Major" and serve as an eye surgeon. We hardly talked about my travels, he didn't ask so I didn't say much about it.

I arrived at the airport in Appleton, WI mid-afternoon and Mom was there to meet me. We were both very excited to see each other and talked a mile a minute! Mom had a million questions and wanted to hear everything I'd seen and done on my travels, and I was bursting to tell her. Dad was out in the barn working when we arrived at the house. Shortly after, he entered the kitchen from the basement stairs and when he saw me he just burst out crying. He hugged me and hugged me and continued to sob. Mom kept trying to soothe him, saying, "Now Floyd, there is no reason to cry. She is home again and safe." I felt so close to him at that moment, realizing how it must have been hard for him to have me be away for so long. (However, I didn't fully appreciate how he must have felt until I had a daughter of my own.)

I absolutely loved being back home. I spent all my time with the family, getting acquainted with my three new nieces (Kerri, Leilani, and Sarah who were still babies, under the age of one), and getting reacquainted with Tammy (now 12), Kurt (11), and Mike (age 4). They called me Aunt Hanny and I very much enjoyed spending time with all of them; playing games like baseball or cards, dancing, riding horse, or catching fireflies. I slept upstairs in the farmhouse Mom and Dad had bought after I graduated from college, so it was a space I had never occupied before, but it was large and felt very luxurious.

My belongings had been shipped to Los Angeles from Iran but there was a ship docker's strike and so all ships had been unloaded in Ensenada, Mexico and trucked up to L.A. From there it was shipped to my parent's address and when I finally got it and went through it I realized that most of my silver jewelry from Iran and Turkey was missing. However, and more importantly, what was there were all my slides from Europe and Iran. I then got the ones developed from my travels through Asia and decided to have a slide show for the family one night. Mom was enthralled and asked many questions. My sisters, June and Audrey, and their husbands, Gene and Marly, seemed definitely interested but probably not quite sure what to think about it all. Dad sat in his comfy lazy boy chair and fell asleep shortly after I started! My first clue that not everyone would be interested in the details of my travels.

Gary and Rosie, with Leilani, had moved to Madison and were living in a large house that they had rented along with some friends in a commune style of the 60s and early 70s. I took the bus to Madison and stayed with them for a while. There were always a lot of people at the house so every night was like a party of some sort. The conversation was lively and fun but I felt like a "foreigner." They discussed local politics, TV shows, and recent news events, and I realized how out of touch I was. And on the other hand none of these people could relate to what I had been through over the past three years. Once again I was experiencing "culture shock," only this time it was happening in reverse. As in India, I sought solitude. Time alone with books and newspapers helped me reenter American life.

After about six weeks in Wisconsin, and spending it mostly with Mom and Dad with no thought about my future, my intelligent, caring mother finally brought up the subject. Funny how I didn't realize until then that I was taking no initiative regarding my future plans. I had returned home and sort of figuratively curled up in a fetal position, living off of my parents! It was nearly May and I had no job nor any specific idea of where I even intended to live. I still had enough savings left to support myself for a while, but the wake-up call from Mom was appreciated. We had fun discussing various options, and in the end I headed to Boston and Washington D.C. where I had friends to visit and rely on for a while. These were the two cities I had thought would be the most international and easiest to feel at home in. Within a week I was on a Greyhound bus to D.C.

Washington, D.C., May, 1972

I called Cliff, whom I knew from Tabriz, Iran, as soon as I got off the bus. He invited me to come and stay in the guest room of the commune he was then living in. He had returned to D.C. after his tour of duty in Tabriz with the American Consulate, had left his wife and lost his job. He was driving a taxi at the time, I think, and was very active in the anti-war movement. My first night in the commune all eight house members gathered for a celebration of the finalization of the divorce of Natasha, Cliff's girlfriend at that time. The dinner was marvelous, great conversation and lots of laughs. Natasha and I became fast friends and through her I met another young woman, Lori, who later became my roommate.

I very much enjoyed being in D.C. It was spring time and the city was green and warm and beautiful. Flowers were in bloom and parks were easily accessible. The commune was off Connecticut Avenue near Dupont Circle and from there I walked everywhere. I explored numerous historical sites as well as some of the funky bars, book stores, and cafes around the neighborhood. I loved the city: the politics, the people, the numerous parks and public buildings, and of course the abundant international presence.

After a wonderful two week visit, I took the train to Boston and stayed with my old college roommate, Helen. I arrived in the middle of May in a snow storm! It was cold and dreary looking the entire week I was there, which contributed greatly to my decision to move to D.C. It was wonderful to see Helen again and catch up on her life. She was working in a job she didn't particularly care for but as always was full of energy and optimism. She had two roommates and was living in a crowded apartment in Brookline. She was dating a doctor at the time and was very much enjoying Boston. She took some time off work and showed me her favorite parts of the city. I really liked the harbor with all the ships, it was so nice being near water again. I also liked the night life and the proximity of so many little bars and restaurants. Boston had a deep historical sense, like D.C. but the people were less diverse, with fewer foreigners and less of an international flavor. Still, in the end, it was mainly the cold and snowy weather that tipped the balance in favor of D.C.as my future home.

Upon my return to D.C., Lori asked if I would like to room with her. She had a lovely little two bedroom apartment just off Dupont Circle on Q Street. This really worked out great for me since the apartment was furnished, I could move right in, and I liked this neighborhood.

I visited Cliff at the commune on a regular basis, but it was my friendship with Natasha that I enjoyed the most when hanging out there. She had a beautiful smile, a great laugh, and always brought energy to a room full of people. Everyone in the commune was active in the anti-war movement, as were Natasha and I. However, it didn't frame the whole of who we were so our approach to it was not as radical as some in the commune, Cliff included. Natasha and I participated in peaceful demonstrations, carried banners, and endured being tear gassed on occasion. In part, some of these demonstrations were against racism and sexism. We marched on Washington along with thousands of others and spoke out against the Vietnam War whenever the opportunity arose. We didn't cross barriers, get arrested, or boycott events like Cliff and others.

One such time was when Cliff decided to boycott a concert by the Rolling Stones being held at the RFK Stadium in Washington that summer. He had gotten tickets and was going to go with Natasha, but then he decided that some of the music of the Rolling Stones was "sexist" and he would not support them by attending the concert. Natasha was rightfully angry at the absurdity of his decision, so she took the tickets and she and I went! RFK Stadium is huge, it holds about forty-five thousand people and was sold out. Cliff was there with a few other guys holding up amateur protest signs by the entrance, hardly noticeable by any of the thousands of young people streaming in to hear the music. And the concert was, of course, amazing! I've always really liked their music and hearing them live was so energizing, from "Brown Sugar" to my favorite, "You Can't Always Get What You Want." The atmosphere inside the stadium got a little tense when people started throwing fire crackers in amongst the crowd! This, added to all the people smoking cigarettes and marijuana, made for a very hazy smelly environment. Cliff's "over the top" decision to boycott the concert was the end of any real relationship with Natasha. Following that event I didn't see much of him, but Natasha and I have remained close friends all my life.

My former student, and friend, Victor, from Iranzamin was living in Washington D.C. and attending American University. We had stayed in contact via mutual friends and had dinner together the night before he left for his summer vacation in Iran where his father was still serving as the German Ambassador. He asked me what he could bring me from Iran and I told him, "The address of Susan Moss." In my lengthy travels I had lost track of her. The last I heard she was working in the UK but a letter sent to that address had been returned to me.

I wanted to teach again, that was definitely my first choice, so I began to look for jobs. I decided that only if I could not find a teaching position would I look for work in research or clinical laboratories. The first job I interviewed for was a position as a biology teacher for a large Catholic high school in northern Virginia, Bishop Denis J. O'Connell. The principal was a Catholic priest, Father McMurtrie, and I liked him from the moment I met him. He seemed stereotypically Irish to me, with a real sparkle in his eyes and a witty sense of humor. That same day I interviewed at a large public high school in northern Virginia. I do not remember anything about that interview really, other than it was with a group of people and seemed very formal. The following day Fr. McMurtrie called me and offered me the job. I accepted immediately. It was early July and school started in late August, so with a contract in hand I had the summer off to do what I wanted to, and that meant spending as much time with my family as possible.

My first stop was Kingston, Tennessee where my sister Jane lived with her husband Dick and their baby girl, Sarah. Jane was a stay at home Mom then, so we had a great time being entertained by Sarah. She liked spending time in her little bouncy seat "walker" where she could scoot all over the main floor of their apartment. She would inevitably approach the electric outlets and move to stick her finger in one while looking at Jane the whole while. Jane would say, "No!" and Sarah's face would pucker up into a sad, sad expression followed by tears and wailing. Jane and I would turn our faces and laugh silently, it just looked so funny! Sarah repeated this attempt to touch the electric outlets many times, I think because she knew it wasn't allowed, she wanted it even more.

I spent the rest of the summer in Wisconsin, going between Madison where Gary and Rosie and Leilani lived, and Hortonville where the rest of the immediate family lived. I especially loved my time with the nieces and nephews, going horseback riding with Dad, and having long talks with Mom.

The summer went by quickly and I was very excited to get back to D.C. and start my new teaching job. My first day of work was an all-day teacher orientation session for the new school year. Fr. McMurtrie started the morning off with a large assembly in the school auditorium. There were around two hundred teachers in attendance and I think well over half of them were priests, brothers, and nuns. A huge difference from the small lay staff at Iranzamin. Fr. McMurtrie had a great sense of humor and a charismatic way of holding everyone's attention. I remember one thing he said was, "If you promise not to believe everything the kids say about me, I promise not to believe everything they say about you!" And as I found out, he had a great relationship with the students, spent considerable time with them, and I'm sure he heard a lot about all the teachers.

My friend Barb (from Hawaii) had moved to Maryland temporarily with her family. Her husband Ken was going through training/orientation for a job he had accepted in Madagascar. This was wonderful for me since I got to spend a lot of time with them while they were there. Ken helped me buy a used car, a small Toyota for $1600 that I bought on installments. Having a car and my own means of transport for the first time in years was more rewarding than I could have imagined. It gave me such a desired feeling of freedom and independence. The school was seven miles from my apartment in D.C., so having a car was essential.

My teaching schedule was probably pretty standard for the time. The day was divided into eight periods of forty-five minutes each, and I taught General Biology in six of the eight periods. One of the periods was my prep time and the other was an assigned duty to supervise study halls. My classroom was reasonably large with enough lab tables to seat twenty-four students, however, in some of my classes there were more than twenty-four students so I had them rotate sitting on the window sills. There was a storage room in the back of the classroom for supplies which was very convenient. Also, it had a small desk and I could work in there when students were not around, and I could smoke in there! Amazing when I think of it now since I'm sure my whole classroom must have smelled like cigarettes.

I loved the students from day one. I started off kind of strict since I wasn't sure how I would maintain discipline with all these American kids and such large class sizes. I only had one classroom rule: Practice Empathy! Don't do anything to anyone (including me) that you wouldn't want done to you. I soon learned that the kids were great, they were kind, they paid attention and they worked hard. On occasion I would tell them a "story" about some event in my travels. They seemed genuinely interested in my adventures and by the end of the year were telling me, "You should write a book!" It was the first time I seriously thought about writing a book, "one day."

Teaching biology was much more fun than teaching chemistry since I knew more about biology in general and could bring lots of real life examples to my classroom. I had plants growing on some of the window sills and I had a big fish tank in the front of my room. I took students on an outing and we brought back some small fresh water fish, snails, frogs, and water insects and plants and built a living habitat in the room. I taught in that same room all six years I was at O'Connell and by the time I left my remaining fish had grown considerably. Some of them were four to five inches long and I had trained them to jump up out of the water to grab the food from my hand. This was an early morning "thrill" for me and my students.

Each morning started with a prayer and general announcements for the day. Sometimes different folks were asked to lead a prayer. I always wondered if I would ever be asked, though everyone knew I was not Catholic. I was in fact an atheist and would sometimes chuckle to myself at the idea of leading a prayer since the only one that came to mind was Janis Joplin's:

> "Oh lord won't you buy me a Mercedes Benz,
> my friends all drive Porsches I must make amends."

One of the most wonderful things about working at O'Connell was that I met Mary. She taught English in a classroom on the floor above me. She was a young, single lay teacher, but other than that we seemed to have little in common. Still, we became good friends and I very much enjoyed her company. She, like Fr. McMurtrie, was a stereotypical Irish Catholic with a great sense of humor and quick wit. She was a devout Catholic but could, with good nature, poke fun of some aspects of her own life, politics in general, and anyone who took themselves too seriously. She was good friends with Fr. McMurtrie, which made sense because they had a lot in common. Mary and I and a couple other teachers started a Friday afternoon "Happy Hour" at the local Boar's Head Inn, a few blocks from school. It was a nice way to get to know more of the teachers, including some of the priests and brothers. The nuns however never came.

Settling into a comfortable life in D.C. was also going well. Sharing the apartment with Lori wasn't always the easiest, but it was workable. She was finishing her Ph.D. dissertation in English Literature which I'm sure was stressful, and this along with her rather high strung personality made life difficult for her at times. She was also juggling relationships with three different boyfriends in the first few months I was there, so we didn't spend much time together.

Victor had returned from Iran with Susan's address. I was thrilled to realize that she was living in D.C. a short walk from my apartment on Dupont Circle! She was living with Alvin and they were busy planning their wedding. He owned his own small graphic art company and was very active in the Democratic Party and in the anti-war movement. Susan was in law school at American University. It was wonderful to see her again and catch up on each other's lives since last we had seen each other. She and Alvin were married in the courthouse a few months later and I served as her "witness."

Midway through the fall, after Lori and I had been sharing the apartment for about four months the landlady threw us out! She claimed it was because Lori had rented the apartment without a roommate and had not notified her of my moving in. However, we thought more likely she threw us out because one of Lori's boyfriends was an African American and the landlady, who lived downstairs, would glare at him disapprovingly every time he came to visit. In any event, we decided to each go our own way. Lori rented a one bedroom apartment up by American University and I rented a small studio apartment in Georgetown. It was really small, but I did like living on my own, and I liked being in Georgetown.

This was an election year, 1972, and all my friends and I were extremely disappointed that Richard Nixon was elected to a second term. He campaigned on a "secret" plan to end the war. None of us believed him. Immediately following the election a large counter inauguration was planned by the protest movement. It would be held on the Mall in D.C. and we would inaugurate a pig! My friend, Bob, from Tabriz planned to come down for the event. He was now in medical school in Boston, and though he was Best Man at Tricia Nixon's wedding, he greatly opposed the war and the administration of President Nixon.

I flew home to Wisconsin for Christmas that year and every year that I lived in D.C. It was always a highlight of my life when as a family we were all together at Mom and Dad's house with great food, lots of decorations, a big tree, and piles of presents underneath. I loved being "Aunt Hanny" to all my nieces and nephews and was grateful that flights were affordable and working in a school gave me a nice long break at the holidays. I would always stop, either coming or going, to visit Tom in Chicago if he was home for the holidays.

As much as I enjoyed being back in America, I missed Iran, and began planning a return trip in the summer. I would get a cheap flight on Icelandair to Luxembourg, trains and buses overland to Israel and then a flight to Iran. Lori had finished her Ph.D., gotten a part time job at the University of Maryland, and was applying for jobs through the University to teach in Heidelberg, Germany. She was hoping to do the trip with me in the summer and then end up teaching in Germany in the fall.

The counter inauguration was attended by thousands of anti-war protestors. My little studio apartment was full of friends from various out of town places who crashed on my floor in their sleeping bags. On the day of Nixon's inauguration we went to the Mall and endured very cold weather, fiery antiwar speeches, and the live squealing pig someone brought for the ceremony. Following this "counter inauguration" we all began a long peaceful march toward the Capital. Halfway there we were dispersed by the police with heavy amounts of tear gas. We all scattered in every direction. I was walking with Natasha at the time and we ran as fast as we could away from there. Never had I experienced tear gas so thick, not even on the streets of Chicago during the 1968 Democratic Convention.

School finished for the year in early June. Lori had gotten the job in Germany and planned to live there for at least a year. I moved out of my studio apartment and moved into her one bedroom apartment. This worked out well for both of us. She left her furniture there which was convenient for her and me. She didn't have to store it for a year and I didn't have to buy any at that time. Lori and I left on a plane for Luxembourg the day after my teaching assignment ended for the summer. We traveled overland through Germany and then down the coast of Yugoslavia to Dubrovnik. The scenery was beautiful and the people were very warm and friendly. However the buses were crowded with exhausted parents, energetic children, caged chickens, bags of worldly goods, a mixture of odors both pleasant and unpleasant, and all of this capped with the ever present loud playing unfamiliar music on the radio. The tickets were cheap but I could see these bus rides were taking a toll on Lori.

We enjoyed the little beaches at the foot of the cliffs along the coast of the Adriatic Sea. We stayed one night in a small inn, met some handsome young men who built a bonfire in the sand and shared a bottle of wine with us. They spoke no English so we could not communicate other than with smiles and head nods in approval. Dubrovnik was an amazing old walled city overlooking the sea. The streets were too narrow for modern vehicles so the bus stopped at the wall and we walked from there. We spent a few days here and we both loved this city. It was such an old city with well-worn stone steps and tiny shops built in a time I can only imagine. We left by bus under the same circumstances that we arrived in, only this time the bus was taking us over the rather dangerous mountain roads of Montenegro to Bulgaria. We rode all night and passed over the mountains in the dark which was probably a good thing. Around 5 a.m. as the sun was rising the bus driver turned on the radio with that loud unfamiliar music, almost a wailing tone in the singing. Lori had had it! She marched to the front of the bus and began yelling in English at the driver. I'm sure he, nor anyone else on the bus, understood what she was saying, but she was so angry I thought we would get thrown off the bus in the middle of nowhere. Everyone was talking and pointing at her. I went up and talked her into calming down, telling her we were in their country and on their bus, which means it's not acceptable to make any demands whatsoever. And certainly not in that angry, aggressive voice! It would not be the first time that our two traveling styles would clash. My "Midwestern nice" was in complete contrast to her "New Jersey assertiveness."

When we reached the Bulgarian border we got on the famous train, the Orient Express, and took it all the way to Istanbul. It was definitely more comfortable than the buses, but also rather amazing in the fact that there were almost no Bulgarians on the train, only Turks on their way home. As we passed through towns in Bulgaria they seemed empty, very few cars, a few shops but no shoppers, and an agrarian landscape with few modern machines. Arriving in Istanbul was a real treat. I love this city, it's still my favorite city in the world, and it was so nice to be back. I really wanted to show Lori around so she could see what a wonderful city this was, but after a few weeks of traveling on the cheap in Third World countries she was focused on the negatives. We only stayed a few days, shopped in the Grand Bazaar and visited the famous Hagia Sophia.

We flew from Istanbul to Tel Aviv and spent two wonderful weeks in Israel. There were a lot of armed soldiers at the airport and military armored cars along the runway. This was the summer of 1973 and it was obvious that security was tight all over Israel.

We traveled throughout the country from North to South and back, and everywhere we encountered places I knew of from world religions or from history. We spent a day at Masada, marveling at the resolve of the ancient people who had lived there and died rather than succumb to Roman rule. We arose early one day and went to the camel and sheep market in Beer Sheva. It took place on the edge of town in a large empty desert area and

I couldn't help but think that this was a scene and an event that had not changed in centuries! We stayed in dorm like facilities on Kibbutzes and met Jews from all over the world living there in commune like fashion, working on farms and in orchards. I was a seasoned traveler at this time in my life and I always slept with my backpack in bed with me and my purse under my pillow. One night as I was sleeping in a top bunk bed in a kibbutz I awoke to find a man in our room rummaging through the belongings of my fellow travelers. I yelled out at him, waking everyone up, and he clumsily stumbled out the door (there were no locks). A number of us went out looking for him but it was dark and he had disappeared from sight. Fortunately he was not able to steal anything in his quick haste to leave.

Traveling around Israel was overwhelming in the sense of its "familiarity," even though I had never been there before. For example, there was the familiar Biblical names of the towns we encountered, like Bethlehem, Jericho, Nazareth, and Jerusalem and sites like the Garden of Gethsemane and the Sea of Galilee. There were also well known Jewish and Muslim sites like the Wailing Wall and the Dome on the Rock. I really enjoyed spending time in Jerusalem. It was like many Middle Eastern cities I had spent time in: the architecture, old narrow streets, small colorful shops with never a price tag on anything since one bargained for everything, and the familiar smells of all the spices, and tastes of the food. But one thing was very different and that was the dress of the local people. In Jerusalem you could see men wearing shorts and sleeveless shirts, and women wearing colorful miniskirts which were popular at the time. In the Middle Eastern Muslim cities people dressed much more conservatively. At first I thought the Israelis must be much more liberal, and that women there were treated more equally, like in Europe, but that changed when I visited a Jewish Temple and saw that women were relegated to the back of the building and did not have an equal role in the service. This was even more noticeable at the Wailing Wall where a barrier was set up preventing women from getting close to the Wall. We all had to stand on one side of the barrier while the men could walk directly up to the Wall, say prayers, and sometimes put little pieces of paper with prayers written on them in the cracks of the Wall.

We returned to Tel Aviv and flew to Tehran. Again the security at the airport was like nothing I had ever seen in any other part of the world. There were no X-Ray machines back then so the security guards went through all ones belongings by hand, checking everything. They even opened tubes of toothpaste and shampoo bottles to check what was inside. It took hours and therefore our flight left two hours late. On most of my travels this would not matter but this particular time Kami was meeting our flight in Tehran and I didn't want him to be sitting at the airport for that long.

We arrived in Tehran at the end of June and the airport was crowded and chaotic. I was elated to see Kami and Vic waiting for us. It felt so good to be back in Iran again and summer is a wonderful abundant time to visit. The fresh fruits and vegetables are the best in the world. Persian cuisine is my favorite and I was very much looking forward to the food. Also, hearing the language again was "music to my ears." It's a beautiful language, not harsh like Arabic or German, but soft and flowing like French. And best of all was knowing I could spend time with my good friends Kami and Vic and Juni who were all in town that summer.

Kami and Vic were living in their new home in a small development next to Farahabad. The home was very modern and had a beautiful pool. I have fond memories of spending lots of time that hot summer swimming and sitting around the pool with Kami and Vic. They had two dogs, a little one and a big one, and they sometimes joined us in the pool. Ahmed was Kami's house servant. I had known him when he worked for Kambiz and he was not one of my favorites. He always seemed sullen to me, and disapproving of Kami's foreign visitors, especially women. Ahmed also openly disliked the dogs, and once when we returned from an outing we found the big sheepdog with the hair shaved off his butt! Ahmed's explanation was that it was a "jin" who had done the deed. We couldn't help but laugh at this ridiculous answer.

Lori wanted to see some of the historical sites of Iran but I had no desire to do anything in Iran but spend time with my friends. And by this time I had little interest in spending time with Lori since she seemed more and more negative to me. I talked to Kami and we decided to take her to a travel agency that did nice long trips around Iran. She chose one that took her to all the highlights and would end up back in Tehran a few days before she and I were scheduled to leave for our return trip to Europe. Kami paid for her trip and we saw her off on a big air conditioned tour bus the next day.

The month went by very quickly. I had a wonderful time seeing my old friends at the Iran American Society, visiting with Juni as often as I could, and of course spending time with Kami and Vic. We rode horses on Farahabad, took his Land Rover on some desert trips, and stayed in one of the palaces on the Caspian Sea. I also went once with Juni to her lovely little home on the Caspian. We talked, ate great food prepared by her cook, and walked along the beach for a few days. Juni loved Iran and wanted to make a difference in the lives of the people. My conversations with her and with Kami were always thought provoking and uplifting, and so I started to think that maybe I would come back to Iran one day on a more permanent basis.

In early August Lori returned from the guided tour that she said she really enjoyed. A few days later we boarded the bus to Istanbul. The bus route went through Tabriz with a short stopover. We didn't stop for a day or two like I would have wanted to. Lori had to be back in Heidelberg where she was about to start a job as an English professor at the University there. Before we started the return trip she and I had a frank discussion about our different traveling styles. I explained that I would be perfectly happy returning on my own. We could go on different buses, or if on the same bus, be in different seats, but I could no longer travel as her friend if she was again critical of the people around us. She was obviously not comfortable traveling alone so I agreed to travel with her. The trip back went very well. It was not always comfortable. It took about a week of traveling overland, first by bus to Istanbul, then by train through Bulgaria, Yugoslavia, Austria, and into Germany. We stayed in cheap hotels at night, some with an abundance of insects. We ate in small cafes along the route and endured the usual crowded, noisy, hot buses and train compartments. I said good bye to Lori at the Heidelberg train station late in the evening and took an overnight train to Luxembourg. My flight to the U.S. through Iceland got me back to Washington D.C. the night before school started the next day.

That fall Gary and Rosie and Leilani moved to Winona, Minnesota where Gary had started a job teaching agriculture classes at the technical college. Josie and Tom had moved back to Wisconsin and were living in Milwaukee where Tom was in dental school. My Tom had been drafted and was serving the U.S. Army as an eye surgeon, stationed in Denver, Colorado. Ginger was in southern California working in a law firm doing secretarial duties and trying to figure out what she wanted to do in life, knowing it was not going to be as a secretary! Susan was still in law school, Natasha still working at NIMH, Juni was back in England attending Oxford University, and Kami was in Tehran working with his brother in a company they had started for big game hunters in Iran.

I started my second year of teaching at O'Connell High School with pretty much the same schedule as I had the year before. This time it was a bit less work since I had a file cabinet full of lesson plans and ideas from my first year teaching there. Still I spent a number of hours each night on preparations: fine tuning the lessons, dropping what I knew didn't work, and adding new ideas. And there was always homework to correct, tests to write, and grades to average for the nearly two hundred students on my class lists. I didn't have time to do this during my prep time at school since I used that time to prepare for laboratory experiments, or to socialize for a while in the teacher's lounge with my colleagues. And we didn't have calculators or computers then, so I did it all by hand and on my old manual typewriter. Also, I had two new duties that year. I was appointed Chair of the Science Department so I was responsible for our monthly meetings, working on the budget, ordering supplies, and making decisions on course offerings for the future. It was during this year that as a department we decided to offer Advanced Placement classes the following year in biology, chemistry, and physics.

And that fall the school added a new girls' sports team: field hockey. This was meant to help even out the number of activities available to boys and girls. I agreed to be the coach, though I hadn't played the sport since my sophomore year of college nearly ten years earlier! I borrowed a book on the sport, rules, drills, etc. from Peggy, the PE teacher, and read it thoroughly before the first day of tryouts. Luckily for me, a new teacher that year, Carolyn, came and asked if she could assist with the coaching. She had played field hockey in high school and was a big help. The girls on the team were wonderful, talented athletes and so fun to work with. That first year there were only a few games scheduled, and some of those got canceled due to rain. Still the girls came to practice every day and worked very hard at getting good at this sport. I coached the team every year, with Carolyn's help, until I left D.C. (Like Mary, Carolyn and I have remained friends and still see each other whenever we can.) We never had a championship team but we won some big games and I loved every minute of working with those girls. One of them had cystic fibrosis, yet she was a great athlete and worked hard at doing her very best. She died from the disease the year after she graduated, and I still think of her and draw strength from her spunkiness and determination. Another was a truly gifted athlete. She was the star of the field hockey team, the basketball team, and the softball team. In today's world I think she could have received a full scholarship to a Division I school in any one of those three sports. At the end of the year we always had a big celebratory Athletic Banquet where each coach would give out their "Most Valuable Player" award. These events were very well attended and was my first experience at speaking to an audience that numbered in the hundreds.

I still very much enjoyed my job and I loved working with these teens, but I assumed it was not something I could do for the rest of my career with the level of enthusiasm needed to be really good at

Me as Teacher/Field Hockey Coach

teaching. Many of the older teachers seemed tired and no longer interested in their work. I definitely wanted to stay in the field of education, but realized I would need some authority to make changes in the whole system that I thought were needed: smaller class sizes, ongoing training for teachers, and the ability to remove teachers who were not passionate about the students and their progress. Maybe as an administrator? Within a few weeks I was investigating graduate programs in Educational Administration. I was working with a two year temporary teaching license in Virginia and would need to take additional college credits in education anyway. My apartment was located very near American University so I decided to apply for admission to the Masters of Education program in Educational Administration to begin in the fall of 1974. I took the GRE that winter and was accepted into the program shortly after. I was allowed to transfer as many as six graduate credits in education so I decided to attend Winona State University in the summer and take the six credits that I needed to renew my teacher's license, and then transfer the credits to my Master's program. I could live with Gary and Rosie and Leilani and enjoy getting to spend time with them again.

I spent some of my social time that winter hanging out with Mary. We went to movies or out to dinner and just talked. I loved her sense of humor so we always had a good time. Sometimes we were joined by fellow teachers, and almost always we went to places in northern Virginia, but not in D.C. Mary was a lot less comfortable in the city than I was, so mostly I spent my social time with Susan and Alvin and Natasha. Since Alvin owned his own business he had lots of friends and business acquaintances. I would often join them at their house where they entertained or at some social event that was happening. Natasha grew up in D.C. so she had many friends and family members in the area. Wherever I went with Natasha she knew people! Mostly we went to clubs to dance and drink. We sometimes took the train to New York City for the weekend. In particular I remember going in the weeks before Christmas when New Yorkers are in a celebratory mood. I remember once riding on the Staten Island Ferry and the people on the boat started spontaneously singing Christmas carols! Of course it was rather late and they were probably full of Christmas "cheer," but it's what I loved about New York. The people are definitely less inhibited than in other parts of America.

Richard Nixon was still president and negotiations were taking place to end the war in Vietnam. However, the Watergate Scandal was all over the news every day since the investigation was ongoing and it became quite clear that Nixon and his aides were behind the break-in at the Democratic Headquarters in Washington D.C. I had a small twelve-inch black and white TV in my apartment that I rarely watched, and I didn't listen to the radio except to play music while driving my car. I got my daily news through my subscription to the Washington Post.

When school ended that year, Tammy and Kurt flew out to D.C. to spend a week with me. I had given them this as a Christmas gift. They were fourteen and thirteen-years-old at the time and it was great having them visit me. When they first arrived I had one more day of meetings at school, so one of my graduating students (Jean, whom I am still in contact with) volunteered to entertain them for the day. She took them to Arlington National Cemetery for a tour. That week Mary's father died suddenly of a heart attack. It was a big shock as he was only in his early sixties. I brought Tammy and Kurt over to her house and they sat quietly in the living room while I helped Mary compute her students' grades so she could get her records turned in on time. Tammy and Kurt were so easy to take care of and appreciative of all we did. They even attended the funeral with me, though I know that was not high on their list. I took them to some of my favorite restaurants, from Vietnamese to Lebanese and much to my delight, they loved the food! We visited all the historical sites in D.C. and took the boat ride down the Potomac River to Mt. Vernon, the home of George Washington. We also went to the big amusement park and rode the scariest roller coaster ever — we all three screamed the entire while! They rode back to Wisconsin with me in my 1971 Toyota. On the bridge crossing the Ohio River between Kentucky and Ohio I got a flat tire! Luckily for me my gifted thirteen-year-old nephew knew exactly what to do and changed the tire all by himself!

Summer was relaxing and enjoyable in Winona. The classes I took were helpful for my teaching career since one was on "Lesson Planning" and the other was on "Developing Science Curriculum." Gary and Rosie were living in a tiny little house right in the middle of town so we could walk to everything. Leilani was now three-years-old and very precocious. I enjoyed getting to know her on a daily basis that summer. I walked her to the park nearly every day and marveled at her speaking ability and the size of her vocabulary. And I learned that she already had her own personality, something she was obviously born with. Her likes, dislikes, and opinions were her own and she made them known. For one thing, she did not like wearing long pants or even shorts. She dressed herself and wore dresses every day, even for our trips to the park where I thought she would be more comfortable in shorts.

My classes were finished by mid-July so after a few weeks on the farm with Mom and Dad and my sisters and their families I flew to Denver to visit Tom. He had the week off and we went hiking in the Rockies. We climbed Pikes Peak and spent some time back in Denver. He was living in a high rise in Cherry Creek at the time. His plans were to return to Chicago, or maybe Peoria, when his tour of duty with the army finished. He did seem to enjoy his work as an eye surgeon and the idea of taking over his father's practice in Peoria appealed to him.

I returned to Wisconsin just in time to hear the news of the resignation of President Nixon. It was a shocking relief. I hadn't believed he would actually resign so it came as a huge surprise. The American support of the war had been winding down for over a year in terms of financial support and troop deployment, but American soldiers were still in Vietnam and dying every day. The Paris Peace Accords had been signed in the spring of 1973 but the war waged on. Gerald Ford became President following Nixon's resignation. The midterm elections of 1974 put more Democrats and more representatives opposed to the war in office. Congress then voted to refuse to provide any further financial support to South Vietnam and the following spring the south collapsed amid crazy chaos at the Saigon airport in which hundreds of foreigners and Vietnamese supporters were evacuated by helicopter. And so, alas, the war in Vietnam ended. A few months later I walked through Arlington National Cemetery and was shocked and saddened to see the thousands and thousands of graves in the Vietnam War section.

In the fall of 1974 I started my Master's program at American University. The classes were held at night, and since I was teaching full time and coaching, I could take no more than 1-2 courses a semester. The whole experience was so different than my full time Master's program at the University of Hawaii where there was a great deal of camaraderie and I got to know all of the students and professors on a personal and professional level. At American University I took courses, studied on my own, and took the exams. Today I cannot name one student nor one professor from my time in the program, whereas from Hawaii I can still name them all.

Teaching and my relationship with the students was still a huge part of my life. I continued to tell my "stories" to every new class and of course they would always ask for more (a distraction from the biology lesson at hand?). Every year in the spring the school had a special week where teachers could offer different "fun" classes. One of the priests, Fr. E. asked me to offer a class on Iran for seniors and so I did. I called it "The Pleasures of Persia" and he talked a group of senior boys into taking it. I didn't know these boys since I only taught freshmen and sophomores at the time. I had a great deal of fun with this course and those boys were wonderfully attentive, interested and curious. I brought in a rug that we all sat around on, I made tea on a samovar, read poetry from Omar Khayyam, played Middle Eastern music, cooked my favorite food, Fesenjun, taught them how to make yoghurt and how to write their names in Farsi, showed them some of my slides and told them endless stories of my two years in Iran.

I offered this course again for the next few years and it became quite popular and was always filled to capacity. One year Juni

My friend, Juni, giving her presentation to my class on the "Pleasures of Persia."

was visiting me during this week and she came dressed in her beautiful Kurdish clothes and did a presentation for the kids. She even did a dance for them. She was definitely the biggest hit of the week!

My final three years of teaching I taught mostly Advanced Placement Biology. Each year more students were interested in advanced placement since if they passed the AP exam at the end of the year they could receive college credit at most universities in America. I then offered a wilderness trip to the Appalachia Mountains in Virginia during this special week instead of the "Pleasures of Persia" course. The wilderness trip was only open to my Advanced Placement Biology students and most of them chose to go so I would end up taking a busload of students on this adventure. We would rent backpacks and tents and go hiking on the Appalachia Trail. I don't think any of these students had ever backpacked before, and I didn't have near enough chaperones. Usually it was just me and maybe two other teachers (neither experienced backpackers or with knowledge of the trail). I would have a park ranger come and talk to all of us in advance to tell us some do's and don'ts, and that was about it for preparation. In hindsight, it's amazing it worked as well as it did!

There were some crazy happenings, like the girl who packed all canned goods to eat because she didn't think she would like dehydrated food. Her pack was too heavy for her to carry so the boys divided up the cans and carried them for her. There was DS, a student who was sure he knew the area and so we all followed him and went twenty-two miles in the wrong direction! And one of my favorite happenings was while telling stories around the campfire at night. One student, PK, swore us all to secrecy and confessed that he had been the mysterious "streaker" at the homecoming football game when he was a freshman! As far as I know no one ever broke the secrecy pact. Anyway, he graduated that June without any consequences.

The summer of 1975 I travelled to South America with Susan. She was now a lawyer and doing some advocacy work for prisoners in northern Virginia. We flew to San Andres first.

Backpacking on the Appalachian Trail

This is a small island in the Caribbean belonging to Nicaragua. We found an inexpensive room in a bungalow by the beach for our first night. Unfortunately it was hot and stuffy in this small room, with no air conditioning and only a small window. We had a very hard time sleeping; Susan described it as trying to sleep "in a coffin!" We went outside and rested comfortably on mats on the beach. Following this miserable experience we decided to be more selective and perhaps spend a bit more on accommodations. We met some interesting senior citizens on this island on a trip to the bank to cash some travelers checks. These were Americans who had retired there because they could live quite comfortably on their Social Security checks. There was a "natural aquarium" just off shore where we experienced some incredible snorkeling. The water was only about four feet deep in this area so I felt very comfortable in the water, knowing if I felt uncomfortable at any point I could just stand up! I did not feel safe in deep water. I could swim but at that time in my life I never liked being in water over my head.

From San Andres we flew to Bogota. It was an interesting old colonial city with Spanish style buildings that looked like they came right out of the Sixteenth and Seventeenth Centuries. We didn't stay here long because it didn't look safe. All the homes and shops had iron bars covering the windows. In the nicer areas of the city there were armed guards posted in front of the homes and some of these homes also had tall walls surrounding them. From Bogota we took a bus to Cali in the southern part of Columbia. This bus took us up over the Andes Mountains and was one of the most uncomfortable bus trips I have ever taken. The driver was seemingly on some serious schedule since he drove fast and made no stops. The roads were not good and they were windy and steep. After about five hours of nonstop riding I really needed to go to the bathroom but there was none on the bus. In my pathetic Spanish I asked if he could make a toilet stop. He loudly said, "No!" After another hour I was desperate and so was Susan. I walked to the front of the bus and made a motion like I was about to throw up on him. He pulled over to the side of the road and stopped the bus. Susan and I got off to pee along the road in a ditch of tall grasses. Much to our amazement nearly every passenger on the bus did the same thing!

We stayed in Cali for a few days. It was really a beautiful city of large parks with flowering trees along well marked walking paths. It was hot and walking among the shade of these trees was very enjoyable. At some point we stopped and sat on a large stone bench to rest. A young smiling man approached, sat down next to us and calmly said, "F_ck all Americans! Go Home!" We left the park immediately, with another negative opinion of the country. Later while eating lunch in a little cafe some small children came to the window. They stood there, outside the cafe, looking through the window at us. There were five or six of them and when we finished eating and got up to leave, they rushed into the restaurant and scarfed down our leftovers before the manager could chase them out. I was beginning to really dislike Columbia.

We next took a bus to Popayan on our way to Ecuador. This was another old Colonial city and we stayed in a wonderful old missionary hotel with spacious rooms overlooking a plaza. From the hotel we could see a large hill in the distance with a big statue on top. We decided to take a walk over there and check it out. It was further than we thought so by the time we got there we were on the outskirts of the city. We climbed the hill and were admiring the statue and the view of the city from our perch when we heard voices. I turned around and realized almost immediately that no one was up there but us and two young men. I sensed right away that they were talking about us. We decided that the smart thing was to leave, and besides, it was beginning to rain.

I started walking back down the path and Susan was right behind me. Soon I heard a commotion and saw Susan trying to keep one of the young men from stealing her purse! We both had shoulder purses and he had grabbed ahold of the strap. She had immediately grabbed the other end and they were in a tug of war over the purse. My instinct was to jump in to help her, until the other young man pulled out a switch blade and flashed it at me. I was wearing my shoulder purse with the strap over my head instead of just loosely on my shoulder. I had gotten in the habit of doing this during my years of travel since I usually carried everything of worth in my purse. All my valuables including my passport, cash, and travelers checks were in my purse. I reacted to the switchblade by pulling my rather large thick leather purse around to the front to protect my body. I started jumping up and down, moving from side to side and holding the purse in front of me. I figured a moving target would be hard to hit, and besides, my jerky body movements were obviously freaking him out. He was just standing there staring at me like I was some lunatic. Actually, I'm sure that's what I looked like! At some point in the tussle over Susan's purse, she let out a loud roar like a lion which startled the guy and he jumped back, letting go of her purse. She and I quickly started running. It was raining harder now and we looked over the edge at the wet grass covering the hill and simultaneously decided to slide down by the seat of our pants. It was steep and as soon as we went over the edge it was easy to slide. The two would be thieves were standing at the top looking down at us as we slid to the bottom. Amazingly, as soon as we got down a police car came driving around the corner and we flagged them down. We tried to explain what happened by pointing at the guys at the top of the hill and acting out the attempted robbery but they did not understand. There were three of them in the squad car, all with rifles. They asked us for the name of our hotel, we told them, and they gave us a ride back into town to the front door of the hotel. Needless to say, we were pretty shaken up by the experience and decided to forgo dinner and just rest in our comfortable, safe hotel room.

We fell asleep and awoke some time later to what sounded like gun shots and helicopters landing! We could only imagine that there must be a revolution or something going on outside of our hotel! We didn't know whether to lock our door and hunker down or run for help. We chose the former, we waited, and soon all was quiet. Next came the sound of men screaming and hollering and it was so close we were sure they were in the hotel. We were too frightened to stay there and not know what was going on, so we got up the courage to walk quietly down the hallway and peek over a balcony into the courtyard. There we saw two teams of young men playing a raucous game of soccer! This was the yelling and screaming we were hearing. We then went down to the front desk to inquire about the helicopters and what sounded like gunshots. We were informed that the hotel was located next door to an army school and this was the sound of their training program. We were greatly relieved to know there was no imminent danger, but we were definitely ready to leave Columbia. We left for Ecuador the next day.

The rain continued to fall and our bus stopped for the night in a small, muddy town in Ecuador. A young man came to our bus and offered to show us to a hotel room. We were the only tourists on the bus, the town was dark, and we saw no hotels in sight so with some apprehension, we followed him. He took us to a small hotel with a few rooms upstairs. There was a woman at the front desk, which made us feel more comfortable. Once in the room we were shocked to see the soft, sagging mattresses of straw on the beds. These beds were so uncomfortable that all we could do was laugh, but at least we felt safe.

Quito was next on our stop. We got a room on the second floor of an old hotel with a balcony overlooking the central market below. It was a great location, and a wonderful place to watch the crowds of people below. One afternoon we were watching when a thief grabbed the camera from a tall male tourist displaying a Canadian flag on his camera bag. He fought with the thief to retrieve his camera, but the crowd turned against him. They were saying he should give him the camera because he was rich and the would-be-thief was poor!

We went to the American Embassy, as was my habit in all my travels, to pick up our mail. I received a birth announcement from my sister, Jane, telling me of her new baby boy, Jason. It was so thrilling, and brought back memories of the night in Nepal almost four years earlier when I received the announcement of the birth of Jane's daughter, Sarah. I now had eight nieces and nephews. My niece, Sadie, daughter of Gary and Rosie, was born the month before I left on this trip. I thought of all eight of them and hoped that one day they too would travel the world and have adventures of their own.

Susan and I journeyed by bus from Quito over the Andes to Punto, a small town on the edge of the Amazon jungle. This was for me a highlight of the trip, and I appreciated the fact that Susan was willing to come even though she was not comfortable in this environment. We stayed in a small hut like building with open windows, no glass, and a door that did not lock. Insects were numerous, and some of them the size of my hand, furthering the discomfort for Susan. We only stayed a few nights, but for me it was glorious.

There were some graduate students there from Harvard, studying nocturnal lizards, and they asked if I wanted to join them on night treks through the jungle to look for new species of lizards. I jumped at the chance! Susan was happy to stay behind in our little room. The researchers and I wore hats with small lights attached to free our hands to catch the lizards. I followed the lead man on narrow winding trails and was impressed as I watched him find well camouflaged lizards on trunks of trees, under leaves, etc. as we walked. He would catch them and put them in individual plastic bags we had brought with us. Soon I was beginning to spot the lizards myself, and through the course of the night I did manage to catch one that they said was a "new species."

The most amazing thing about the jungle was the noise level. There were so many creature sounds, from screeching to whistling to heavy panting and it was so loud at times it was disorienting. Once I slipped on some wet leaves and caught myself by placing my hand in what I thought was soft moss on a tree trunk. It started moving and then I realized it was a large clump of furry caterpillars! Another time, the researcher in the lead stopped us all and yelled, "Don't move!" He then pointed to an area a few feet to our left, and there, strung between tall trees was the biggest spider web I had ever seen! It was huge, like maybe ten feet by twelve feet, and thick. He picked up a piece of wood the size of his hand and threw it into the web. Instantly thousands of spiders converged on the wood, covering it. He said these were "colony spiders" and were poisonous. Their web could catch birds, and even small monkeys, for their communal meals.

We returned to the village around two or three in the morning with a satisfactory catch of about eight to ten lizards, half of which they believed were newly found species. The village was poor, with few modern conveniences. There was an open air restaurant though, which had tables with plastic table clothes and vases of plastic flowers. These plastic flowers really amazed us since the surrounding jungle was full of beautiful flowering trees and bushes. There were little shops in the village that did sell objects from the jungle, most impressive to me were the insect collections. I purchased a few large colorful well preserved beetles and one huge hairy tarantula. I knew my students would love them!

We left the same way we arrived, by bus going up and over the Andes to Quito. The bus stopped at a tourist spot, identifying the exact location of the equator. There were beautiful well marked trails here and since the bus stopped for quite a while Susan and I were able to take a nice long hike. In Quito we took a plane to Cartagena, Columbia to end our vacation together by spending a few nights in a beach resort. We stayed in a rather modern hotel right on the sea. The food was good and they served real brewed coffee. It was a relaxing relief after days on the road. Susan needed to get back, so she left after a few days and flew back to D.C. Since I had the entire summer off, I decided to stay an extra couple weeks. I spent my days on the beach reading books, sun tanning, swimming, and eating fresh fruit. I spent my evenings in this large crazy bar/night club. It was full of young people and they always had live music. I met some pretty wild young women and we had a great time finding boys to dance with. I enjoyed their company, and each night they would save me a spot at their table. Their English wasn't good and my Spanish was worse, but smiles and music and dancing created the friendship.

On my flight back to Washington D.C. I was seated next to an older woman with a large bandage on her hand. She told me that while in Bogota two thieves told her to hand over her diamond ring and wedding band that she was wearing. She said they were too tight and she couldn't get them off. The thieves then produced a sharp knife and cut her finger off to get the rings! Her story left me weak kneed and speechless. I've thought about her on and off over the years, and right or wrong, her traumatic story along with my own feelings about Columbia that summer have kept me from ever wanting to go back there.

I spent another three years teaching at O'Connell High School. Unfortunately, for reasons I didn't understand, Fr. McMurtrie was transferred, promoted to a position of "Monsignor" whatever that meant, in the fall of 1976. The assistant principal in charge of school discipline was promoted to the principal's job, and so an assistant principalship became available. I was nearly finished with my Master's Degree credits in Educational Administration so I decided to apply for the job. I thought it would be perfect for me. I loved the students and believed that disciplining young people was easy when there was mutual respect. I didn't get the job, didn't even get an interview. I remember the comment by the new principal, which was something like this: "How would you maintain discipline? You need to be able to throw kids up against a locker now and then in order to keep them in line." Since I had no intention of "throwing kids up against a locker" I knew I was not the right person for this job, but it started my mind thinking: *Where did I want to go next?*

Lori stayed in Germany, met John a fellow English teacher, and they were married. I kept the apartment. Living in Washington D.C. was perfect for me. Natasha and I started a weekly happening at a local establishment near her condo in the Adams Morgan neighborhood. It was an easy way to meet up with friends on a weekly basis without anyone having to host a party in their home. We designated this one bar and established Wednesday night as the time we would always be there to meet and greet. It worked out wonderfully. Natasha named it our "Salon Night" — as in the days of the French artists, writers, and musicians who would get together for entertaining chats. Some Wednesdays there would only be a few people who showed up, other times it would be crowded with all our friends. I met many really interesting people there. We would talk and drink and smoke all evening. I was on a tight budget since I had graduate school to pay for and I needed to save money for my summer travels. I never drank more than two drinks, and one was always an Irish Coffee.

Christmas of 1975 I flew home as always, and this year I gave my parents a gift of plane tickets to come visit me in Washington the following summer. So in June of 1976 Mom and Dad flew to D.C. for a ten day visit. I was still living in my one bedroom apartment with my parakeet. I gave them the bedroom and I slept on the sofa. They seemed to really enjoy every place I took them, including the places closely connected to my life. I took them to O'Connell High School and showed them my classroom. We visited Mary and her mom in Virginia, walked around the campus of American University, and dined with Susan and Alvin and Natasha. We of course visited some of the famous historical sites too, like the Smithsonian museums, Monticello, and Mount Vernon. I then drove them to Delaware to visit Natasha's mother, Helen, and her stepfather, Sergei, at their beach house. This was a place I dearly loved and Natasha and I went there often. We had a great visit with her parents, and my dad was amazingly impressed with Sergei. Somehow these two men, one a Midwest farmer with an eighth grade education and the other a learned scholar/ professor from Russia connected with each other. My dad spoke of this encounter for years thereafter. On the drive back to D.C., along a country road in Delaware we got in a car accident. Mom was in the front seat next to me and Dad was in the back seat. I was wearing a seatbelt but neither of them had their's buckled. When a car turned right in front of me, I hit it broadside. Mom's head went through the windshield. It was a very nerve wracking ride in the ambulance on the way to this small town hospital since Mom seemed to be bleeding a lot. The EMT riding with us assured us it would be okay. He said there are lots of capillaries in the scalp and it may look like a lot of blood but it's not dangerous. After stitches in her head and on her knee she was released. My car was totaled so we went to pick up a rental car. Dad was surprised when they would not rent a car to him. He carried a lot of cash but no credit card. I, on the other hand, had very little cash, but I did have a credit card. I rented the car and we drove back to Washington for the last few days of their visit. Mom was a real trooper though her eyes were somewhat blackened and her knee was so sore it made it impossible to visit the Capital Building with all its steps or other hard to get to places that we had saved for the final days of the trip. I had gotten tickets for a Bluegrass concert at the Wolf Trap (an outdoor concert hall) in Virginia and we did go to that. The manager there was very nice and arranged for a wheelchair for Mom so we were all seated down front!

After Mom and Dad flew back to Wisconsin and she visited her own doctor she had to have the stitches removed and replaced since it had become infected. Still, in the end everything worked out okay. The woman driver in the other car was declared 100% at fault so her insurance company paid me for the loss of my car and paid Mom's medical bills plus a stipend for pain and suffering.

I stayed in D.C. until after July 4th since I wanted to participate in the big celebration on the Mall for the two hundredth birthday of America. Susan does not like crowds so she didn't come, but Natasha and I were there for the entire day. I brought with me my last pack of cigarettes. I had made a resolution on New Year's Eve that I would give up smoking on the 200th birthday of America. It would be my gift to myself and my country. No more stinking, noxious cigarettes to destroy my lungs nor pollute the air!

The Mall was packed with a few hundred thousand people. We brought a picnic basket and blanket and found a comfortable spot to enjoy the festivities. Everyone was in a good mood, friendly, and ready for a shared celebration. Folks passed "joints" around as well as food and drink. There was live entertainment throughout the day with big name musicians like Johnny Cash. The fireworks in the evening were wonderful and long lasting. They displayed a laser beam from one end of the mall to the other. It was hyped all day. I had never seen such a thing before and I don't know what I was expecting, but it didn't seem that spectacular — just a long greenish colored light beam. In the early evening Natasha ran out of cigarettes and started borrowing from me. I had rationed them all day, not wanting to run out before the celebration ended. Now with both of us needing cigarettes I knew it would be close. We left around 11:30 p.m. and went back to her apartment, there were two cigarettes left in the pack. As we sat there together and smoked, I thoroughly enjoyed the last cigarette of my life!

The next day I flew to Tennessee to visit Jane and her family. This was a good place to be since they didn't smoke. I knew it would be difficult in D.C. where all my friends were smokers. I hadn't told anyone in my family that I quit, so they were all pleasantly surprised that summer when I visited without bringing my nasty habit into their homes. After a few days in Tennessee I flew to L.A. Ginger was living with her brother, Jay, in a nice big house in Huntington Beach. She had warned him about my chain smoking (which Jay did not like) and they were both very glad it would not be an issue. Ginger got me a job at the law firm, transcribing documents. With headsets on I typed all day. The money was a big help, since I only got paid during the nine months I worked at the school and had to save and plan ahead for summers. This summer job worked great for me, and besides, I got to spend over a month with Ginger catching up on each other's lives and enjoying sunny California together.

One night we went to a wonderful old Mexican style hacienda / restaurant. The place was absolutely gorgeous with live plants, colorful paintings, adobe walls, and a Mariachi Band. The special of the night was "peach margaritas." Peaches were in season and very fresh and delicious so we ordered a pitcher of peach margaritas for the two of us. We had a wonderful meal, finished off the margaritas and went out to the parking lot to find Ginger's VW Bug and drive home when we realized we were absolutely drunk! Luckily we were smart enough to go back inside, borrow the phone and call Jay to come and get us.

We spent time on the beach watching the surfers and sunbathing. We drove around and viewed some of the famous spots in the area like Malibu and Hollywood, and she introduced me to date milkshakes. One weekend we drove to the desert in Arizona, saw the Grand Canyon from the North Entrance and slept on blankets under the stars along the Colorado River. It was a relaxing, wonderful summer.

I flew back to Wisconsin from California and visited all the family members again. Audrey and Marly and the kids (Mike and Kerri) had planned a car trip to Washington D.C. so I rode out with them. They had a full sized van so it was a fun drive. I played cards and other games with the kids on the way out. In D.C. besides seeing all the sites, they drove me to a Toyota dealer where I bought a new car. It was a chocolate brown Toyota Corona with an eight-track player. I loved that car!

Quitting smoking was not easy. When I got back to D.C. all my routines reminded me of cigarettes. A cup of coffee in the morning and I longed for a cigarette. The same for reading a book, finishing a good meal, and most of all when drinking in a bar with friends. To begin with, most of my friends still smoked. One had quit eight years earlier and he told me that he still craved cigarettes! This was not what I wanted to hear since I was hoping the urge would soon be gone. But I stuck to my promise and to this day I have never smoked another cigarette. For me the urge was nearly gone after about six months, and over the years I have grown to hate being around cigarette smoke and am grateful that it is now pretty much banned in most public places in America.

The following summer I drove my new Toyota across country, all the way to California and back. That summer, 1977, was Mom's sixtieth birthday. I picked her up in Wisconsin and drove her to California with me. It was a wonderful trip. I did all the driving and we were very much on the same page regarding travel. We arose early and drove along interstate highways when there were more deer visible along the road than there were other vehicles. We stopped early, by around 4:30 or 5 p.m. each night since by then I was tired. Whenever I asked Mom what she wanted to do or what direction she wanted to go in, she always answered, "I'm good with anything. You decide." And truly, everything pleased her. More than once she responded with her famous quote, "What more could you want?"

Mom and I went all the way to California together and stayed with Ginger and her Mom. We had a great time. The four of us went to Sequoia National Park and then to Yosemite, which were both beautiful. Mom flew back to Wisconsin and I stayed for a while longer and then slowly drove back across America on my own. It was a "freedom drive" for me in many ways. I had great music to listen to on my eight-track player since I brought all my eight-tracks with me. I listened to Janis Joplin, K.T. Oslin, the Eagles, Neil Young, Dylan, and Emmy Lou Harris among others, and their music made me feel powerful and excited about future possibilities. I started thinking about going out and seeing the world again. I could finish my Master's Degree in Educational Administration and get my principal's license by the next summer, so what would stop me from looking for jobs internationally? The more I thought about it, the more excited I got!

Back in D.C. I was in my routine again, teaching school, coaching girl's field hockey, attending classes at American University, and going to my weekly "Salon" nights with Natasha. This was my sixth year in Washington, D.C. and things were the same in my daily life, but not inside my head. I began to plan and dream about all the places in the world I still wanted to see. I joined the National Geographic Society and went to their Friday night presentations which were each about a different place on the planet, from Peru to Pakistan and everywhere in between. By Christmas I knew this would be my last year in Washington. I needed a new adventure! In January I notified the school that I would not be returning in the fall. I contacted ISS (International School Services) and put in my application for a job in administration or teaching science overseas. ISS is an organization that interviews and hires for about five thousand schools around the world. Next I created a chart, a matrix of sorts, to prioritize where I might want to go. I listed criteria that were important to me and then assigned points (one to three) for each item based on how important it was. For example, location: Europe got three points since it was high on my list. The Middle East got one point since I had already lived there. Warm weather also got three points, as did a location by the sea, a language worth learning, and the job itself. I preferred something in administration since I thought I was ready for it. If teaching, I preferred something in biology rather than chemistry. The amount of pay was on the list, but I only rated it as high as two, not a three.

Job offers started arriving in my mailbox in late February, early March, and I felt like a kid in a candy store. They came from Guatemala, Greece, Zaire, Barcelona, Norway, Jordan, India, Bangladesh, Malaysia and many more. Every day there would be a few more, and these were not inquiries, they were actual contracts! All I needed to do was sign one and send it back and I would have a job for the following fall. Some I discarded almost immediately. Zaire because they were having riots at the time. Bangladesh was an administrative position, headmistress of an all-girls school, which sounded very intriguing until I got to the part that said that as a single woman I would need a full time body guard and it would be included in my benefits package. Barcelona quickly moved to the top of my list since it met all my criteria, except for a concern about the pay. The contract included a Stateside telephone number to call if I had questions so I called to ask if the pay was really enough for one to live on in Barcelona. The answer was "No, you would need to use some of your savings." I was shocked and appalled to think a teacher would be worth so little that they could offer a non-living wage. Besides, I had no savings. Norway on the other hand was offering a very generous salary, much more than I was making in America. However, it was not a warm climate and I didn't think Norwegian was a language worth learning since in the world not many folks speak it. The semester went by and I had not made a decision. The offers kept coming, but none seemed right.

At the end of the school year the students at O'Connell High School voted me their "Top Banana" award which was really a wonderful honor since it came from a vote of the entire student body. I added it to my resume and continued to pour over the contracts I was receiving. I now had two piles: Not a Chance! and Maybe. In early June I received an invitation along with a plane ticket to fly to Houston to interview for a position with the Aramco Schools in Saudi Arabia. I wasn't real interested in Saudi Arabia at the time, but a free trip to Houston could be fun, so I went. The experience was quite wonderful. I stayed in a nice hotel along with about a dozen other teacher candidates. They gave an interesting presentation about Saudi Arabia and the Aramco Schools that were run by the oil company and located in the Eastern Province along the Arabian Gulf. The interviews went well. I met the Superintendent, Jack DeWaard, and was very impressed. I flew back to Washington the next day and started thinking about my criteria: A warm place, near the sea, a language worth learning, and a job teaching life science. And the big bonus was the pay and benefits. They far exceeded anything I ever thought possible for a teacher. The only negative really was the fact that it was in the Middle East where I had already lived. Still, I loved the Middle Eastern cultures and began to think what a pleasure it would be to be back, especially so close to Iran, making it easy to visit my friend, Kami. The day after I returned to Washington Mr. DeWaard called me and offered me the job. I immediately said, "Yes."

The rest of the summer was a flurry of activities involving moving, getting a physical and dental clearance, new passport with a work visa from Aramco, giving my plants, fish, and parakeet away to my students and friends, and organizing for movers to come and pack up my belongings for shipment to Saudi Arabia since my contract included payment to ship all my things. Most important I spent time with my friends, Susan and Natasha and Mary before I left. Went to the beach house a few times with Natasha and her Mom. Tom flew out and joined us once for a long weekend. He was now living in Peoria, having taken over his father's ophthalmology practice. And of course I went to Wisconsin to say good bye to all my family. I drove my wonderful car that Dad had said he would buy from me. That worked out great for me since it allowed me to pay off the rest of the car loan and have a little money in the bank. I opened a bank account in Hortonville and gave Mom power of attorney over the account. This is where my checks from Aramco would be deposited.

Tom and I met in Madison for a visit and then drove down to Peoria to see his family. He bought me an expensive new set of luggage as a going away gift. I think we both realized that our relationship would not last. I was so excited for a new adventure and he was settling into his own medical practice.

CHAPTER 9

RULE # 9: Die Hopefully

Study religions, all religions. Just because you were born into one religion does not mean you cannot learn something from others. Develop your own philosophy of life and spirituality. Follow Cicero's advice: "Live joyfully, die hopefully."

SAUDI ARABIA, 1978-1984

I flew to Houston for a four day orientation at the Aramco headquarters in mid-August. I was booked into a beautiful hotel and enjoyed every minute of my stay there. Each day was filled with presentations on what to expect in Saudi Arabia (also known to Aramcons as "the Kingdom"), the culture, the religion, the climate, the oil industry, day to day living, amenities provided by the Company, and much more. I met Kathy during the orientation and we became quick friends. Her husband was already in the Kingdom and she was on her way to join him.

While in Houston my Persian friend, Juni, flew in to visit me. It was a wonderful surprise. She had come from Alaska where she had been vacationing and we got to do a lot of reminiscing and late night talking. Also, my friend Barb's husband, Ken, was in Houston interviewing for jobs in Africa. He and I went out one night and reminisced about old times, laughed a lot, and talked about our upcoming adventures. (They did end up going to Algeria.)

I did some last minute shopping in Houston after realizing that it could be difficult buying clothes and shoes to my liking in Arabia. This turned out to be a very good idea since by the following spring the one pair of sandals I bought had pretty much worn out.

The plane ride over took almost an entire day. We flew to New York first and then on to Dhahran. Kathy and I did a good job of talking almost the whole way. She has a great sense of humor and kept me awake and laughing for most of the flight. We flew over much of Saudi Arabia in daylight and I was amazed at the vast areas of nothing but desert sand, crisscrossed by empty roads and miles of pipeline. We arrived in Dhahran around four o'clock in the afternoon. The airport was small and we exited the plane right onto the runway. As I left I was hit by a rush of hot air and assumed I had stepped behind the jet engine of the plane. However, I soon realized that the plane was parked and that what I was experiencing was the normal hot summer wind of Eastern Arabia.

I was met at the airport by Jess Arceneaux, the principal of Dhahran Junior High, and my new boss. He was from Louisiana, but had been living and working in Dhahran for many years. Over the next six years I came to like and respect him more and more. I learned so much from him and remain very grateful that I had the opportunity to work for him. He taught me the art of patience, and of listening to all sides of a story before making a judgment. I eventually became his assistant principal and, at first, my style of administration tended to be much faster paced than his. I just wanted to get things done and move on. Jess was a bit older and a lot wiser and would always think things over before making a decision. I learned to really appreciate his style, and made an effort to adopt it as my own, since snap judgements are rarely the best. Besides, except in emergencies, any decision can always wait at least one day.

We drove from the airport, dropped my suitcases off at the shared housing unit I was assigned to, and then went directly to a house party being held that night for all school personnel in Dhahran. I was tired and jet lagged but this was a nice opportunity to meet my fellow teachers. At the party, I was also introduced to "brown" and "white." These were the two types of alcoholic beverages available in Dhahran. It turned out that many Aramcons had private stills in their back "storage sheds." These sheds had been built by the Company during the 50s and 60s for the main purpose of distilling alcohol! Prior to that time many a novice had accidentally caused fires/explosions in their homes. Employees had also been issued pamphlets titled "The Blue Flame" that explained how to properly distill alcohol. Due to tighter controls on alcohol use in the Kingdom, these pamphlets were no longer being issued by the time I arrived. The "white" was a basic alcohol meant to mimic a vodka, and the "brown" was aged in oak caskets and meant to mimic a bourbon. I ordered a "white" with tonic water and discovered it was actually pretty good. By the end of the evening I had met most of my new colleagues, the Dhahran Junior High teachers, and many support staff, elementary teachers, and Central Office Administrators. I liked them all. They seemed adventurous, and right at home in this new environment.

The next day I slept in and met my three roommates, one American and two British gals. Like everything connected to Aramco, one's nationality played a part. As an American I got my own room as did the other American, Sharon. The two British gals had to share a room. Pay scales were also based on nationality. As single American women, Sharon and I were "dollar hires" and paid the same as our male counterparts. My friend Kathy, as a married American woman, was called a "casual dollar hire." Although she was also paid in dollars, her salary was reduced by 40% because she could work only with the permission of her husband, and, since this permission could be withdrawn at any time, she was deemed worth less in the work force. Our British roommates were paid on a British pound scale (lower than a dollar scale), Saudi professionals were paid on a Saudi riyal scale (similar in value to the dollar scale), Filipino accountants on a Filipino peso scale, Indian house servants on an Indian rupee scale and so on. I believe that at the bottom of the pay scale were the Yemenis, who did yard work.

A week after I arrived in the Kingdom, I went on a planned trip to the beach at Half Moon Bay with a bus full of teachers. Half Moon Bay was a beautiful spot on the Arabian (also called Persian) Gulf. It was about a twenty to thirty minute drive from

Dhahran and over the following six years I came here often. This first trip was memorable because I had a very strange experience. It was hot, really hot, maybe 110F, and the water in this bay was also very warm, probably close to body temperature. The water was very salty and I was shown how to float on my back — arms bent, hands behind my head, legs stretched out — and to just lie there, like resting on a bed. I tried it and was amazed. It worked! I relaxed and floated like this for a while, realizing that I was weightless, I couldn't hear as my ears were just below water level, I couldn't see because my eyes were closed with the bright sun shining right down on top of me, and I couldn't feel anything since the water was as warm as my body.

A few moments later "I" was "floating" in the air, looking down at my body, and seeing the water and the other teachers nearby. The "view" and the strange sensation lasted only a few moments and then, suddenly, my whole body jerked and "I" found myself once again floating in the water. It was a very real and vivid experience that started me questioning who I truly was. How could I have been in two places at once — both in the water and in the air — looking down at my own body floating there in the water? What a strange way to start my new life in Saudi Arabia. I didn't know anyone well enough with whom I felt comfortable discussing the experience, and, especially since they were my professional colleagues I certainly didn't want them to think that I was really weird. It brought back memories from India that I had not thought about in years, and also books I had read by Carl Jung, and books on Buddhism and Hinduism. I soon discovered the Dhahran library and began searching for information on "out of body" experiences.

Classes started and I was teaching three sections of seventh grade life science and two sections of eighth grade earth science. This presented me with two challenges, one was learning to relate to twelve and thirteen-year-olds, and the second was teaching earth science. This was my weakest area in the field of science. Other than some college coursework in biomes, meteorology, and soils I had little background in this subject. Once again I became a regular at the Dhahran library, and happily, since it was run by the oil company, there was a wealth of information on geology. The science department consisted of three classrooms, a nice sized office, a storage room, a rather large greenhouse, six teachers, and one aide. We had ample equipment and supplies and our class sizes were small, between twelve and sixteen students, so the teaching situation was really ideal. My students were mostly American, about 70%, along with 20% Arabs, and 10% from the rest of the world. I began the year feeling uncomfortable and out of my element trying to relate to such young students. I missed my high school seniors who were adult-like and easier to talk to. However, by the end of the first trimester I was in love with these middle schoolers. They were less inhibited than high school seniors and kept me entertained by saying the darnedest things! They were funny and fun loving, and best of all, most of them seemed interested in science.

I walked to work every day and was amazed at how humid it was. Sometimes my hair felt wet by the time I arrived at the school, which was only about four blocks from my house. It was truly a very hot climate and Dhahran was situated near the Arabian Gulf so that water was constantly evaporating into the air. The roofs of the cars were what rusted, not the underside, as happened in the Wisconsin winters when they salted the roads.

In September I met Rick. He was a young guy from Indiana and, as I recall, was a friend of one of the teachers. I can't remember how I even met him, but he had a big influence on my life. He was an engineer and had a Company car assigned to him. One weekend he drove me to Hofuf, an old Arabian city in the oasis a few hours south of Dhahran. The town looked ancient and classically Arabic with a huge covered bazaar selling everything from carpets to truckloads of fresh dates. On another occasion we went in four wheel drive across desert trails to a watering hole where we saw large herds of goats and camels left seemingly unattended. On the evening of September sixteenth (my father's 63rd birthday) we drove to some sand dunes not far from Dhahran, and watched a total eclipse of the moon! We were sitting on top of a dune with nothing in sight but a three hundred sixty degree circular view of flat sand colored earth. It looked so strange, as if I were sitting on a different planet looking at someone else's moon.

Rick was important in my life because he was a Rosicrucian, and he started me on a path of investigation into entire realms of ancient philosophy that I had never before considered. I had never even heard of the Rosicrucians. He loaned me books and magazines that explored different views on the history of the universe, the purpose of life on earth, and reincarnation. He introduced me to a number of diverse authors, from J. Krishnamurti to Edgar Caycee. I only knew Rick for about two months, but I have continued to read and study the ideas of the Rosicrucians, the Sophists, and many others. Slowly, over the years, I have established my own "spiritual" philosophy.

Rick was never a "date," just a friend. Dating was an issue for me in Saudi Arabia since the ratio of single men to single women was so disproportionate. There were so many different men asking me out that trying to gracefully refuse a date was difficult. I could say, "Oh, I'm sorry but I am busy this weekend" and get a response like, "Well how about next weekend? followed by "How about three weeks from now?" Sometimes I made errors in judgement and accepted a date that I later regretted. Following a few bad dates I decided to keep my life more simple. I actually enjoyed being single. I felt strong and independent and wanted to stay that way. To maintain this commitment I went into Al Khobar, the nearby Arab town, and had a gold ring made for myself with the word, 'Zimmer' written in Arabic on it. I loved this ring and wore it every day for the next six years.

I did meet a couple guys, one Arab and one American, both of whom I dated on a casual basis for a few months. Ihsan was a horticulturalist and he helped me set up the greenhouse for my science classes. He was soft spoken and kind, with interesting stories to tell of his life in Saudi Arabia. The other man, Wayne, was a petroleum engineer from Alabama, handsome and very knowledgeable about geology so he was a big help to me in teaching my earth science classes. In fact, he actually taught a few of the classes for me!

In October I received notice that I could move into a housing unit of my own. It was a small, three hundred sq. ft. flat that looked a lot like a hotel room with a small kitchenette. In fact, everyone in Aramco called this building the "Holiday Inn." It was for single females only and most of them were British. I happily took one of the rooms even though it was small, and further from the school, I much preferred having my own place. I was still good friends with Kathy, and she and her husband started hosting Wednesday "steak nights" in which about six or seven of us would gather to grill steaks and eat, drink, and talk. I very much enjoyed these gatherings since they were always filled with laughter. The other friends who came, Jack and Nancy, and Steve, were upbeat, funny and told great stories.

Weekends in Saudi Arabia were Thursday and Friday, not Saturday and Sunday, so Wednesday nights were the beginning of our weekend. These parties were always at Kathy and Richard's house since the rest of us were all new and had very small or remote housing assignments. We each took turns hosting by buying the steak and providing the rest of the food. Richard had grown up in Saudi Arabia and since his father had worked for Aramco back in the 50s and 60s, he was therefore already an expert at making "white" and "brown." And I started making my own wine! A fellow teacher had given me some recipes and instructions/equipment for the process. The most difficult part was obtaining the proper wine yeast, which was obviously not available in Saudi Arabia. I made my first batch using blueberries, fruit juice and baker's yeast and it was pretty awful.

The "Haj" (annual Muslim pilgrimage to Mecca) was coming up and since we all got a five day vacation at that time, travel plans were a major topic of conversation. Kathy and Richard decided to join an Aramco trip to the Philippines. I planned a trip to Iran to visit Kami. This was part of my reason for choosing Saudi Arabia to move to. I wanted to be closer to Kami so I could see him more often.

The five day Haj vacation began in mid-November and I had purchased plane tickets to Tehran, obtained my Iranian visa, and was very excited to see Kami. Unfortunately demonstrations against the Shah had begun in the streets of Tehran that fall and shortly before my scheduled flight, serious riots broke out. All flights were cancelled and so I remained in Saudi Arabia for the Haj. I was really disappointed about being unable to see Kami again and Iran. I spent my five days of vacation at Half Moon Bay and had a relaxing time on the beach. I decided I would fly home to Wisconsin for Christmas and then visit my friends in Washington, D.C. I could easily take two weeks off and I now had the money to do it.

My trip home was amazing in a number of ways. To begin with, my flight went through Cairo and Paris, then Chicago and Appleton. I had a long layover in Cairo so together with a few other Aramcons on the flight we decided to take a taxi into this exotic city. It was exhilarating and just what I had imagined when I made the decision to go abroad again. I felt so "free" and so happy to be an "expat" again. We toured the city for about five hours and then returned to the airport for the flight to Paris, where we did the same thing. And then, nearly a full day after I had left Dhahran, I arrived in Appleton, completely thrilled with my new lifestyle and also completely exhausted.

Christmas with the family was, of course, wonderful. The whole family was gathered there, and now there were nine nieces and nephews for me to enjoy. Gary and Rosie had a baby boy, Nicholas, born the previous February. He was now ten months old and the perfect age to bounce around. Tammy was now eighteen and attending the UW in Madison. Kurt was seventeen and a senior in high school. Mike was ten years old and I think he still considered me his "girlfriend." He painted me a Green Bay Packers figurine for Christmas. Kerri, Leilani, and Sarah were all seven years old. They each had a distinct personality, and yet played well together and I loved watching them. Sadie and Jason were just three years old, both blonde and blue eyed, and as cute as could be. All in all these nine young beings brought me immense pleasure!

After the Christmas holiday I flew to Washington, D.C. to spend the remainder of my vacation with my friends. Susan and Alvin hosted a party for me at their home, enabling me to see a number of friends in one night. Juni was in town, having arrived from California where she was attending graduate school at Stanford. Cyrus was living in D.C. at the time, working at the World Bank. (I like to credit myself for getting them back together!). We talked late into the night about the problems in Iran and the fear that the Shah would fall. Kami had left Iran for medical treatment in Denver, but the rest of his family were still in Iran. Same for Juni and Cyrus and many others of my Persian friends; they were mostly living abroad, but their families were still in Iran.

Tom flew in to celebrate New Year's Eve with me. We had a good time, and attended a number of parties together with Natasha and other friends. We dressed up (suits and ties and fancy dresses) and went to many different places, the biggest of which was the newly converted Union Station downtown. There was music and dancing and lots of food and drinks. When I left D.C. for my flight back to Dhahran a few days later, I knew that this time I was really saying good bye to Tom. Whatever feelings I had once had for him were now gone. I was so happy and excited with my new life in Dhahran, and I was experiencing a feeling of complete freedom and independence with a strong desire for new knowledge and new directions.

While in D.C. I had gone to a bookstore in Georgetown called "Yes," and I stocked up on great reading material that Rick had suggested. I also visited a special store that sold products like wine making yeast especially packaged for smuggling into Arabia! Each package was falsely labeled with names like "Baker's Yeast" or "Baking Powder." I was now anxious to go back to Saudi Arabia to start a new chapter in my life of being truly "single," wearing my new gold "Zimmer" independence ring, and ready to take on lots of new adventures.

Ten days later in Dhahran I met Don! Aramcons typically went to the central "mail room" at the end of each work day to pick up our mail. Each one of us had been issued a mailbox there and, this being the era of snail mail, it was our main means of communication with family and friends back home. It also was a social gathering place where we would meet and talk to other employees, catch up on news, and check out rumors at the end of each work day. On January 13, 1979, I was sitting on a brick ledge in the courtyard of the mail room area with Kathy, sharing stories of our day. Her husband Richard joined us, and shortly after, he recognized Don in the crowd. He and Don had attended high school together in Rome, Italy and had not seen each other since. He introduced us and the four of us talked for quite a while. Don had just arrived in the Kingdom that day, a new Aramco hire.

The following week was my turn to host the steak night at their house and Kathy called to ask if it would be okay to invite Don to join us. I told her that was fine with me, I'd just buy an extra steak. The night of the steak dinner, Ihsan, my Arab friend, was my date. The evening was enjoyable as always. The next day Kathy called to ask me what I thought of Don. I replied, "Don't ever invite that guy again!" She was shocked and asked, "Why?" I answered, "It's those blue eyes. I'm afraid I could fall for him, and right now I just want to be independent!"

I did see Don a few times in the coming weeks, by the mail room, or in the dining hall; each time it seemed that he was with a different woman. I remember thinking, *How does he do it? There aren't that many single women here!* A month later I went to a party with Wayne and his fellow workers at TradCo. This party was hosted by him together with his coworkers, so we came early since Wayne needed to set up the "bar" and help serve drinks. A few hours later Don came walking in with a date — Karen, a business hire from Dallas — on his arm. I had met her a few times before at some other social gatherings. Again I was amazed to see him with yet another woman! The party was fun, I knew almost everyone there. We played backgammon, drank, ate, listened to music, and danced. Later in the evening I was in the kitchen getting a drink from Wayne at the "bar" when Don came up behind me and started kissing me on the neck! He obviously had a few drinks and didn't know that Wayne was my date. Don followed me out of the kitchen and asked if I wanted to take a walk outside to get some fresh air. We walked all over the neighborhood and talked. We left our dates at the party that night and we have been together ever since.

I learned that he loved travel and adventure, and that he had an interesting international background. He and his twin brother, Dan, were born in Reykjavik, Iceland, in 1948. His mother, Heida, was from Iceland and his father, Gilbert, was an American. They met while Gilbert was working at the U.S. Airbase in Iceland after the war. They were married and lived there until Don and Dan were starting school in the first grade. Don's father had taken a job with Aramco in Saudi Arabia and the family moved there in 1953. At the time neither Don nor Dan spoke any English. In the years that followed they went to English speaking Aramco schools through ninth grade, making many return trips to Iceland as well as vacations in Lebanon, Europe, and America. For high school he and Dan went to a Catholic (though neither were Catholic) boarding school in Rome, Italy and following graduation they moved to America to attend college in Missouri where

Don and me shortly after we started dating

Don's father owned a ranch. Don did not enjoy college, he was tired of schooling in general and wanted to do something more "adventurous" and "meaningful." He dropped out of college and joined the U.S. Air Force in 1967 at the beginning of the escalation of the Vietnam War. (He went back to college later, in Florida, and received his Bachelor's Degree, but not until after six years in the Air Force and a tour of duty in the Vietnam War). Don is a PJ above all else. PJs (Air Force Pararescuemen), are an elite group of highly trained men whose motto is "That Others May Live." His membership in this "brotherhood" and the training, missions, and camaraderie experienced during those years are a huge part of who he is.

Don was very athletic and involved in nearly every sport Aramco offered. He and some of his friends/colleagues formed a softball team and played in the Dhahran league. They named their team "The Arabian Knights" and they played once or twice a week. I went as often as I could and watched the games from the stands and got to know the other girlfriends/wives. Don was also on the tennis ladder playing competitively at least once a week, and he played basketball with a Dhahran team that competed against teams from the local University of Petroleum and Mining. I would sometimes accompany him to the big gymnasium at the University and watch them play teams of varying nationalities, from the Philippines to Saudi nationals.

His favorite sport was scuba diving and he became an officer and was very active in the Dhahran Dive Club. He also learned to sail after getting a small sunfish sailboat from friends of his parents. He bought an old, almost neon colored green suburban that we called "the green machine" and he would tie the sunfish on the top. We spent many weekends driving to Half Moon Bay to sail. A friend, Ira, came with us the first time. He was an avid sailor and said he would show Don how to sail. To launch the boat, he had Don get in it, and then he simply pushed it off and said "good luck!" That was the end of the instruction, but in no time at all Don was sailing the boat around the bay.

I took my first trip with the Dhahran Outing Group (known as

Don and his Green Machine

the DOGS) in April, 1979. This was a five day trip to Syria and I went with my teaching colleague, Cathy. It was a wonderful trip. We visited historic sites and spent time in Aleppo and Damascus. (They were beautiful old cities and it's sad to imagine what they must look like today, in 2017). I had not been back to Syria since being held captive there ten years earlier. Seeing armed soldiers walking on rooftops was my only reminder of that time, since the people I met on the streets and in the shops were friendly and hospitable like most Middle Easterners. I loved the big covered bazaars built hundreds of years ago and still selling much of the same type of merchandise: gold and silver handcrafted items, carpets, wood inlaid boxes, backgammon sets, and furniture, samovars, copper pots and pitchers, spices, exotic perfumes, and camel bags and saddles. Many Aramcons on the trip were serious shoppers and the organizers had said that because the plane was chartered, we could purchase and bring back whatever we wanted. Cathy bought wood inlaid tables and chests. I only bought a wood inlaid backgammon set and some hand blown tea glasses. I was new at this Aramco life, and later, I regretted not having bought more!

The school year was on a trimester basis so the students were off basically for the last week of November and all of December, the last week of March and all of April, and the last week of July and all of August. The school employees got one of those time periods off each year and it was called repatriation or simply one's "repat." All Aramco employees were required to leave the Kingdom for their annual "repat." During the other two time periods we offered tutoring to help kids catch up on what they had missed if their parents had a "repat" during the school year causing them to miss five to six weeks of classes. We also offered "fun" classes during these break periods so the kids would have something to do if they were in the Kingdom when school was not in session. Cathy, my fellow science teacher, was very creative and gifted. She came up with great ideas for fun classes. We team taught many of them and all of them were popular with the kids.

One of these classes was petroleum geology. I loved this class since I myself got to learn a lot about the oil industry. We took the kids to various departments within the company to learn what they did. We also took them on a helicopter ride to visit an offshore oil rig and on a small company plane ride to the main drilling sites in the Rub-e-Khali (the "Empty Quarter" of Saudi Arabia). Another class we taught was oceanography. In this class we took the kids to Half Moon Bay to study the sea life there. We also took them to Jurayd Island, sailing on Arabic dhows, and we camped out there for a few nights. Don and other members of the Dhahran Dive Club would come along to help as chaperones and to teach the kids about the beautiful coral reef and also to give scuba diving lessons to those who wanted to try it.

Once Cathy and I were invited to visit some Saudi Arabian science teachers, up on the "Tapline" (the oil pipeline that traversed Saudi Arabia), and to attend an annual camel race. Of course we accepted; we flew on a Company plane to Qaysumah where we were met by two Arab science teachers. They took us to their home where we met their families and spent the night. Their home had the traditional two main rooms, one for the women and children and one for the men. Cathy and I were invited to have tea and dinner and conversation in the men's section since they all spoke English and the women did not, and at night we slept in guest rooms in the women's quarters with the women and children.

At the Camel Races with a Fellow Science Teacher

The following day our colleagues drove us far out into the desert to witness the annual camel race. This was truly an amazing event. There were a few hundred camels with riders in the race and the race was about forty kilometers long. Many Arab men and children were camped around the area near the finish line. Very few women were in attendance, or if they were there, they stayed inside the tents. The race took place in the afternoon, lasted for hours, and was followed by a big feast and ceremony in which prizes were given to the winners. The King sent two of his brothers to attend the event as his representatives.

Cathy and I were invited to the feast and we were the only women in attendance. The meal was served on large trays placed in the center of hand woven carpets set out on the sand. Each carpet could accommodate about eight people and we sat around these large trays filled with camel meat and rice that we ate with our fingers. We joked that we were eating "the losers" of the day's race! For dessert fresh oranges were served along with tea. After the meal there was dancing by the men who formed long lines moving in unison to Arabic music. The winner of the camel race was presented with a brand new baby blue Mercedes Benz! The science teachers had told us that these people were Bedouins who lived their lives in the desert, moving their herds of camel and goats as needed for food and water, and that this prize would probably be driven until it ran out of gas and then would be left in the desert! We spent one more night in the home of our new friends and flew back to Dhahran the next day.

I thoroughly enjoyed teaching in Dhahran for a number of other reasons. First of all, I loved my students. I still look back through the yearbooks I have saved from those years and enjoy remembering them all. Some I remember more than others, like Rana (definitely a teacher's pet), and Michael, Todd, Sami, DR and DH and many more—likely it's because there's a story in my mind about each one. Also, my fellow teachers were really excellent. I came there thinking I was a great teacher, but after working with these colleagues, I knew I still had a lot to learn. Cathy was my closest mentor. We both had a good relationship with our students, but she had teaching strategies that I didn't know about. She taught me how to set up learning stations with hands on activities, coupled with instructional strategies from basic to advanced, and then organize students into cooperative groups where they could move around the room from station to station and learn from the activities and from each other.

Also, Cathy and I both really liked Saudi Arabia and we worked together to try to instill this into our students. On a few occasions we took them on overnight camping trips in the desert. We brought a telescope along so the students could watch the movement of the planets and constellations throughout the night. We worked to identify animal tracks in the sand, and the desert insects and plant life. We taught them to beware of scorpions who liked to hide under our canvas tent floors in the heat of the day to stay cool. On one such overnight camping trip a strong "shamal" blew in. This is a desert sand storm wherein winds from the north blow so strongly that it brings visibility to near zero. One of our students got lost and wandered about for four to five hours before some local Bedouin tribe found him and brought him out to a highway and a team of searchers. By that time we had many groups including the Saudi military looking for him. This event was truly one of the most frightening days of my career in education.

Another wonderful thing about teaching in Saudi Arabia was the amount of resources available to us, from high quality telescopes to Company helicopters and planes at our disposal. And, as a teacher, I was allowed to fly to New York City for the National Science Teacher Convention one year. On that particular trip my sister, June, and my mother flew to New York and joined me for a wonderful five days in the city. When not in sessions at the convention, the three of us played tourists and had a great time taking in all that New York could offer. My mom was thrilled to experience this huge city and she wore us out! I realized again that if she had been given the opportunity she too would have been a world traveler.

And finally, teaching in Saudi Arabia was made wonderful because the administrators were so highly competent and supportive. They encouraged me in my desire to take on leadership roles. I was made Chair of the Science Department in my second year, and after three years I became the Assistant Principal at Dhahran Junior High, the first female to fill this role. This was a position that I had worked hard to prepare myself for and I was very excited to have this opportunity. It was my first step into the world of school administration.

Living in Saudi Arabia was rewarding in another important way: the friends I made. Don and I met so many wonderful young people with whom we shared much in common. To begin with, they were adventurous. Who else would travel half way around the world and love this life style. There were a few folks who came only for the money and were habitual complainers, but we avoided those people. We had parties on the weekends in different friends' houses and held friendly competitions on our homemade wines. (One year I won a prize for my white wine that I had named White Diamond). With our friends we traveled around the country, camped in the desert, took dhow trips to the islands in the Arabian Gulf, and sailed in Half Moon Bay. Some learned how to scuba dive. I also took up scuba diving and this was one of my greatest physical accomplishments.

In the summer of 1979 after we had been dating for a few

months, I went on my first repat. I started in Europe by spending a few days in Spain with my friends Ginger (fellow teacher) and Alan (her boyfriend). I loved being back in Europe and the three of us had fun trying to find restaurants open before 10 p.m.! We stayed in Madrid for a while and then visited Granada before splitting up. I flew to the States and they to England. After visiting family and friends in Washington. D.C. and Wisconsin. I met up with my old friend Ginger (now still living in California and getting ready to start down the path to become a doctor) and together we traveled to Costa Rica.

This is a country I had wanted to visit for a long time, known as the most stable country in Central and South America. Don's father, Gil, had been contemplating the idea of retiring down there and this gave me a good excuse to check it out. The nice weather, beautiful beaches, and relatively inexpensive living conditions had led to the growth of many American retirement communities along the coast. Ginger and I rented a VW Beetle and took off driving to see the country. We really had no specific plan other than to see as much as we could. We drove through the cloud forests in the mountains and down the Pacific coastline where we found beautiful resort style housing communities, occupied almost entirely by foreign retirees. The rain storms in the afternoon were torrential! I had never seen rains like this before, not even in Hawaii or India. At times the wind would be so strong the heavy rain would move horizontally. We took refuge in the beautiful bar/restaurants along the beach and enjoyed the uniqueness of it all with rum and coke.

Lastly we went to the Caribbean side, drove over the mountains from San Jose, and headed to Limon, a major city on that side of the country. As we approached the town, traffic came to a standstill. Looking down the road we could see a car on fire and an angry mob of men heading our way. They were yelling loudly and tipping cars over as they approached! Luckily we were driving a little VW Bug so we made a quick U-Turn and headed away from town. A few miles out of town we encountered a roadblock. A man came up to our car and told us that the road was closed and that we should head back toward town. He said that there was a small resort we could get to via some dirt roads. He said it was not safe for young women to remain where he was because, "Maybe we drink de rum, and den no safe no more for de ladies!" We followed a dirt road to the north side of town and found this resort in the middle of a banana plantation. When we arrived only a few people were there, but soon more and more foreigners began arriving, followed by the mayor and other officials from Limon. This resort became the safe haven and communication headquarters for the local officials as they sought to control the riots that were taking place in the city. We learned that the United Fruit Company workers had started a strike for higher wages and were making their demands known in a somewhat violent way.

On the other hand the resort was quite nice. It had a large open-air bar and restaurant with just a thatched roof covering, no walls, so we could enjoy the tropical breezes which were wonderful. There were a number of small bungalows to rent and Ginger and I took one. And, the resort had a lovely large pool that was only four feet deep from end to end. We stayed there for three days, while the riots continued to rage in the city. I took advantage of the time by practicing my swimming. I would swim back and forth along the length of that pool to see how long I could do this without touching the bottom or the sides of the pool. I soon realized that I could swim for an hour and more without needing to stand up or grab the sides of the pool for support. This gave me a great deal of confidence, knowing there was no need for such a strong fear of deep water.

The resort had a telephone and we were allowed to make a call to the U.S. so I took the opportunity to call my friend Susan in Washington, D.C. to ask her to try to contact Don in Saudi Arabia to let him know that if we were delayed much longer in Costa Rica, I might miss my flight back to Dhahran. Don later described this call from Susan as "frantic," beginning by her saying, "I don't want you to worry, but Ruthann is stuck in Costa Rica in the middle of some riots." Of course, that did raise his anxiety a bit! As it turned out when we tried to leave three days later, we came upon an overturned truck blocking the road to San Jose and thus had to turn around and go back. We asked and gratefully learned that we could detour around that portion of the blocked road by driving on a dirt path through the banana fields. This was quite an adventurous drive, but it did lead us around the blockade and back onto the one highway crossing the mountains to San Jose. With very little time to spare, I did catch my flight back to the States and then on to Saudi Arabia,

Don met me at the airport and informed me that he had signed me up for scuba lessons that would start in less than two weeks! Until I met Don, I had been afraid of deep water. I could swim, but I stayed in shallow waters, only about four feet deep, so if I got scared I could always just stand up. I had finally gotten to the point where I felt I could venture into deep water to swim and snorkel, but I had not even considered scuba diving. The lessons were to be taught by Don's good friend and former roommate, Mike. I received a packet of information describing in detail what each lesson would cover, beginning in the pool, and ending with an open water dive in Half Moon Bay. The day before each lesson Don would meet me in the pool late at night, with no one around, and patiently go over each upcoming activity with me. He brought his own diving equipment for me to practice with and all went smoothly.

There were about twelve people in the class and my dive buddy was a young woman from Texas who could swim like a fish. She sailed through all of the pool activities, which included diving to the bottom in ten feet of water to retrieve an object, and swimming around the pool with just a regulator in your mouth and no face mask. None of these tasks were easy for me and I'm sure I ranked at the bottom of the class, but I did manage to pass each requirement. The final class was a trip to open water where we had to perform all these tasks in twenty-five feet of salty water filled with wonderful sea critters. I was very much looking forward to an actual scuba dive in the sea, but my dive buddy was extremely nervous about it. When we made our inaugural descent to the bottom, we encountered many beautiful colored fish and a sea snake. That did it for her, she panicked and started to rush for the surface. Luckily the instructor stopped her and made her do the necessary slow ascent. She did not pass the class and never did get her certification. She told me that she just did not like being so close to all the strange sea life, and I wondered why she ever wanted to scuba dive in the first place. The sea life was the only reason I had wanted to conquer my fear and learn to dive. The instructor became my dive buddy for the rest of that open water dive and I received my PADI certification.

For the remainder of my time in Saudi Arabia, scuba diving was a big part of my life. Don and I took as many opportunities as possible to go diving. My first big dive after receiving the certification was in the Red Sea, near Yanbu on the western coast of Saudi Arabia. The Dhahran Dive Club sponsored a week-long trip there during one of the Eids (religious holidays). Don was an officer in the club, so he drove out there with other officers and instructors in Aramco-owned four wheel drive vehicles, carrying all the equipment, including a generator to refill the scuba tanks each day, and the camping gear. I flew out with our friend Frank, and I carried with me a surprise birthday cake that I had baked for Don.

We set up camp on a sandy beach just a few feet from the sea. There were about fifteen divers in all, mostly couples, each with their own tent. Don and I had purchased a rather large tent at a Dhahran garage sale and it was very comfortable and big enough to hold us and all of our gear.

The diving there was the best I have ever experienced. The Red Sea off the coast of Arabia is totally unspoiled since tourism is not allowed in the country, and for the most part the Arabs were not into scuba diving. Where we camped we could simply walk into the water, swim out about twenty yards, and then drop down off an eighty foot amazingly colorful wall of coral. It was like nothing I had ever even imagined before. From that first dive I was hooked. I felt like I had entered a new planet, one of science fiction, it was so damned beautiful and other-worldly.

There were giant cone shaped sponges, bigger than me, in bright colors like purple and yellow. I saw clams that looked large enough to swallow me whole! And the fish were too numerous and varied to really focus on. They appeared as a swarm of moving colors, shapes and sizes as curious about me as I was about them. Some would swim right up to my face mask and look me in the eyes! In the nooks and crannies of the eighty foot deep coral reef were numerous bright green eels, seemingly shy until some of the divers started offering them pieces of sea urchins that they had broken open. The eels then quickly slithered out of their holes and snatched the food. Some were large, maybe six feet long and about eight to ten inches in diameter. The coral was multicolored and provided a great camouflage for the various species of fish. I learned early on not to touch the coral when I nearly stuck my hand into a brightly colored, venomous scorpionfish. Touching their spines can be very painful. And on the sea floor, there were sting rays to watch out for since they were half buried in the sand and well hidden. And of course we did see sharks, mostly small hammerheads cruising the bottom, but sometimes larger ones came swimming by. We stood still and watched until they left. None seemed too interested in us.

The first day we just did one dive in the afternoon, because it was following a day of travel and setting up camp, and we were tired. Don was already half asleep in the tent when I went to wake him up. His birthday was the next day and I had gathered everyone around our campfire for his surprise cake. He was groggy and kept insisting he wanted to sleep. I finally got him up and outside the tent. He was definitely surprised!

I did two dives every day after that and each one was a new miracle of awe. It was almost too much to take in during such a short time span. I tried to soak it all into my visual memory to last my lifetime, and it has. I can still "see" that beautiful coral reef and all that it held. Don and some of the other advanced divers also did night dives with headlamps to guide their path. It was a year later before I would brave a night dive.

Frank and I rode back with Don in the company vehicle, in a

carpool with a number of the other divers. It was a long drive and Don and Frank took turns driving. Our first stop was in Turaif, which is a mountain town and well known in Saudi Arabia as the site of many OPEC meetings. There was one huge, fancy hotel in town that accommodated these meetings. We decided to stop there for lunch. After five days of camping with no fresh water to shower in, we were sticky from salt water and smelly from sea critters. The first thing we did was use the restrooms to try to wash up a bit. I changed clothes in there and threw the ones I was wearing in the trash can. Feeling somewhat better we went to the beautiful dining area for lunch. The host and the waiters were very gracious though I am sure we all still looked pretty grungy. We were seated at a large table and enjoyed a delicious meal with china and crystal.

Frank had a great sense of humor and was well-known and well-liked in Dhahran. He could always make me laugh. He and Don were both very entertaining, which made the ride actually enjoyable. At one point when we stopped for gas, Don parked in the far dark corner of the lot, walked to the front of the vehicle and proceeded to take a leak. Frank jumped in the driver's seat, turned on the light and backed up a bit. There stood Don, in the spotlight! Never a dull moment.

Don's parents (Gil and Heida Faber) were living in Al Khobar, Saudi Arabia at the time, which was only about a thirty minute drive from Dhahran. Gil owned and ran a small company called Handyman. Working with an American partner,

Heida and Gil in Saudi Arabia

and the obligatory Saudi partner, the company repaired items like household appliances, air conditioners, fleets of cars, and more. During the course of the five plus years that Don and I were together in Arabia, I met and spent time with most of his family. Don's sister, Berta, was in boarding school in Rome but returned to Saudi Arabia for holidays. His brother, Bruce, came over and worked for a while with Gil, and also with another company in the area, TradCo. And Don's twin brother, Dan, also came over and worked for Gil for a while, so I got to spend time with most of the family. Only Brian (Bruce's twin) was not in the Kingdom during those years but eventually I did meet him and his family while vacationing with Don in Florida.

Having family members nearby was a very nice bonus. We had dinner together on many weekends and we jointly celebrated holidays and birthdays. Heida would come to the Aramco compound often to play bridge in various bridge clubs and to swim in the pools. She tried to teach me how to play bridge and even bought me a bridge table cloth with bidding instructions printed on it! She was a master bridge player and I was pretty much hopeless. Heida also regularly returned to Iceland to spend time with her elderly parents and other family and friends.

Heida was a traditional cook, much like my mom, but with different recipes based on her own cultural heritage. She made wonderful lamb dishes, in particular I loved her leg of lamb which she roasted in a marinade of coffee with cream and sugar. My favorite dish was her Icelandic pancakes. She never used measurements, just mixed things together until it "felt right," so I could never figure out how to make them. One time before she came over to make the pancakes at our house I measured all the ingredients in advance, then after she left I measured what was left of them all, and 'voila', I had the recipe!

Life in Saudi Arabia was fulfilling. We were very active, both physically and socially. We had many good friends and there were always parties and events going on. Our closest friends were Ike and Alice. Don had known Ike while living in Florida and had gotten him a job with Aramco. We were also good friends with Dan and Diane, Ginger and Alan, Kathy and Richard, Jack and Nancy, Marge and Folke, Cathy and Dan, and Frank, Steve, Jim, Dave, and many others. (We are still in contact with some of these folks after more than thirty years). We bought a sailboat with Dan and Diane, a sixteen foot catamaran, and sailed it often on weekends at "the Yacht Club" in Half Moon Bay. This was a marina owned and operated by Aramco so sailing from there was easy. Catamarans are made of two hulls with a canvas platform stretched between for passengers to sit on. When speed is picked up the catamaran can lift up on one hull and go faster. The thought of it was frightening to me since it seemed to me that it would surely tip over. The first weekend we had this boat I brought a picnic basket imagining a nice gentle sail on the Bay. The water there was never rough and always fun to swim and sail in. Don and Dan took the "cat" out first and had a great time sailing it around faster and faster on one hull. Then they came to pick up Diane and me. We sailed for a while and it was thrilling, the winds were high but the water was relatively calm. They then decided to try to bring it up on one hull but it completely capsized, catapulting Diane and me into the water! So much for our picnic! In time we mastered the art of sailing a catamaran and had hours of fun with it over the next five years.

The Dive Club sponsored regular trips by Arabian dhows to Jurayd Island and Jana Island in the Arabian (Persian) Gulf. These were exhausting but wonderful trips. The boats left early in the morning for the slow motorized trip to one of the islands. It took about three hours and we usually saw schools of dolphins on the way and sometimes giant sea turtles. When we did see them, some of the divers, Don included, would jump in to swim with these creatures. The dhows would anchor off the island near the beautiful coral reefs and we would begin our dives from there by jumping off the boats in full gear. We each brought two scuba tanks so we could do two dives. Sometimes we did overnight trips to the islands and the dhows would then dock on the shore of the island and we would camp for the night.

Don and me on Jurayd Island

On my first overnight trip to Jurayd Island with Don we were awoken around 2 a.m. to the sounds of a giant sea turtle that had come ashore to lay her eggs. We quietly snuck up on her in order to watch this amazing event. The turtle worked away digging a large hole in the sand with her flippers and spraying us with the sand in the process. When she deemed the hole was large enough she began laying the eggs, over fifty of them for sure, and then she carefully covered them up and slowly and clumsily made her way back to the sea. This whole process took many hours so we didn't get much sleep that night.

It was on Jurayd Island that I did my first night dive. Night time in the sea is quite different since few creatures are moving about. Most of the fish actually sleep by staying still in the water, so I was able to pick them up and hold them and they didn't wake up! Some nocturnal creatures like shrimp and crabs would be scurrying about, feeding on the bottom, but mostly it was quiet and peaceful, giving divers the chance to see the fish and coral close up with little movement.

The Company often brought in entertainment from the States, live bands for dances, sometimes well-known entertainers like Kris Kristofferson, and they also sponsored events like the Jingle Bell Run. This was a five mile run around Dhahran right before the Christmas break. One year there were newsmen there from the States, and I was later informed by a friend back home that she had seen me on the evening news, participating in this run!

Early on, the President of the Company invited all the Dhahran teachers to his home for a garden dinner party. The hit of the evening was his cordless phone. None of us had ever seen such a thing and couldn't imagine how it could work, especially as he allowed us to use it to call family and friends in the States! How could we talk to family in the States when it was not even connected to a phone line? The phone was passed around from person to person during the entire evening and we were all agog at its magic!

The school system was also a source of entertainment. We planned parties and celebrations for any and all occasions. Teachers, in general, are a creative bunch and so these events regularly included humorous skits, musical performances, and comedic impersonations. Don was always amazed at the elaborate plans/entertainments at these events, saying, "No one in the corporate world ever does this!" Two of the teachers played guitar, sang, and wrote very funny lyrics to "Hi ho! Hi ho! It's off to work we go!" poking fun of all the nationalities represented in Aramco. Arabic lessons were also offered through the school by some of our Arabic teachers. I took these lessons in the beginning hoping that I could learn this language, but I may as well have been studying Arabic in Washington D.C. since almost no one spoke Arabic in Dhahran. Everyone spoke English.

The Company provided free bus service into the local town, Al Khobar, and I went often, to shop, eat local foods, and just enjoy the local sights and smells. Even here, all the shopkeepers could speak English. There were numerous small gold shops in the "suq" (shopping area). And there were tailors to make "thobes," the long robes worn by men and the long sleeved, floor length dresses for women. I selected some materials and had a few made for myself. They were loose and comfortable and made visiting the local, conservative towns of Arabia easier. The gold suqs were my favorite. In the 1980s gold jewelry was very popular for both men and women and Al Khobar was full of these small shops from which to buy rings, earrings, bangles, necklaces, and gold coins and other medallions. In Saudi Arabia it was illegal to sell gold jewelry under eighteen karat, anything under this was considered "fake gold." We always marveled at the fact that the shops were small, with no security, and had glass windows displaying gobs and gobs of eighteen and twenty-one karat gold jewelry. Theft was not an issue in the Kingdom since the penalty for stealing was to have one's hand cut off! There weren't many other stores of interest to shop in. Music stores and book stores carried mostly Arabic language merchandise and these were highly censored. Clothing stores were scarce and their conservative styles were not what I would have chosen. This meant that for birthdays and holidays we gave and received mostly gifts of gold jewelry. After six years in Arabia I had a rather nice collection of gold.

I only lived at the "Holiday Inn" for about eight or nine months, because in the summer of 1979 Don was issued a six hundred forty sq. ft. house and we moved in together. The house was located in Dhahran Hills, a new housing development that was about three miles from the school. He often had a Company car assigned to him so I would drive the "green machine" to work. The muffler was really loud and we had the red and white sail boat strapped to the top so everyone could see and hear me when I arrived. For Christmas that year Don got me a new muffler! That "green machine" remained our means of transportation until 1982 when King Khalid died and King Fahd took over. It was customary for the new King to present all the people working in the country with a gift; Don and I each received a bonus of one month's pay and this was enough to enable us to buy a new car. In the local town all purchases were made in cash only. We took the bus into Al Khobar carrying a brown paper bag full of Saudi riyals and returned home with a new Subaru 4WD Station Wagon!

We moved one more time during our stay in Arabia and that was to a larger house assigned to Don. It was about one thousand sq. ft. and was very comfortable. Housing was assigned based on time spent in the country and your rank in the Company. Don had received promotions and so after three years he was assigned this house. Meanwhile, I also received an upgraded housing assignment based on my promotion to Assistant Principal and it was a 700 sq. ft. house diagonally across the street from Don's house. This worked out perfectly for us. We stored things in my house and rented it out to a bunch of guys for their Wednesday night poker games. I think they paid us about $700 per month for that privilege.

Much of our time in Arabia was spent planning for trips, both short and long, to take advantage of the many holidays on our calendar and of course for our annual "repats." There was a small library in Dhahran, operated by Aramco for the employees. The book collection wasn't large but we were grateful for it. They had copies of all the world airline schedules in three huge volumes and these were a godsend. Don and I spent many a night there planning these trips. Each year the Company gave each employee the cost of a round trip full fare plane ticket to their home base for "repatriation." This usually amounted to about $3,000 for each of us. With careful planning that amount would pretty much cover the whole trip — airfare, hotels and meals for five to six weeks.

The first "repat" that we took together was in April of 1980. We flew first to Thailand, then Australia, New Zealand, Tahiti, America, and then back to Saudi Arabia on a six week round the world trip. The focus of this trip was the South Pacific: Australia, New Zealand, and Tahiti where neither of us had been before. We loved Australia and the Australians. They were friendly and fun loving. We did typical tourist things in Sydney, like visiting the Opera House and taking the ferry to Manly Beach. We also did local things like finding funky old bars, where we ate at long tables with lots of Aussies and then danced on the table tops when the meal was finished. We rented a jeep and drove along the coast, visited a wildlife sanctuary where we hugged some koala bears and petted the kangaroos. We flew to Cairn, a city near the equator in the north, and then rented a private helicopter to Heron Island where we stayed for three days and did a lot of scuba diving. Heron Island is right on the Barrier Reef and the diving was excellent. Each dive would last about forty-five minutes, the average time a diver takes to use up all the air in their tank. Don, however, is so relaxed underwater that his air would last him an hour and a half. While the divers and most instructors surfaced and boarded the boat after forty-five minutes, Don and a few of the instructors continued underwater for another thirty to forty minutes. Each day we did two dives and the thing I remember the most is the huge schools of manta rays, numbering in the hundreds! Sometimes I would be above them, watching as they scurried along the bottom. Other times I'd be standing on the sea floor watching as these huge schools would pass above me.

We left the island the same way we arrived, by a private helicopter. I sat up front next to the pilot and Don sat behind me. It's an estimated ninety minute ride and coming over all had gone smoothly. On the return trip a storm came up and the sky and sea both turned a very dark grey color, such that I could not distinguish between the sea and the skyline. It looked as though we might be flying straight into the water at any moment. Then came the lightning and thunder and a very heavy rainfall. I was beginning to feel panicky. The pilot was busy checking all his gauges and I didn't want to interrupt him with stupid questions so I turned around to ask Don if he thought we were safe, knowing that he had flown many helicopter missions during his military career. As I turned around I saw that he was fast asleep! *"Hmm,"* I thought, *"if he can sleep through a storm like this in a loud, shaking helicopter, then it must be safe!"*

Our next stop was New Zealand. We spent all of our time on the South Island and were in awe of the scenery. We rented a jeep and drove from Christchurch to Queenstown to Milford Sound and everything in between. We hiked in Mt. Cook National Park and took a small private plane ride to the snow covered peaks. We visited grass covered plains filled with deer and other wildlife, we walked through fern forests, and explored the beaches along the western coast that were home to piles of driftwood and colonies of seals. We hired a guide, put on spiked boots and walked atop glaciers, We took a boat off of Milford Sound and viewed some of the most spectacular tall rock formations which emerged straight up out of the ocean that I have ever seen. All in all, it's not that big of an island and yet it had the most diverse and beautiful scenery imaginable for such a small country. And we didn't even make it to the North Island!

We flew to Tahiti next and spent a week at the Club Med on the Island of Moorea. It was very laid back and a perfect way to end our "repat." Most of the tourists there were French or Australian or Tahitian. The women were all topless on the beach which was a surprise. There were two other American couples there and we quickly became friends. They were from Wyoming and Idaho and, like me, the ladies did not feel comfortable going topless. However, after about two days we all said, "What the heck! We look more out of place with a bikini top than without it,," so we took them off! At a Club Med you buy beads from the office and these are what one uses for "cash" to purchase drinks. Don and I each got a large string of beads to wear around our neck and purchase drinks with. After dinner and watching the show with our new friends we all went to the bar. I got the first round and it cost about half of my bead necklace. Our friends got the next round and the same thing happened to them. Then Don went up and got a round of drinks and came back with only four beads missing! After that we sent him up to the bar each time to get the drinks. The bartender was a nice looking young Tahitian woman with long dark hair and a grass skirt with a big flowery top. She worked there every night and Don continued to be favored by her. On our last day at the resort we took a boat to one of the smaller islands for a snorkeling trip and a picnic organized by the resort. Don's bartender friend was on the trip. After lunch she and the other waitresses did some Tahitian dances and then at the end of the performance they took their tops off. It was then that we realized that they were not women, but men! We were told that in Tahitian culture sometimes baby boys were raised as girls!

We flew on to America, me to Wisconsin and Don to Florida, to visit family and friends before heading back to Saudi Arabia. And so ended our first long "repat" together. In the years that followed we had many more wonderful trips. We circled the globe and stopped in fabulous places like Bali, Indonesia, Sri Lanka, Germany, France, Spain, Austria, England, Iceland, Italy, Western Australia, the Caribbean, Egypt, Bahrain, Cyprus, Tanzania, Kenya, Mexico, and numerous places in the USA. We went scuba diving, horseback riding, sailing, whitewater rafting, hiking, mountain climbing, camping, and skiing. This was a very active and adventurous time in my life.

We also very much enjoyed traveling within Saudi Arabia, especially when diving in the Red Sea was part of the adventure. Once we drove across the Rub-e-Khali (The Empty Quarter) in southern Arabia in a caravan with three other couples. Each couple was driving a four wheel drive vehicle so we could help each other out when we got stuck in the soft red sand. Each vehicle carried an extra tank of gas since we knew gas stations might be difficult to find. The vehicle Don and I were in was a borrowed older jeep with no air-conditioning and airplane tires and a handmade extra gas tank. We rode with the windows rolled down since it was very hot outside and endured incoming sand. There were no roads so we simply traveled by compass, always heading west with the goal of reaching the Red Sea. We camped at night in what looked like the most desolate, uninhabited spots on earth, and yet there were always signs of the Bedouin tribes who passed through these areas. Like a goat carcass hanging in an acacia tree. We were of course not the only vehicle travelers to take this route as there were other tracks in the sand.

We camped the first night in a large open desert area with not even a dune around. The only thing visible on the horizon was a lone gas pump! It was locked and there was no one around but we camped nearby, assuming the owner would show up, and he did!

Camels near our campsites and along the road.

As it was getting dark a lone man appeared, having walked across the sands from somewhere unknown to us. He had a key to the gas pump and we filled up our tanks and paid the man the fair price he asked. He thanked us graciously and disappeared into the night. The next night we camped by a "wadi." These are dry river beds, containing water only when rare heavy rains come, sometimes causing flash floods. Along the wadis there are tamarisks and acacia trees, bushes, and cacti providing some shade and sticks to build a fire with at night. It was a beautiful campsite with a billion times a billion stars in the sky. The next day, another hot day, we began to smell gas as we were driving. Upon investigation we found that our handmade gas tank was leaking so we had to empty out all our scuba gear to get to the fuel tank and then empty out the tank. We commented on how glad we were that neither of us was a smoker. Could have had disastrous results!

Our destination on this trip was near the southwest corner of the Kingdom. We set up camp on the beach by the Red Sea and had a glorious five full days of scuba diving and snorkeling in the giant colorful reef just a few meters off shore. We also fished from an inflatable raft we brought and had delicious fresh grilled seafood every night. We carried our own generator, compressor, and dive tanks so we could each do at least three dives a day. This equipment was mostly owned by the Aramco Dive Club, of which we were all members.

Don ready to dive

On the return drive we decided to cross the Asir Mountains, if we could find the road, instead of going back through the desert. We headed north on a new highway, beautifully paved, and with freshly painted center lines. After about ten to fifteen miles the road abruptly came to an end and we bounced off into the sand! There were construction workers nearby and we tried to ask them how we could get to the highway over the mountains but they did not understand English. They didn't speak Arabic either but then Don realized they were speaking Italian! So in the Italian he remembered from high school years in Rome he got some directions and we decided to give it a try.

The Italian spokesperson knew one word in Arabic which he kept repeating. "Khatar!" Which we knew meant "dangerous." We found the road but it looked more like a camel path than a road. We continued on this "road" and indeed it eventually wound its way up the mountain. As we approached the summit we were stopped by Saudi soldiers. The approach was so steep that our jeep started to roll backwards! I quickly jumped out and put rocks behind the tires. The police came and inspected each of our vehicles, looking for illegal items such as weapons, alcohol and walkie talkies (only military and police were allowed to carry this kind of equipment in Arabia). We had no weapons but were carrying both of the other items in each of our vehicles. The alcohol was in capped glass tonic water bottles. One of our friends had a bottle capper, for just this purpose, and the alcohol we brought was the "white" which looked just like tonic water. The soldiers did not even take a second look at these "capped bottles." They did find our walkie talkies and a conversation ensued about these. They tried using them and couldn't get them to work so they decided they were "toys" and allowed us to continue. The reason they were there on top of that summit was to check for contraband coming over the mountains since we were very close to the border with Yemen. Later on the descent our brakes gave out and Don used the emergency brakes until we could stop and repair them. Without further problems we made it back to Dhahran two days later.

Don and I did not always get vacations scheduled together so I also took trips with various friends. Once my friend Natasha from Washington D.C. and I met in Cairo and traveled in Egypt for about ten days. We visited many of the famous ancient ruins along the Nile, in Luxor, and the Valley of the Kings. We rode camels around the pyramids and listened to guides trying to explain their significance in limited English. Mostly what we were told was that these places "were very, very old." It was a great trip and spending time with Natasha was always pleasurable.

Another time I went to Jordan with my friend Kathy (her husband, Richard, was unable to come as was Don) on a DOG'S trip sponsored by Aramco. Most memorable was our visit to Petra. We rode horses through the narrow passageways and spent a day just in awe at the vastness and beauty of this place. I felt the same as I did in Egypt to see these huge, marvelous

Me on camel (my favorite animal) on a trip to Egypt
with my friend, Natasha

structures. How could these ancient peoples build this? In Jordan we also went scuba diving in the Red Sea, followed by a visit to some Palestinian camps near the border with Israel. Here there were thousands of people living in temporary structures all these years later, still looking back at their former homes in Israel. We were invited to swim in the Dead Sea but the smell was so putrid I only got as far as putting my feet in.

I went to England one summer on a short trip to visit my old college roommate, ML, and her husband. Both were now professors at Oxford, he in astrophysics and she is plant physiology. They had a cute little home near the university and seemed to really be enjoying their life style. He loved cricket and was on a local team so ML and I went to watch him play one day. Six hours later the game was still going on. She had brought a picnic blanket and some snacks. When the game ended I had no idea who won since I had no understanding of this game. I did however get in a few short naps.

Don and some of his friends went on a different DOG'S trip to Austria to ski. He had skied a few times in Italy while in high school but had not skied in years. This trip was the beginning of what would be the next thirty-plus years of being an avid skier. The following year he and I flew to Breckenridge, CO for a ski trip with Dan and Diane. They all could ski, but I was a beginner so I took a private lesson for my first day on the mountain. The instructor was great, and with patience and care I learned to ski down the beginner slopes by the end of that day. As I later learned, he was a former classmate of Don's from Rome! We spent a week in Breckenridge and though I was still a beginner skier by the end of that time, I felt pretty comfortable on the green runs. Since Dan and Diane and Don all wanted to ski the blue runs I did try these but usually ended up falling a number of times. From Saudi Arabia, in the years that followed we returned to Breckenridge to ski, as well as other ski resorts in France, Austria, California, New Mexico and Utah. (NOTE: We still love to ski and now own a condo in Keystone, CO and ski on a regular basis).

In August of 1980 my niece, Tammy, was getting married in Wisconsin and though this was not my scheduled time off I received permission to take ten days and fly home. It was a very memorable ten days because not only did I get to enjoy the wedding and see all my family again, but I also flew to New York City and attended the Democratic National Convention! Susan's husband, Alvin, was one of the organizers of the convention so he got badges for Susan and Natasha and me. The badges gave us access to the entire convention floor and I was ecstatic! (I still have mine). Jimmy Carter was running for re-election and he did receive the nomination, but Ted Kennedy was also running and he gave the most exciting, energizing speech. I liked Jimmy Carter and thought his heart was always in the right place, I just was worried he would not get re-elected and of course that's what happened. Still, I will never forget how thrilled I was to be part of the process that week, seeing all those delegates, meeting Ralph Nader, and having rooftop dinners with all the interesting people behind the scenes of the Democratic Party.

The following spring, Don and I had our second "repat" together and this was another around the world trip, but this time in the other direction. We flew from Dhahran to New York City and then I went on to Washington, D.C. to stay with my friends and he went to South Carolina to visit Pete and his wife, Debby. Pete was a fellow PJ (they served together in Vietnam) and close friend of Don's. I later flew down to North Carolina and met up with Don and Pete. We drove from the airport in Pete's van with lots of amenities including Bloody Mary's! We drove to this nearby lake property and joined Debby and the girls. We looked at some property on a lake and near a golf course as a possible joint investment. It was a beautiful area for swimming, boating, and fishing in the lake. We later did decide to go in on this purchase but it never made us any money. Meanwhile we had been doing the same thing in Arabia, which was listening to various proposals on investments. One was to buy thirty acres in Maui with beachfront but remote and used as a cattle ranch. We decided against this. (Too bad, since this was later developed and would have made us a bundle of money!) Another was to invest in apartment buildings in Austin, Texas near the campus. We thought this could be a great investment so we chose this. So did a number of our good friends. (This project later went bankrupt due to corruption and we lost our investment.) A third choice was to purchase almond orchards in California, which we also turned down. (I don't know if these ever made money.)

We left North Carolina to visit our families, me to Wisconsin and he to Florida, and then we met in Denver for a few nights before flying on to Australia. This time we visited the western part of Australia. We stayed in Perth on the ocean. We both really liked this town and being near the sea. What amazed us the most were all the farms with flocks of sheep that went right down to the ocean. We rented a jeep and drove along the coast through lots of small towns where surfing was the popular sport. Neither of us tried it as the waves were too high for beginners. We also drove into wilderness parks nearby to see lots of kangaroos before flying on to Bali, Indonesia.

Bali was a beautiful island with perfect beaches and a gentle lifestyle. The people left little offerings everywhere for the gods. These little baskets or bundles of flowers or sweets were on the streets, floating on the water, and next to buildings and farms. We took a taxi from the airport to our rented bungalow from the Oberoi Resort. When we arrived, being used to Middle Eastern protocol we started bargaining with the cab driver regarding the price since we were told that in Bali this was the norm. After haggling back and forth for a short while we realized that translated into dollar currency we had been arguing over about ten cents! We gave the man what he asked and got out. Our bungalow was gorgeous and right on the beach. It's probably still the best accommodation we have ever rented. We had our own little garden and pool with fresh fruit cocktails delivered every afternoon. The bungalow itself was stunning, filled with carvings in teak wood, colorful paintings, large plants, fresh flowers, and a huge bathroom in which the shower was without a roof. It was right on the beach and so we had a relaxing week of swimming, sunbathing, and a few side trips into the mountains to see local villages with wood carvers who did the beautiful artwork. These little villages were filled with monkeys who were not afraid of humans. I learned this the hard way when I thought they were cute and I would give them some nuts. When the nuts were gone they came after me! I had to run to the car for safety and once inside they climbed on the roof and pounded on the windows!

While in Bali one of our friends from Arabia, Dave, was there at the same time. He was there to buy a whole load of batik clothing like shirts, dresses, etc. to ship back to America and sell. These clothing items were super cheap in Bali and he thought it would be a good business deal. I'm not sure he ever really made any money on this venture. Mainly he was just hanging out on the beaches and perhaps enjoying the "magic mushrooms" that were available everywhere. They were even advertised on menus: do you want regular mushrooms in your omelet or "magic mushrooms?" Dave was also a scuba diver and Don did a dive with him while there, but I had to leave earlier and get back to Arabia. Don went from Bali to Sri Lanka where he did some recruiting for Aramco.

I became the assistant principal in 1981 and took over a little office near the teacher's lounge in the junior high school. Having been hired from within I already knew all the teaching staff, but one of my responsibilities was to be in charge of the grounds crew. These were all young men from India, Pakistan, and Sri Lanka. None had ever worked for a woman before and when their leader, Mohammed, brought me out to meet them all, I could see they were nervous and uncomfortable with a woman in charge. I decided that it would work best if I stayed in the background and ran all of my requests, suggestions, compliments or complaints through Mohammed. He spoke excellent English and did not seem at all uncomfortable around me. My first or second week on the job I was working late one night when one of the acoustic ceiling boards in my office came crashing down. Along with it came a very frightened, seemingly vicious feral cat! I called Mohammed and he and his crew climbed up in the attic and discovered an entire colony of wild cats living up there! I took a deep breath and decided I should keep a journal since this job was likely to be filled with lots of surprises.

I got to know the head of security very well, he was usually in my office at least once or twice a week and we became good friends. It was mostly small stuff, kids sneaking into someone's alcohol supply or getting into a friend's house while they were away on "repat" to have a little party. Sometimes it was more serious like taking their Dad's car without permission and driving out of the camp through the security gates! Depending on the situation it was either he or I who would spend time with the parents and the student to get things quieted down. There were a few times when a student would get kicked out of the country. In some cases, the parents would leave too.

I had some humorous encounters with student discipline too, and one of my favorites was with Todd. He was sent to the office by the PE teacher but he wouldn't tell me why he was sent. The teacher had kind of a crusty old military style. He called the boys "men" and would say things loudly like, "Form a line, men!" I eventually convinced Todd to tell me what he had done to get sent to the office. He said the teacher brought out a rack to hold the soccer balls and asked the kids to help by picking up all the balls. When the kids were too slow in doing it, he yelled "Rack your balls, men!" And Todd said, "So I did."

In the spring of 1982, Don and I did our third "repat" together. We started out by flying to Europe to do some skiing shortly before the resorts in the Alps closed. We flew to Zurich and took a train to Val d'lsere in the French Alps. There were a few ski runs still open so Don skied for a short while. I didn't since I was still too much of a beginner to ski in these conditions. We stayed in a small hotel nearby and were the only guests there, but we were still offered a fixed menu dinner that we were grateful for since everything in the area seemed closed. They brought in a tray on wheels and it was full of cold cuts and various breads and cheeses. They spoke no English so we couldn't communicate with anyone there. The meal seemed fair enough given the fact that they were getting ready to close for the season. We ate a little of all of it and sat back to finish our wine when they came in with a huge entree of roasted rabbit with potatoes and carrots! I was already stuffed but we realized they had prepared this just for us so we had to eat it. We knew now that the first cart was meant to be an appetizer, not the whole meal! We did the best we could with the rabbit, slowly over the next hour, and once again sat back to finish the wine. Then in they came with the dessert, a large piece of cream cake for each of us. I could barely look at it but realized again that I had to eat it. We asked for coffee and then slowly over the next hour we ate the cake while sipping the coffee. That night there was no way I could fall asleep. I was so full that my stomach ached and I had to wait for hours for my body to digest that humongous meal.

The next morning we took a train back to Zurich and flew to the States. We visited family and friends, he to Florida and me to D.C. and then Wisconsin. I had given my parents the gift of a trip to Knoxville to visit Jane and family and then on to Florida and a time to meet Don. So the three of us left Wisconsin together on this trip. We spent a few days in Tennessee with Jane and then flew to Jacksonville where I rented a car and we drove down along the coast, stopping a few times so Dad could put his feet in the ocean. Neither Mom nor Dad had ever touched sea water. We met up with Don the next day in Orlando and had a big lobster dinner. After a few more days of touring Florida together they flew back to Wisconsin, and Don and I flew back to Arabia.

By the end of my first year as assistant principal there were over seven hundred students in the junior high. I was beginning to feel overwhelmed and worked at least one day every weekend. The Company was in a big growth spurt and new employees were arriving every week. The Board of Education and the superintendent agreed to hire an additional administrator and so a second assistant principal was added to the staff. This was a tremendous help to me. The new assistant principal, Joe, was also hired from within. He had been a physical education teacher and was promoted to the position. He and I divided up the job and were a perfect complement to one another. He organized and oversaw all the extra-curriculars, the ground crew, and the intersession schedules between the trimesters. I did the academic schedules, teacher evaluations (along with the principal) and the student discipline and attendance. The student schedule was computerized with a very complicated system. It was the same program used by Michigan State University with over twenty-five thousand students at the time. It took me a long time to get really proficient using it for our needs, and this was all done on a main frame computer system where the schedules would be printed out in "The Towers," which is what we called the Company Headquarters. I eventually learned to enjoy the process and helped do the schedule for the other Aramco Junior High Schools in Udhaliyah, Ras Tanura, and Abqaiq.

In 1982 an "Eid" fell in early October so Don and I took advantage of the timing and flew to Munich for the Oktoberfest. It was truly a fun loving festival and I definitely felt close to my German roots while there. There were big beerhalls with polka bands and loud singing Germans. Huge steins of beer were served along with sausages and sauerkraut. I loved it! From there we flew to Mallorca to stay with Danish friends from Arabia who had retired there. They had a beautiful home in the mountains, overlooking the sea. Don's aunt and uncle (Magga and Arni) from Iceland were vacationing there at the time so we visited them too. We rented a car and took them on a tour of the island. As we were leaving the city I asked about our gas level not knowing how frequent the opportunity to fill up would come. Don said not to worry, we still had a quarter of a tank. About fifteen minutes later as we were driving in the country our car ran out of gas! Turns out the gas gauge did not work. Fortunately there was a little bistro there in the middle of a vineyard so Magga and I stayed there and drank wine while Don and Arni walked back for gas.

Sometimes we spent the holidays in Dhahran and had nice celebrations with our friends. Some of our friends had been with the Company a long time and they had beautiful big homes. Some came when we did but as a married couple, and married people were issued bigger houses than single people so they also had nice accommodations. The practice of "house sitting" was common and on occasion Don and I did house sit for friends which was fun, especially when there was a yard with a hot tub. The weather did cool down in winter to about 60F so a hot tub felt great. We still went to the beach in the winter but did not swim in the sea until early March. The weather in Dhahran was in general hot, really hot. In the summer temperatures of 120F and greater were common. Rain almost never happened. The first year I lived in Dhahran it didn't rain at all. During the second year, I was riding the bus into Al Khobar one day with a few teachers and we thought we saw large plumes of smoke. We believed there was a fire somewhere until someone finally said, "I think those are clouds!" They were right. Later that day it rained and we all talked about how amazing it was to not recognize a cloud since we had not yet seen one in Arabia.

There were beautiful big swimming pools in Dhahran and everyone enjoyed these. Don and I swam laps often and ate a pile of super salty French fries when we finished since the heat really sucked the salt out of one when exercising. In fact there were salt tablets available at most of the water fountains and reminders to drink lots of water and replenish your salt. Sometime in 1983 the Saudi government decided to be stricter on life in Dhahran. Until then within the boundaries of this Compound we lived much like one would in America. We could wear shorts or any other attire acceptable in America. Women could drive. I even had a Saudi driver's license. Dhahran was only about three miles wide by three miles long so I couldn't drive far. And men and women openly worked and played together. In 1983 they segregated the swimming pools. Women and children were assigned a specific pool for use and men a separate one. That was the end of Don and I being able to swim together. And because the women's pool included all the children, there weren't really free lanes for me to swim in on my own. As changes like this began to occur, Don and I started to think about the possibility of leaving.

By 1983, after five years in Arabia, I had earned the right to go on a "sabbatical" to further my training/education. I went to Utah for about two months, worked under the direction of the Utah State Department of Education, and visited a number of schools around the state with state supervisors who evaluated teachers. While there I took six credits in Teacher Evaluation/Supervision through Brigham Young University. On that occasion Mom and I drove out there together (using the car I had sold them when I left America) and she stayed with me for a week. During that time Don flew in for the beginning of his "repat" and met up with Mom and me. The three of us went to Park City where Don and I did some skiing and Mom got to ride the chair lift with us, another new experience for her. After Mom left, Don flew on to Lake Tahoe and more skiing.

I started my sabbatical with the Assistant Secretary of Education who showed me around the state. He was a Mormon, as was everyone in the high positions in education in the state. He said he didn't think it would be possible to move up in any government office in Utah without being a Mormon. One night

I met some prior teacher friends of mine from Aramco who had returned to Utah. We went out to dinner at a nice restaurant and they brought a bottle of vodka with them. This was how the system worked. You brought your own alcohol if you wanted it and the restaurant would provide the set ups. It was illegal for the restaurants to sell alcohol but they could use yours to mix your drinks. The problem was, you were not allowed to leave with an open bottle so you either drank it all or poured it out! We did not pour it out. Fortunately there were six of us to share in the task.

Don returned to Utah after a few weeks in California and we drove down to Bryce Canyon which is one of my favorite spots on the planet for natural beauty. We rode horses down into the canyon and I loved the experience. We then drove back to Salt Lake City where he flew on to Florida to visit family and then returned to Saudi Arabia. I continued to work with Utah's Department of Education, visiting a number of school districts around the state doing teacher evaluations with state administrators. All in all it was a good experience and I learned a lot from these Utah educators.

At the end of my sabbatical Gary, Rosie, Leilani, and Sadie rode the train out to Salt Lake City to join me. We traveled together around Utah a bit, including a visit to Bryce Canyon, and rode horses down into the canyon. Rosie is not a fan of horses or steep narrow trails so this was not a high light of her trip! They drove the car back to Wisconsin and I flew on to Dhahran, ending my two month stay in the States.

I arrived back in Dhahran in late June, and Don and I began to talk more seriously about the possibility of leaving Saudi Arabia. In August I celebrated my fortieth birthday and Don surprised me with a marriage proposal and a diamond ring! He joked about my having to meet his Icelandic relatives and get their approval before he could marry me. He also promised me that for our honeymoon we would climb Mt. Kilimanjaro! He knew this was something I had thought about since high school when I read Hemingway's The Snows of Kilimanjaro."

We talked a lot about our future plans during the coming

months and thought that by the following fall we would leave Arabia and start a new adventure together somewhere else. We would ship all our belongings to our house in Spring Green that Gary was building, stay there a short while, and then move on to San Francisco most likely. Golden Gate University had a Master's program in International Business that Don was interested in. We expected to be there a few years and then move abroad again somewhere, wherever Don found a job.

We contemplated getting married in the fall of 1984 and leaving shortly after. Getting married in Saudi Arabia was impossible since there was no such thing as a secular wedding, only Muslim ceremonies. Over the winter we wrote to various embassies in the area inquiring about the marriage policies. We knew it would be possible in Israel but we were not allowed to travel to that country and ever return to Saudi Arabia. The Saudis did not recognize Israel as a country. In fact one year at the school a teacher ordered inflatable globes for her classroom and when they arrived they had been censored. Israel had been physically cut out. Unfortunately this ruined the ability to inflate the globes! Most countries we heard back from had a minimal residency requirement, like six weeks, so that would not work. One of our friends told us about Cyprus. He had gotten married there a few years before and said it was easy and there were no residency requirements.

In December I had my "repat" and started the vacation out with a ski trip to Austria with Aramco friends, Richard and Ann, and their children. It was a wonderful skiing experience. Richard and Ann were always fun to be with and their children were naturals on skis. As I recall, Ann didn't ski but Richard and I tried our best to keep up with the kids even though they had never skied before! I flew back to Wisconsin for Christmas with the family. Don had been in Florida visiting his family and then flew into the little Appleton airport to join us for the holidays and meet the rest of my family. The day he arrived it was thirty degrees below zero! My dad brought his sheepskin coat to the airport for Don since he was arriving from Florida with only a light rain jacket. We had a big party at June and Gene's house and invited all the cousins to meet Don. Don remembers it as a time when all the talk was on the Green Bay Packers, and trying to get cars started at the end of the evening. The men went out to keep the engines plugged in or running, and meanwhile their beer froze inside the cans within minutes of being outdoors!

We did not tell anyone that we were planning on getting married before coming back to the States in the fall. The possibility of going to Cyprus would be our own private wedding. We planned to have a traditional wedding in Wisconsin in the spring of 1985 and shared this news with everyone.

The rest of the year in Saudi Arabia went by quickly. Some of our close friends had already left, like Kathy. She and Richard divorced and she was back living in Texas and had remarried. Jack and Nancy decided to leave because their oldest son was finishing ninth grade and there was no high school available for foreign students in Arabia. All had to leave the Kingdom for boarding school or return to their home countries and stay with relatives. This was often a time when parents would choose to quit their jobs and return home with their children. Marge and Folke were planning on retiring. Ginger and Alan had gotten married and moved to Texas. Frank left unexpectedly and Dhahran was definitely not the same without him. My science teacher friend Cathy had met Dan, an airforce pilot stationed in Saudi Arabia, and they had married and left Dhahran. Dan and Diane had a baby, Jesse, and we knew they probably wouldn't stay much longer.

Don and I spent much of our time making our plans for the coming fall. We wrote to the Ministry of Marriage in Cyprus with an "official" request to get married there. We used Aramco stationery, had it signed by friends attesting to the fact that we were both single and of age, and then we used Saudi postage stamps by the signatures to make it look really authentic! The request was accepted and we made plans to go there over the "Eid" in September. We then made plans to visit Egypt and Kenya and Tanzania upon leaving Arabia. Most important was getting our permits to climb Mt. Kilimanjaro. My sister June and her husband Gene asked if they could join us in Egypt. Neither had ever traveled abroad before and June really wanted to do some adventurous trips. So we put that in our plans, to meet them in Egypt after we climbed Mt. Kilimanjaro.

In June of 1984 we took our last "repat" from Aramco. We went to Wisconsin for a party my brother Gary held at the house he had been building for us. It was far from finished on the inside but the outside was done along with a beautiful big deck. It was on twenty-six acres of land joining his farm and stood on a high hill from which we could see for twenty miles. It was a wonderful party with friends who came from all over. We had sent Gary money every month and with it he had been building this house.

After the party we flew back to Dhahran by way of Iceland and I got to meet many of Don's family members, in particular, his Afi and Amma, Heida's parents. This was a wonderful visit and I very much enjoyed getting to know these kind, gentle people. His Amma had been ill for years with some sort of inner ear issue causing serious vertigo. She almost never left the house or her bed. She was the whitest person I had ever seen from lack of contact with the sun. His Afi had been diagnosed with cancer but was doing remarkably well. He had a sparkle in his eye and spoke to me in Icelandic even though he knew I could not understand a word. I think he really wanted to talk to me, as I did to him, but we didn't know each other's language.

The Eid al Adha came in early September in 1984 and we had a five day vacation so this is when we flew to Larnaca, Cyprus, rented a car and drove along the coast to Limassol where we stayed in a beautiful hotel right on the beach. The next day we visited the Ministry of Marriage in Limassol to schedule the ceremony. We were then told that the rules had changed and we would need to go to Nicosia to get our license and that it may not be issued. Cyprus is a divided country, part Greek and part Turkish. We were mostly on the Greek side but did cross the border which meant encountering armed military personnel on the road and on rooftops. We quickly drove to Nicosia and waited inside a government office for a few hours hoping the license would be issued. Finally a polite, soft spoken man came out with the official signed document. We were greatly relieved and thanked him sincerely. It was then sealed inside an envelope using a jar of old fashioned paste. Everything in this office was done by hand, no computers or even typewriters.

We drove back to Limassol, arriving at the Ministry of Marriage just before 2 p.m. The Minister took the license and said he could marry us, but would have to do it in the next ten minutes because the office was closing at 2 p.m. for five days to celebrate the annual Wine Festival in Cyprus! So we got married right then. His secretary became the witness and she was actually emotional during the ceremony, even shedding tears on our behalf. The minister's English wasn't so good so it was hard to understand all that he said, though we did hear more than once a warning against committing adultery. Later Don liked to tease that he wasn't sure we were really married since it was "all Greek" to him! After the vows were witnessed they brought out a thick old, old book with narrow lines and recorded our marriage in there by hand. We looked at this book later and saw that weddings had been recorded in there going back over two hundred years!

Well this wasn't the ceremony we had planned but we were now married and we were ecstatic that we had somehow pulled

Cyprus Wedding September 5, 1984

this off. I was a "wife" and I had a "husband." It felt so strange to think of at first. Back in our hotel room was the wedding dress I had planned to wear. It was light mint green, pure silk, short, and tightly fitted. I still have it but I've never worn it. Our friends, Dan and Diane, had a bottle of champagne delivered to our room and it was waiting for us when we got back to the room. Don poured two glasses and we drank a toast! In the bottom of the glass was a gold wedding band. He had bought these in Al Khobar before we left and had planned to surprise me with it at the ceremony, but of course there was no time to retrieve it so instead I nearly drank it! And how did we celebrate that night? We went to the Wine Festival of course!

The next day we drove to Paphos, had a beautiful lunch in a garden under grape vines and then visited an ancient amphitheater nearby. We later drove to the north shore and visited the Baths of Aphrodites. We had to hike along a trail to get there and then realized that if we wanted to go into the Baths we would have to do it with our clothes on since our swimsuits were back in the car. It was getting late in the day and we didn't have a hotel for the night so time was a factor. We decided to just walk into the water and get wet! We arrived at a small inn by the sea just as it was getting dark and luckily they had a room because by this time it was cooling off and being in wet clothes was not very comfortable.

For a honeymoon night, the room was a hoot. There were two small cot like beds, on opposite sides of the room and they were nailed to the floor! The shower was outside of our room, on the deck, facing the sea. It was a closed in area except for a few open windows, but the water was hot and felt great. That night we had a very delicious dinner, served outside under the stars in a lantern lit setting by the sea. Dinner consisted of freshly caught fish served with a Greek salad that I wish I could replicate, and of course a really nice bottle of wine. A truly memorable evening. The next day we drove back to Larnaca and caught our flight to Dhahran. My old boyfriend, Wayne, was on the flight! We all talked for a while and told him that we had just gotten married in

Cyprus. A while later a bottle of champagne arrived at our seats — a congratulatory gift from Wayne.

As soon as work started and the offices opened at Aramco after the Eid we went to headquarters and told them we had gotten married and showed them our license. This meant I was let go, as policy required, because now I was a "casual hire" as a wife. Since the Company policy had this requirement for married women, there was a cash benefit to us, when we left. Also, I had thirty days on my current contract at my regular pay and we gave notice immediately that we would be leaving at the end of the thirty days. This had been our plan from the beginning.

My last month in Saudi Arabia was wonderful. Ike and Alice had a great going away party for us and invited everyone we knew. And the teachers at the junior high had a wonderful farewell party for me complete with hilarious skits. They gave me a video copy of this, which I still have, and two gold bangles which I wear all the time along with the ones Don gave me as gifts. The Saudis that Don worked with had a farewell party for him too, at one of their homes. It was very traditional and we loved it. We ate Saudi style, men in one room, women in the other, and by sitting on the floor on carpets eating food off a large tray with one's hand. After the meal the women had henna decor painted on their hands and they did it for me too. It was a lovely good bye party and made me so glad that I was privileged to know these people.

Movers came and packed up all our belongings to be shipped back to the States. We listed Gary and Rosie as the address to ship everything. We each packed one suitcase and that's what we had with us when we left Arabia. We left Dhahran on the night of October 7, 1984 with mixed emotions. We were very excited to begin the next adventure of our lives, but leaving Saudi Arabia was saying good bye to this country forever, since one cannot go there on a tourist visa. We had quit our jobs with Aramco and did not plan to work there again.

We left on a flight to Nairobi, through Jeddah. In Nairobi we stayed in a fabulous, opulent old hotel that reminded me of what Africa must have been like in the colonial era. From there we left on an arranged safari to The Governor's Camp a few hours away. This was a comfortable yet rustic place in the middle of a huge wild animal habitat. Tents were set up in a circle in an area of the savannah where large herds of migrating animals came through. There was a river that ran by the camp too. In the middle of the circle was a large tent that served as a restaurant and another that was a bar. Night and day there was a huge bonfire always burning in the center of the camp. As soon as we arrived we were taken out for a ride through the savannah by jeep with a driver and a guide riding shotgun. We had prearranged to have this available to us for a private safari. There was no roof and no windows so visibility was great and we had the entire jeep to ourselves. We took lots of pictures and it was at a time when we had a very expensive camera with interchangeable lens so we could do some good close-ups.

On this first ride we came upon a pride of lions eating a Cape buffalo, the problem was the buffalo was not dead! The guide explained that the older lions were teaching the younger ones to hunt, and keeping the buffalo alive as long as possible. They would put their mouth over the mouth of the buffalo to suffocate it until it grew weak, then let go, while the young continued to eat this animal from the rear end. It was making me sick to watch it. This event was happening very near our campsite so when we returned for evening dinner we could all hear the moans and groans of that buffalo! I voiced my concern to the guide about how close the lions were to our tents and he said that really they were not to be feared since "humans killed by lions in Kenya was very rare." He said the most dangerous animals to humans were the hippopotamus. After which we drove along the river and sure enough, there were many of them soaking in the mud, within easy reach of our camp!

Our tent contained two cots, two lanterns for reading and a small writing desk. It reminded me of something I would have imagined David Livingstone himself would have occupied. However, attached to the back of our tent was an additional small tent that was a real bathroom with a toilet and a private shower with hot water!

The first night in the tent I had a very hard time sleeping. I kept having all these dreams about being out in that savannah with no place to hide and surrounded by a herd of hippopotamus or roaring lions. There were Maasai warriors who carried spears and torches and walked the perimeter of the camp and we were told that they stood guard all night. Sometime in the middle of the night I woke up to a strange grunting sound right close to the canvas tent by my bed. I got up and walked to the tent flap, opened it slightly and looked out. It was really dark and there were no Maasai warriors anywhere in sight! The bonfire was still lit and when my eyes adjusted to the darkness I could see that the creatures near our tent were zebras.

We spent five nights in that camp and each day we went out by jeep with our same driver and guide and cruised the bush for animals. It was a spectacular experience and we were lucky enough to see thousands and thousands of migrating wildebeests, zebras, and gnus. There were also herds of elephants and giraffes, some hyenas, rhinoceros, warthogs, vultures, and every other critter that roamed those plains. On our last day of the safari we even saw a cheetah, which they said was the most difficult to find. I think what amazed me the most was the massive size of these herds, and the impact on these countries with the annual migrations.

Tanzania was next and our plan to climb Mt. Kilimanjaro. The border between Kenya and Tanzania had only recently opened so travel between them was still questionable. We had round trip plane tickets from Nairobi to Kilimanjaro Airport on a Tanzanian airplane. The first thing we encountered was an issue getting our bags checked. The airline officials just stood there and looked at our two bags and refused to load them. After a while we realized they wanted "baksheesh," a common practice of bribery in the Middle East, so Don handed them the equivalent of a few dollars. They picked up one of our bags and put it on the plane, and stood there. So, Don got a few more dollars out and they loaded our other suitcase. This is the one and only time in all my years of travel where a bribe was needed to load luggage.

We had hired a Tanzanian government agency to make all the arrangements for our stay and the climb, since there were some pretty strict requirements. The agency had a van meet us at the airport so all was well until we were loaded inside and the van would not start. The driver yelled out for assistance and a bunch of young men came running over and they pushed the van until it started. We got used to this since during our entire stay this was the method of starting the van! The hotel was at the foot of Mt. Kilimanjaro located in a small village near a thick green jungle environment. The room was nice enough but very dated. It did include a bathroom with running water. The only problem was it was not dependable and was never hot, not even warm! The room had an old fashioned wall-mounted telephone from the British colonial period, but that didn't work either.

The next morning our guide, Frank, came to the hotel along with his sixteen-year-old son. The government required one guide for each climber and these were to be our guides, and they were wonderful! They each carried a large pack, while we were told to carry nothing. They had all our food, drink, and extra clothes in their packs. We started the climb right from the hotel, walking on a path that took us along a river and into the jungle. I was excited but apprehensive because I wasn't confident that I could really do this climb. It's about nineteen thousand four hundred feet high, and though not a technical climb, the altitude is what prevents many people from reaching the top. Coming from Saudi Arabia at sea level there was no way to train for high altitude. As soon as we started the walk we met a woman and her guide coming toward us. She was excited to tell us that she did this climb and made it to the top to celebrate her seventieth birthday! I was totally impressed and my confidence level went up greatly. I figured if she could do it for her seventieth birthday, surely I could do it for my fortieth!

The first day's walk was easy and beautiful. Mostly we were walking under a canopy of trees with Colobus monkeys chattering and swinging in the branches above. We walked slow and steady all day, exited the jungle into a savannah like area above the tree line. The weather was great, sunny all day which gave us gorgeous views once we exited the trees. The first night we stayed in huts along the trail, built there specifically for climbers. Our guides cooked a simple meal of a vegetable like soup with bread and hot tea. Our hut had two wood cots with a thin mattress and blanket. There was an outdoor toilet set up inside a central tent. That night there were two other climbers there, American dentists who lived and worked in Mali, and this was their second climb up Kilimanjaro. I slept pretty well that night except for the sound of rats, or maybe they were mice, scurrying around the ground under our cots.

The second day we hiked again, slow and steady, resting when needed, through terrain that became ever more bare. Visibility was again spectacular with great views of the snows above us and the jungle below us. That evening we stayed in huts near the edge of a big drop off. In fact, the hut with the toilet was perched out over the edge so there was no need to empty the contents! I was very tired and after dinner of the same menu as the night before,

Camp site on 2nd day of climb with a view of the snows of Mt. Kilimanjaro

I fell right to sleep, hoping I would not need a bathroom break in the dark, and I didn't!

The third day got colder, but visibility was still great. The trail made many more traverses since the climb was getting steeper and now the ground was brown and bare except for a scattering of rocks. We were nearing a tundra biome by the time we stopped that evening for dinner, and we stopped early, around three o'clock. This was the last campsite before the final approach to the summit. There were no huts here, but rather one small bunk room that could accommodate about twelve people. We were now at about sixteen thousand five hundred feet and I was feeling a bit nauseous. We met some young men from Switzerland who were headed back down, without having reached the summit. They were too ill with altitude sickness to finish the climb. We drank tea and ate a very light supper and then tried to get some sleep in the bunk beds. Frank woke us up at midnight to make the final ascent and reach the top by sunrise. There was a full moon and it was quite cold when we started off. We were the only ones on the trail. This last three thousand feet was extremely difficult for me since I needed to rest often, got sick and threw up often, but because my vision was still good it was not dangerous for me to keep climbing. Altitude sickness that reaches a level of blurred and double vision means it's time to turn back. Don felt okay so that was good, and he had much more stamina than me. I was told before we started the climb that I should rent some hiking boots, but when I tried them on they were very uncomfortable and heavy. I chose to stick with my sneakers and was very glad I did, since I don't think I could have managed one more ounce of discomfort! I was also very grateful for the cold air, it felt so good and continued to bring me extra spurts of energy. As dawn was creeping up over the plains of Africa I stepped on the famous snows of Mt. Kilimanjaro! I felt almost other worldly. I sat down in the snow and watched the sun come up, thinking I could almost see all of Africa from up there! The top of Kilimanjaro is an old extinct volcanic crater and there was an option to walk around the crater but I was far too exhausted and still too nauseous to consider this. I started back down the mountain with Frank's son as my guide, while Don and Frank continued on the walk around the crater. As soon as we reached the bunk house from the night before I started to feel much better. I drank more tea and rested until Don arrived and we headed further down the mountain. The hike down was much faster and we made it in two days, which is the typical climb. Three days up and two days down. We were very pleased with our two guides and gave them a very nice tip in U.S. dollars which thrilled them. They told us they were going to walk to Kenya to buy some things like sugar which was impossible to get in Tanzania. It was obvious that Tanzania was far less developed than Kenya, and poorer. We witnessed people waiting in long lines for a can of gasoline. There were no proper working modern conveniences, and everything seemed to be in need of repair from roads to power lines.

When we got back to the hotel we both took a long shower even though the water was cold it felt good. We then slept for about twenty hours, after which I felt amazingly great. No muscle aches or stiffness of any kind. The only physical discomfort came from my big toes, because on the way down the mountain my toes kept sliding into the end of my sneakers and I lost both of my big toenails. Fortunately, the weather was warm and I could wear my toeless sandals for the next few weeks.

The following day we tried to get through to the airport to confirm our flights, but were told the flights were full and we were not booked on them. Hmmm, needed more baksheesh? We decided to hire a car to drive us to the border, and we would walk back into Kenya. The driver arrived in a beat up old 1950s car and insisted on being paid in dollars (of course). He then made a stop in this strange parking lot with a dilapidated old building in one corner where he could exchange the dollars on the black market for much more Tanzanian currency than the banks would give. He got out and walked into the building, leaving Don and me in the car. Soon a police car came driving up and parked not far from us. We both thought we had definitely made a big mistake and would be arrested for having all this dollar cash in our money belts that we had not declared. We were sweating it out for about fifteen minutes until our driver returned as if nothing was wrong, and we drove away! He took us to the border on the Tanzania side and left us there. We went through the passport check and walked about two hundred yards to the Kenyan side and went through the passport check there. We were not the only tourists doing this and there were cars lined up on that side of the border waiting for us. We bargained with one of the drivers for a ride to Nairobi and hopped in. It was a big old Cadillac, old but comfortable, and we were safe and on our way. The drive took almost all day, and the scenery was mostly desert with numerous signs of the severe drought this area had been experiencing.

We spent the night in the same luxurious hotel we had stayed in before, enjoying hot showers and proper drinks at the old colonial style bar. The next day we flew to Cairo in time to meet my sister, June, and her husband, Gene, at the airport. We stayed in Cairo, at the Hilton on the Nile and enjoyed being tourists and taking in as many sites as we could. My favorites were the Museum of Antiquities and the Grand Bazaar. The museum was a great introduction to all that we would see as we traveled to Luxor and the Valley of the Kings. And the bazaar was full of all the old familiar smells and sights and sounds that I love so much in the Middle East. June and I were interested in bargaining for jewelry and perfumes and rugs and everything else that drew our attention. Each shop keeper would offer us a cup of tea, as is the custom throughout the Middle East. We had a wonderful afternoon going from shop to shop and enjoying all the hospitality of the shopkeepers. All the while, we didn't realize that Gene was very uncomfortable and afraid that these guys had ulterior motives. That they would put something in our tea so they could take advantage of us, steal our money, kidnap these two white women, or whatever! Don and I were completely oblivious to these notions since we were in familiar settings having spent years in the Middle East drinking tea wherever we went.

We flew to Luxor and toured the famous ruins. Near an ancient site surrounding a pond there was a giant statue of a scarab. Our guide told us that the scarabs were symbols of fertility and ancient Egyptian ladies would walk seven times around a scarab statue with their spouse to ensure a pregnancy. We thought this was pretty funny, so laughingly we carried out the ritual and walked around that scarab seven times.

Two months later I was pregnant, and so began another wonderful adventure in my life!

EPILOGUE

I am seventy-three years old now and over thirty years have passed since I left Saudi Arabia. Don and I returned to America and settled near Spring Green, Wisconsin, where my brother, Gary, had built us a house. We had sent money to Gary for this purpose during the years we lived in Arabia and so we came back to a beautiful home, with no mortgage, on twenty six acres of land in the country. We had deer and wild turkey, possums, raccoon, squirrels and skunk for our closest neighbors. We returned in November and snow soon covered our land. It was a huge change from the desert sands of Saudi Arabia. We held a wedding reception for family and friends in April of 1985.

Our House in Spring Green, WI

Our Wedding Reception in Wisconsin

Our beautiful daughter, Amelia Jara Faber, was born August 8, 1985. She is named after my grandmother (Amelia) and his Icelandic grandmother (Jara). Don started an Agribusiness Company (Midwestern BioAg, Inc.) with Gary and two other partners. I took a position teaching biology and chemistry at

Don, Amelia Jara, and me, 1985

Highland High School, in Highland, WI. Two years later I was the Superintendent of the Highland School District and very much enjoyed my six years there. I will be forever grateful to the people of Highland who helped make this possible. The year was 1987 when I became Superintendent and I had just finished my sixteenth year in education, thirteen years as a science teacher and three years as an assistant principal. I really had no idea of all the responsibilities of a school superintendent in Wisconsin but I loved the Highland School District, wanted to be their District Administrator, and believed I could be a fast learner and that there were many resources available to me in the community and in the state. I started work on my Ph.D. at the University of Wisconsin in Madison in school administration that fall.

I brought Amelia with me to Highland to the home of Marvalene. She was a wonderful woman and it gave me a great sense of relief to know that Amelia was being well cared for and was just a few blocks away from me. The other two days a week Amelia was in daycare in Madison. Don's parents had rented a townhouse in Madison and we spent a lot of time there with them. Don was attending night classes to finish his MBA and I had night classes for my Ph.D., so we stayed at their house at least two or three nights a week. We grew more and more fond of living in Madison, and so by 1988 we actually spent more time at the townhouse in Madison than we did at our home in the country.

As a teacher and administrator in Highland I told many of my "traveling" stories to my students. They always seemed very interested in hearing about the strange places I had been to and suggested that I should write a book one day. I had heard this before from past students and always planned to do this, but hearing it again started me thinking more seriously about it. At the end of my first year as superintendent in Highland I gave the address at the graduation ceremony and focused it on my Rule #1 to live by: Have an Adventure! At least once in your life.

Amelia's first day of kindergarten

When Amelia started kindergarten in 1990 we moved to Madison, where we had a home built. Commuting to Highland left me little time to spend with Amelia during the week so I left my superintendency in Highland at the end of that year with some sadness. I took a part time position as Director of Instruction for the Deerfield Community School District in Deerfield, WI and started a graduate assistantship at U.W., Madison. I finished my Ph.D. in Educational Administration in 1994 and in 1995 I became the superintendent in Deerfield when the then superintendent, Ed Van Ravenstein, was called to active duty in Bosnia. I spent a very enjoyable and rewarding career as Deerfield's Superintendent of Schools until my retirement in 2006. All together I spent fourteen years as a school superintendent in Wisconsin and had the privilege of working with a total of twenty-eight dedicated board members, many, many caring and talented teachers and administrators, and numerous skilled and dependable support staff members. All of these people along with every student in our system made my career so enjoyable. I have often stated that being a school superintendent is the best job on the planet!

A gathering of my family for a reunion in Spring Green, Wisconsin, 2011

Meanwhile, Midwestern BioAg did very well, expanding onto farms throughout the country and creating a number of "spin off" businesses throughout the years. Don finished his MBA at Edgewood College in Madison and spent his career as CEO/CFO of the Company. They sold the Company to investors in 2014. Gary stayed on board while Don stepped aside and is spending more of his time with Bio-Vet, Inc., one of the "spin off" companies.

Over the twenty-five years that we lived in Madison we had the opportunity to spend time with my family. This was a wonderful occurrence for me since I had not lived near them for twenty years. It gave me a chance to reconnect with my siblings and parents, cousins and aunts and uncles, and to watch my nieces and nephews grow up, get married, and have children of their own. Another bonus was the connection we made with Don's Icelandic aunt, Agnes, and her family in Minnesota. They were wonderful and welcomed us into their "clan," giving Amelia a strong bond with cousins her own age. We also spent many vacations in south Florida where Don's brothers live with their families: Bruce and Maria with their two sons, Jason and Jesse, and Brian with Justin and Brigitte. We watched their children grow up along with our daughter, Amelia, during many trips back and forth between Florida and Wisconsin.

I stayed close to my old friends over the years. Natasha came to Iceland with us one summer and we explored some of the exotic scenery there on a long road trip with music that she brought along for the occasion. Susan moved to Wisconsin! This was an especially wonderful bonus for me and we had years of great times together. After I retired I reconnected with Dee, my college friend from New York and she, Susan, Natasha, and I became a foursome who gathered together once a year for our annual "reunion."

And then there were the twenty-eight different people who lived with us over our years in Madison. Some were people we didn't know, they were friends of a friend or family member who needed a place to live for a while. Some were Icelandic relatives who came for a few months or a year to be in America. Some were former students who stayed for a summer or a semester while at

Above: Susan and me
in Madison

Right: Natasha and me
in Iceland

Below: Me With My Good
Friends: Susan, Dee, and Natasha

the university. Some were close friends of our daughter. And some were friends or family members who just wanted to be in Madison, usually to attend the university. In any event, these guests were another bonus over the years, and wonderful for Amelia since she was an only child and enjoyed extra people in our home.

We continued to experience exotic adventures and included our daughter in our travels from a very young age. We called our small family "The Unit." She had her first plane ride at four months and her first trip abroad (to Iceland) at eight months. She started boarding school in ninth grade at the Wayland Academy in Wisconsin, where she initially met Eric, her future husband. She transferred to the Leysin American School in Leysin, Switzerland her junior and senior year and graduated in 2003. She was a competitive skier in both high school and college. She did a Semester at Sea while in college and circled the globe on a university ship visiting many countries along the way. She spent summers in Iceland as a young child, staying with her grandparents, and she spent summers in Costa Rica and Ecuador while in college as an exchange student. She is fluent in Spanish and speaks some Icelandic. Together the three of us have traveled extensively visiting most of the States in the U.S. and many countries from Morocco to Vietnam, Thailand, Turkey, Oman, Iceland and most of Europe, Central America, Mexico and Canada. She too is a certified scuba diver. We have raised her to be a world traveler and to not be afraid to take risks.

In September of 2000 Don took me on a surprise vacation to the panhandle of Florida, where he had lived for part of his military career, to celebrate our sixteenth wedding anniversary. I fell in love with the region and while there we bought a lot and signed a contract for a vacation home in Sandestin. It was a rather spontaneous decision but a great one. We enjoyed numerous vacations there over the next fifteen years, as did many of our friends and family members. I loved those white sand beaches, warm gulf waters, and the easy going southern culture that went with it. We sold our home there a year ago, but are grateful for all the wonderful times spent there.

With Amelia and Don in my Favorite City, Istanbul

I have continued to follow my Rule #1 by having real adventures. I think the craziest one I've done is jumping off a mountain peak in the Alps on a hang glider! (With an instructor of course). Some of my other fun adventures have been riding Segways through downtown Denver and Seattle, doing a hot air balloon ride over Tucson, riding a donkey up a steep cliff on the Island of Santorini, hopping on the back of a motorcycle taxi in the crazy traffic of Ho Chi Minh City, snorkeling with sea lions off the coast of Mexico in the Sea of Cortez, riding an elephant through a jungle near Phuket, Thailand, and attending Barack Obama's first inauguration along with millions of other cheering supporters.

At Obama's Inauguration

Paul, Mary, me, Don, Robin and Bill at Machu Picchu

Me and surprise visitor at Machu Picchu

Don and I also had wonderful adventures with our good friends, Paul and Mary, and Bill and Robin. The six of us (one time known as The Rumrunners!) have shared a lot of laughs together. We rode camels and camped in the Sahara Desert of Morocco and hiked and camped in the Amazon jungle of Peru, spent weekends at Paul and Mary's Lake House, vacationed in Sandestin, and attended a number of sporting events from Badger basketball to Packer football.

Over these past thirty years we have made many trips to Iceland and have very much enjoyed spending time there with family members. Don's sister, Berta, lives there with her husband, Kristjan, and their children, Siggi-Dan, Heida Mist, and Gustav. At the turn of the century, January 1, 2000, Don, Amelia, and I were in Reykjavik, Iceland and it was a most wonderful place to bring in the new millennium. We spent ten days there celebrating the event with our Icelandic family and friends. I felt a great deal of emotion just thinking about a new century, but especially entering a new millennium. I thought about what it must have been like on January 1, 1000 when many people thought the world was coming to an end. And to realize that there were some folks one thousand years later of the same belief. In March of 2000 my Mom passed away and my Dad followed eleven months later. Don's mother passed away in the year 1994 and his father eleven years later in 2005. Losing one's parents is definitely a huge milestone in life, and though we are prepared for it all our lives, it still leaves a large hole in one's life. I often wish I could see them again to ask questions and tell them my thoughts. Harder still was the passing of Don's twin brother, Dan. He died of cancer in 1999 at the age of fifty. We took his ashes to Iceland for burial in the family plot.

My sisters and I started a tradition of doing a "Sister Trip" each year, and have now completed fifteen trips! These have been very enjoyable experiences and have brought us many laughs, fond memories, and some exciting times. We have traveled from New Orleans to Boston to Branson, Missouri to Vancouver, to Greece and many other fun places. We've had some interesting experiences like getting lost on a Greek island and sailing the

Sister Trip: Golfing near Whistler Mt. in Canada, Me, June, Audrey, and Jane

"Titanic" (as my sister Jane called it) on the Mediterranean Sea. This was a cruise ship that we sailed to Turkey on. Our first night at sea was stormy and I awoke sometime in the night to feel the ship heaving from side to side. I was sleeping in a small cot in a cabin shared with Jane. The ship was rocking so much that first my feet would be way up and next my head would be way up, as waves splashed against the portholes. I began to feel like I was receiving a wonderful massage on my whole body as the ship moved to and fro, and then I felt like I was being rocked to sleep like a baby. When I awoke the next morning, Jane said, "How could you sleep through that terrible storm last night? I thought we were on the Titanic and were going to sink!" When I told her about my "massage," she said, "You are such an optimist, you see the world through rose colored glasses." She explained that she is not a pessimist, but a realist. We continue to share, with humor, the differences in our perceptions of various experiences. The year I retired, for my final graduation speech as superintendent, I told this story and suggested to the graduates that if they could not see the world through rose colored glasses, they should buy some!

Thailand with Amelia

Belize

Vietnam

Morocco

Don and me in Spain

Bryce Canyon with Amelia

Amelia, a school SLP

Amelia graduated from U.W., Madison and went on to graduate school at the University of Colorado in Boulder. She is now a Speech and Language Pathologist (SLP) for the Jefferson County School District. She got married in 2013 to Eric Larimer, also a world traveler and adventurer. She and Eric, and our new granddaughter, Anita, live in Golden, CO. Anita is named after my mother. She is only two years old but already showing a very adventurous spirit! Don and I bought a house in Golden to be near them and we moved here nearly two years ago. We also enjoy spending time at our condo in Keystone, and ski every winter.

Amelia & Eric's wedding

Last fall we spent a month vacationing in La Paz, Mexico on the Baja Peninsula. Don had gone there last summer to check it out for possible future beach vacations. We all fell in love with it, so much so that Don and I bought a house there in the Costabaja Resort. Another adventure is about to begin. We will be expats again for part of our life!

Anita, age 2

Hiking in Colorado, Maroon Bells

Enjoying time in beautiful Baja, Mexico on the Sea of Cortez

REFLECTIONS

These are some of my afterthoughts, tidbits of advice, beliefs, flashbacks, opinions, realizations, regrets, feelings of gratitude, ponderings, wishful thinkings, and hopes.

1. I still remember a presentation back in high school (1961) when the presenter promised us that one day we would have a watch that would be a time piece, telephone, and TV all in one. My iPhone pretty much proves he was right. I haven't purchased my iWatch yet, but I'm definitely going to. Only now I am also wanting a honeybee-sized drone to run errands for me, spy for me and answer all my questions. And I want my own flying suit so I can fly on my own without booking tickets on a crowded plane or fighting traffic in a city!

2. Key people in my career-life that I owe a lot of thanks to, in chronological order. Thank you!!! I could not have done it without you. You were the key decision makers who believed in me.
   *Dr. Ivan Buddenhagen, Professor, University of Hawaii, Honolulu
   *Dr. Herbert Uemura, Pathologist, Children's Hospital, Honolulu
   *Dick Irvine, Headmaster, Iranzamin International School, Tehran, Iran
   *Fr. James McMurtry, Principal, D.J. O'Connell H.S.
   *Jack DeWard, Superintendent, Aramco Schools, Saudi Arabia
   *Jess Arceneaux, Principal, Dhahran Junior High, Saudi Arabia
   *Vince Ramsden, School Board President, Highland, WI

*Dr. Marvin Fruth, Professor, U.W. Madison
*Dr. Paul Bredeson, Professor and good friend, U.W. Madison
*Ed Van Ravenstein, Superintendent, Deerfield, WI
*Gary Borgrud, School Board Member, Deerfield, WI
*Brad Gleason, School Board President, Deerfield, WI

3. I look at people differently now, based on their age. When I see a teenager I am realizing that inside that beautiful young being lives not just a seventeen year old, but also a twelve year old, six year old, two year old, and all the other stages that provided the experiences and memories that created the person who is now seventeen. Carrying that thought to the elderly brings a profound recognition of the significance of this truth and how little attention is given to it. I am seventy-three now, but it's not like I used to be fifty and I used to be thirty or seventeen. I am still all those ages! I may look seventy-three on the outside, but on the inside I still feel like a "girl," a "daughter," a "student," a "free spirit," a "hippy," a "teacher," a "wife',," a "superintendent," a "mother," a "grandmother" and much, much more all at once.

4. I believe in "angels." I have two: my husband Don, a former Air Force Pararescueman (aka Guardian Angels) and an invisible angel I think has always been with me, I just didn't know it until I moved to Saudi Arabia. I call her Sars. I'm not sure what brought me the realization, but now it just seems obvious. Much more so than the thought of a "god" or any other "holy" figures. I have been a Unitarian Universalist for the past thirty years, because I am definitely interested in spirituality, just not any specific religion. Most organized religions seem so

archaic and barbaric in their beliefs. For example, a god that is a "loving father" sending his children to a burning hell forever for not believing in him? Even if they have lived a kind and loving life? Sick! I am in awe of scientific findings on the size and age of our humongous universe, which leads me to accept the possibility of things that I cannot see or understand. I hope there is a god, because a god who created this wonderful world would be kind and loving, not egotistical, petty and vengeful.

5. It's the music! Writing this book has taught me how important the music was in my decision-making processes over the years. In the 60s folk and rock music were full of "Ramblin" songs, riding freight trains, "feel like I gotta travel on," "500 miles from my home," "going away with no words of farewell," "Spanish boots of Spanish leather," and so many more. In the 70s it continued with songs of faraway places and reasons to go: lyrics like "walking down a country road," "you might even find it in Katmandu," "bound for places I'm not known to" and so many more! It definitely helped me romanticize the path I chose to take. And later, the Beatle's song, "Let it Be" and John Lennon's "Imagine" helped soften my being. I owe a lot to many wonderful musicians including Woodie Guthrie, The Kingston Trio, Ray Charles, the Rolling Stones, The Eagles, Joan Baez, James Taylor, Janis Joplin, Willie Nelson, The Who, Jimi Hendrix, Rod Stewart, Peter, Paul, and Mary, Arlo Guthrie, Kris Kristofferson, Bob Seger, Leonard Cohen, John Prine, and so many more, but especially Bob Dylan! Of all these musicians, Dylan by far made the biggest impact on my life, starting with "The Times They Are a Changing."

6. My first serious encounter with yoga was in Vietnam about a dozen years ago, and it has been an amazing help to my physical well-being ever since. I believe that the core strength and balance it has given me are the reasons I can still ski today, and ski better every year.

7. While sitting on the sandy beaches of Hawaii and discussing existentialism with my friend, Kami, I came to understand what a positive philosophy this actually could be. It allows one to live day to day, recognizing how insignificant a life is and in the grand scheme of things how really short it is, like the snap of a finger. This being the case, how silly to worry or get stressed out about things even smaller and shorter lived. This is my optimistic interpretation of existentialism.

8. I regret that I did not have enough deep adult to adult talks with my parents. The conversations we had were mostly parent to child or child to parent, even when I was in my fifties and they in their eighties. I wish I could have spoken to them as a close friend, asking them how they felt about personal things, their decisions in life, their biggest pleasures, any regrets, how they coped with losing parents at such young ages, and so much more. If I had written this book earlier I may have come to this realization before they passed away.

9. I did not know how deep and strong love could be until I had a child. There is nothing else like it in life. It is unconditional and so powerful that it supersedes anything humanly rational.

10. I am extremely grateful that in my lifetime Barack Obama was elected President of the United States. It has given me more hope for the future of our wonderfully diverse nation, and feelings of love for my fellow countrymen. I have so much admiration for President Obama that my husband calls him "the other man in my life!"

11. I wish I could repay all the people who were helpful to me as I traveled around the world; complete strangers who invited me in, offered me rides, food, friendly conversation, and a place to stay. I don't even know all their names, but I can still

remember some of their faces and stories. I like the idea of "paying it forward" — that I can do.

12. One of the smartest things I ever did was follow my inner voice and wait until my perfect life partner, Don, came along.

13. The thing I am most proud of in my life are my friends. If you can judge a person by the quality of their friends then I am a rock star!!!!!

14. The most important obligation on our entire planet is the care of ALL the children, their safety, health, and education must be our number one priority.

15. My advice to K-12 educators gained from my thirty-five years in this field:

    A) Ban most "homework!" It wastes our kids' precious time. Instead, for after school we should encourage adventures, activities, play time, family time, social gatherings, etc. I wish I would have come to this realization at the beginning of my career.

    B) Alter our curriculum to include the study of a foreign language beginning in kindergarten. American children should be bilingual like children in other developed countries.

16. To all the readers of this book: Please write the story of your life. It is your legacy, and will be added to the collection of human knowledge, and needs to be available to your contemporaries and the generations to come. It doesn't have to be an entire novel, but the "story" of your life, and as much advice as you would like to share.

17. In my next life I think I will be an entomologist.

Me skiing in Keystone, Colorado, January, 2016

MY RULES TO LIVE BY

1. HAVE AN ADVENTURE!

2. KEEP A JOURNAL

3. PRACTICE EMPATHY

4. LIVE JOYFULLY

5. ENJOY AND SUPPORT THE ARTS

6. LEARN THE ART OF LETTING GO

7, DON'T JUDGE!

8. BE A LIFE LONG LEARNER

9. DIE HOPEFULLY

10. BE POLITICALLY ACTIVE

11. FOLLOW YOUR INTUITION

12. IT'S ONLY MONEY

www.ingramcontent.com/pod-product-compliance
Lightning Source LLC
Chambersburg PA
CBHW041955080526
44588CB00021B/2751
9781943650613